ARE YOU TENSE?

ARE YOU TENSE?
The Benjamin System of Muscular Therapy

TENSION RELIEF THROUGH DEEP MASSAGE AND BODY CARE

BY BEN E. BENJAMIN, Ph. D.

PHOTOGRAPHS BY RICHARD BLINKOFF

PANTHEON BOOKS, NEW YORK

Library of Congress Cataloging in Publication Data

Benjamin, Ben E., 1944–
Are You Tense?

Includes index.
1. Relaxation.   2. Stress (Physiology).   3. Muscles.
4. Exercise.   5. Massage.   I. Title.
RA785.B46   613.7′9   77–88778
ISBN 0–394–49511–X
ISBN 0–394–73499–8 pbk.

Line drawings by Bonnie Warwick
Anatomical drawings by Carol Ann Morley
Anatomical illustration on page 57 (Figure 1-3) by Steven Baker
Book design by Kenneth Miyamoto

Manufactured in the United States of America

468975

TO ALFRED KAGAN

for his warmth and guidance throughout my career

CONTENTS

ANATOMICAL DRAWINGS

FOREWORD

Common sense tells us that practically everyone suffers from too much tension. Ben Benjamin's work explains tension in understandable terms and describes a practical method for its elimination.

As Chief Physician for the Pain Rehabilitation Unit at Massachusetts Rehabilitation Hospital, I have had many of my staff work closely with Mr. Benjamin for the past two years. These people have been trained in his methods of deep massage, body care, and tension-release exercise. His work has been a decisive factor in many cases. Because of the success of his techniques, they have become an integral part of our program. I have personally seen the value of his tension-control techniques applied to our group of hospital patients suffering from excess tension and accompanying pain.

The material presented in this book is of tremendous practical importance to all people who are subject to excess tension and especially to those with the accompanying symptoms of pain and injury. The greater value of the techniques described in this book is that they can actually alter your life by reducing or preventing the buildup of excess muscular tension. It is a fact that less tension means a healthier body. I heartily recommend a serious consideration of this book and its underlying principles both to the public and to professionally trained medical persons.

NATHANIEL HOLLISTER, M.D.
Massachusetts Rehabilitation Hospital
Boston, Massachusetts

PREFACE

This book provides a comprehensive approach to coping with and alleviating everyday tension. Its aim is to help those who want relief from their own tension and to serve as a text to accompany training in muscular therapy.

During the past fifteen years I have helped thousands of people to live free from tension and pain. The results I have achieved have led hundreds of people to study with me, both privately and in intensive seminars in more than twenty universities and colleges. Although I have taught more than two thousand people basic deep massage, I have trained only twenty people thoroughly in the techniques of muscular therapy, because of the length of time it takes to properly learn it.

My own interest in learning to reduce tension began at fourteen, when, in rigorous dance training, I received an injury that was diagnosed as severe enough to permanently end my dancing career. Upset at this possibility, I sought treatment with Alfred Kagan, well known for his deep-massage techniques that benefitted thousands of dancers. His assessment of my injury was startlingly simple. My problem was due entirely to excess tension. To my amazement, after three weeks of treatment I was able to dance without pain.

My interest in Mr. Kagan's work grew and four years later I began training in deep massage with him. At nineteen, under the constant guidance of Mr. Kagan, I began my own practice in New York City. During the next few years, I studied privately with several doctors to learn about muscular tension and how it relates to the emotions and to physical pain.

After four years of private practice, I created, through Project Head Start, an extensive program using movement to break down tension in children. Some time later, teaching at the Fifteenth Street School, based on A. S. Neill's Summerhill, I further developed the tension-release techniques that I had formulated in Project Head Start.

By 1967 I had combined this experience, as well as study in voice, speech production, body alignment, and movement techniques in my own method, which I call the Benjamin System of Muscular Therapy. At this time I began teaching workshops and classes in California and New York and started training people privately in the use of my techniques. Since 1967 I have devoted an increasing amount of time to teaching in addition to my private practice.

More recently, I have directed an extensive training program for the Pain Rehabilitation Unit now located at the Massachusetts Rehabilitation Hospital in Boston. This program, developed and administered by Dr. Nathaniel Hollister, surgeon and psychiatrist, is an individualized program, using various therapeutic methods to treat patients whose problems range from complete debilitation to simple chronic pain. I trained Dr. Hollister and many of his nursing staff in the use of my methods.

The Pain Rehabilitation Unit is based on a premise that is fundamental to my work: that the individual should be encouraged to do something constructive about his pain rather than remain a victim of it.

In 1975 the Muscular Therapy Institute was established. Formal training to become a certified muscular therapist is provided at the Muscular Therapy Institute, which now has training centers in New York City, Boston, and Washington, D.C. In order to maintain a high standard of professionalism, a nation-wide Muscular Therapy Board of Examiners is currently being organized. Therapists will be certified by the board and will prominently display their certificates.

Throughout my career I have not hesitated to borrow from diverse sources in the formulation of my own methods, and in this book I try to give credit where it is due. Primary among those to whom I am indebted is Wilhelm Reich, M.D. Although I never met him personally, I have read many books and journals written by him and have attended lectures given by doctors and workers associated with the American College of Orgonomy. Through these books and lectures I have gained a knowledge of biological energy and muscular armoring that has provided me with a sound theoretical basis for my work.

Muscular therapy is not orgone therapy, nor is it any form of psychotherapy or physiotherapy, and it should not be confused with them. Furthermore, it is not intended to be a substitute for any of these, nor for medical treatment, although it can be a useful adjunct to them. (Of course, if you are in doubt about your own fitness, you should first consult a physician to be certain that the exercises described in this book are compatible with your physical condition.) Muscular therapy is a practical therapeutic approach to reduce physical tension and muscular pain through body re-education.

BEN E. BENJAMIN
Muscular Therapy Institute
910 West End Avenue
New York, New York 10025

ACKNOWLEDGMENTS

It gives me great pleasure to thank all the people who helped make this book possible. I shall always be indebted to the late Dr. Simeon Tropp for the generous sharing of his vast knowledge, as well as for his guidance and encouragement.

I am also indebted to Peter Dogan. If it were not for him this book would never have been written. Together we drafted two original chapters. With this in hand, I was able to find an interested publisher, and thus give life to an idea that had been germinating in my mind for years.

I am deeply grateful to and wish to thank the following: Joseph Blitman, Mary Butler, Sanford Goodman, James Robinson, Charles McGlaughlin, Leon Prochnik, Allen Graubard, Carol Benjamin, and Peter Christ for the part they played in the early stages of the book; Elaine Sommers for allowing me to use some of her exercises; Carol Hess, Sandra Genter, Naid Sofian, and Aileen Crow for their helpful criticisms of chapter 5; Carol Ann Morley for her clear and accurate anatomical illustrations; Bonnie Warwick for her imaginative drawings; Kenneth Miyamoto for his sensitive design of the book; Richard Blinkoff for his wonderful photographs and infinite patience and dedication to a seemingly endless job; Erika Bro, Carol Hess, Gilda Mullette, Deborah Darr, and Joseph Blitman, who appear in the photographs; Professor Alfonso Solomini for his technical clarification of the anatomical material; Irene Dowd and Ellen Boyers for their endless help in writing and rewriting the finer details; Terry Jackson for her help in the last stages of refinement of the manuscript; Robert A. Dew, M.D., Nathaniel Hollister, M.D., Barbara G. Koopman, M.D., Ph.D., and Bryn Waern, M.D., for their painstaking review of the final manuscript for medical and technical accuracy; Alice Warwick for her endless patience in typing manuscript after manuscript; Ruth Turner, who, as my administrative assistant, gave valuable advice, while managing to keep the project moving forward in an organized way; and Leonard Smith, whose remarkable objectivity and sensitive criticism helped bring the final manuscript to completion.

And finally, I give my heartful thanks to all my students for the knowledge and pleasure I have gained through teaching them.

ARE YOU TENSE?

Chapter 1 · TENSION

Are you tense? Your tension and what you can do about it is what this book is all about.

Everyone suffers from tension and tension-related problems at some time. Many people accept this tension and its accompanying problems and resign themselves to living with it. Others try to escape from it by taking pills, other drugs, or alcohol. Hypochondriacs deal with it by talking about and dwelling on it, insomniacs lie awake with it, and others suffer and don't recognize the problems until serious symptoms develop. The most common health problem in this country is tension.

A client once said: "I always thought my legs were strong and healthy because they were tight." This reflects the distorted attitude most people have about their own bodies. The person who makes such a statement has a lot of excess tension. This kind of muscle tension has nothing to do with strength. This tension is, in fact, unhealthy.

Each joint is surrounded by a system of muscles that cause it to move. The muscle functions by contracting and shortening, expanding and lengthening. In everything we do the muscles are constantly expanding and contracting, tensing and releasing. Without appropriate muscle tension, we could not stand, move, or even breathe. Tension is produced when muscle fiber contracts. A certain amount of muscle tension, called muscle tone, is necessary. But when a muscle is not in use, it should relax. If the muscle fiber remains contracted, *excess* tension, which can be a serious danger to health, results. Maintaining excess tension uses up tremendous amounts of energy that should be available for normal functioning. In this book the word *tension* refers to excess tension.

I have formulated two categories of causes of excess tension—mechanical and emotional. These causes are of course interrelated, and it is often difficult to know the precise origin of tension. But, with enough experience and knowledge, one can usually determine whether the major causes are mechanical or emotional. Excess tension caused by mechanical factors can be alleviated by muscular therapy; whereas excess tension caused by emotional factors requires a different and sometimes difficult approach, for example a psychiatric one.

Mechanical Causes of Tension

This excess tension is produced by bad physical habits, poor posture, incorrect body alignment, accidents, injuries, and operations.

Faulty habits, for example, cause a large and unsuspected amount of tension. Sitting with tightly crossed legs, regularly carrying a heavy briefcase in the same hand, and constantly wearing high-heeled or tight-fitting shoes and clothing are but a few of the daily habits that cause tension. Once recognized, these habits often are easy to correct, but unfortunately they usually go unnoticed.

Environmental factors are another major cause of mechanical tension. These are frequently beyond our control. Walking daily on concrete is hard on the legs. City noises of construction, subways, and traffic assault the ears and cause the muscles of the head and neck to contract. Mass transit is often crowded, unsafe, and unpleasant, and driving in city traffic is a nerve-racking experience.

Jobs also have a hand in creating tension. Some build tension in particular areas of the body—secretaries are often tense in the arms and shoulders; mailmen, in the legs; singers, in the throat.

It is virtually impossible to avoid all excess tension, but mechanically caused tension can be alleviated by recognizing and avoiding harmful habits.

Emotional Causes of Tension

Chronic repression of emotion results in chronic tightening of the muscles. This is called armor. (I have taken the concept of "armor" from the work of Dr. Wilhelm Reich.)

Reich discovered that armor is caused by the specific inhibition of emotional expression and that the inhibition of the particular emotional expression could always be traced to specific muscle groups usually occurring in segmental rings along the vertical axis of the body. For example, in order to hold back crying impulses, one often contracts the muscles of the throat and neck, front and back. In order to hold back the expression of rage, one might involuntarily tighten the neck, the arms, or the shoulders.

Armoring usually begins in infancy or childhood. Many parents do not permit the expression of a child's natural impulses. Children are full of life and run and jump and make noise, often for hours on end. But parents, and indeed society in general, make them contain their impulses in the only possible way —by tensing the muscles. It is natural for children to express their emotions, often loudly and forcefully, which many adults find hard to tolerate. A crying child is comforted with, "There, there, stop crying." To stop crying, the child must squeeze the muscles around the eyes, tighten the throat, raise the shoulders, and, more important, control respiration by tensing the chest and diaphragm.

A child who is *forced* to stop crying gets angry, but anger can evoke more parental disapproval than crying does. The child, thus, has no choice but to bury the anger deep in the muscles: hitting and kicking impulses are repressed by tensing the shoulders, arms, and legs; crying and yelling are controlled by tensing the jaw, throat, and chest. Children put a lid on their emotions, and dull the pain from physical traumas such as beatings by tightening the buttocks and legs or clenching the jaw and tightening the muscles of the head.

Armor can be produced in response to withdrawal of love or to negative parental attitudes that may be communicated through a look or a gesture. These expressions cause confusion in the child, which in turn causes a form of armor in the head and eyes.

Thus, layers of tension begin to form at an early age and later develop into chronic armor. People not only lose the ability to release tension but even become unaware of it and of the impulses and feelings they were originally suppressing. The result may be lifelong problems.

I have found that there are analogous counterparts in the mechanical realm of tension and pain. Reich's concept of segmental rings of armor can also be applied to tension produced by mechanical causes.

For example, when there is tension in the lower back, there is almost always corresponding tension in the abdominal area.

As I have already stated, armor is not what the Benjamin System of Muscular Therapy treats. However, if we are to understand and to treat the body in a coherent way, we are obliged to come to grips with all the forms and causes of tension. By clarifying the meanings of and differences between armor and mechanically caused tension, we can make a precise distinction between the two. Were we to proceed without this analysis of Reich's discoveries, we would find ourselves constantly confusing mechanically and emotionally caused tension.

Tension as a Function of Time

Tension can also be viewed as a function of time. For example, compensating tensions caused by a leg injury will, if not treated, increase over a period of time. The result will often be a new problem—more severe than the original one. In order to identify tension as it varies with time, I have created two categories: *current tension* and *residual tension*.

Current tension has been present for a short period of time and feels as if it lies in the superficial muscles. It is generally not lasting and can be either mechanical or emotional in origin.

Residual tension is deep tension present over a long period of time. Deep residual tension is more serious than current tension but can also be either mechanically or emotionally caused.

Think of the body as a reservoir. The deep water out in the middle of the reservoir is residual tension. The current tension is the shallow water lapping around the shore. If the reservoir is almost full, only a little need be added to cause an overflow, but if it is almost empty, its contents can be doubled or tripled without flooding the surrounding countryside.

Pain occurs when the reservoir overflows. This means that the current tension added to the residual tension caused an overflow. A body with little residual tension can sustain considerable current tension without pain, but a person who is full of residual tension is constantly on the threshold of pain. Some-

times even a slight twist or bump can result in a strain or sprain, because muscles with deep tension cannot absorb the jostlings and little shocks they continually receive in daily life.

Effects of Excess Tension

Doctors are aware that tension contributes to serious diseases. Problems such as heart disease, asthma, eczema, colitis, ulcers, boils, sciatica, and back pain, to name a few, are tension related. However, most people are not aware of how tension affects them and how very destructive it is.

Tension causes pain. Tension is the cause of scores of daily "ache" complaints—from "Oh, what a headache!" to "My aching back!" Generally, if we suffer from chronic muscular pain, regardless of how we got it, we have too much tension. This book, however, is not concerned with organic pain caused by disease.

Tension uses up energy. People who are chronically tense use the bulk of their energy to hold their bodies tight. Walking around with excess tension in the body is like carrying a backpack filled with lead. People who are tense feel more sluggish and need more sleep.

Tension restricts movement. If you are tense, your range of movement is limited and you may feel stiff. Perhaps you can't throw your head back to look at the ceiling or turn your head before changing lanes on a highway without pain. Maybe you can't bend down to pick something up without difficulty or dance as freely as you would like. Rigid muscles do not move easily.

Tension reduces blood circulation. When you pinch a straw, fluid will not pass through it. Similarly, when muscles contract around blood vessels, circulation is less efficient. Even arterial blood vessels have muscles, and the inhibition of circulation is often due to spasms of these involuntarily controlled vascular muscles. Thus, poor circulation is often due to excess tension.

Tension reduces the ability to breathe deeply. Tension in the muscles of the chest and spasms in the diaphragm muscle prevent full expansion and contraction of the chest cavity and thereby restrict breathing. When we can't breathe deeply, respiration, which brings oxygen and energy to the cells and removes carbon dioxide, is impaired. If carbon dioxide is not efficiently removed from the cells, the blood and tissues become acidic. Dysfunction may result. It is a dangerous circle. If we are too tense we cannot breathe properly, and if we do not breathe properly our muscles cannot relax.

Tension inhibits the expression of emotion. When muscles are rigid, expression of feelings is difficult. The phrase "being up tight" is an accurate description of someone who is tense and therefore unable to express himself. The muscles are indeed held tightly.

Tension interferes with sensation. Mild pressure on nerves blocks sensory and energetic impulses. Decreased sensation is particularly common when the neck is very tight. Tension in effect deadens the messages sent and received by the central nervous system. Severe pressure on nerves, of course, produces pain.

I once treated a young woman whose lack of body awareness was almost total. Her legs were especially cut off from full sensation and were covered with bruises from bumping into things without realizing it.

In her first treatment, she lay face down on the table as I gently massaged her calf. I lifted her lower leg up and supported it in my hand. "Relax your leg," I told her, "don't hold it up."

"I'm not holding it," she protested.

Suddenly I released it. Did it drop? No. It stood there like a flagpole. There was so much tension in her leg that she held it up without knowing it.

At first her treatments were not particularly painful, but after a few weeks she began to complain of considerable pain. "I don't understand why treatments that are supposed to relax me are causing more and more pain," she told me.

I explained that she was becoming more aware of sensations in her body. It was actually the initial relaxation of her muscles that permitted her to sense how tight she was. She had been so contracted that perception of her own pain had been blocked. As she loosened up through treatment, her awareness of sensation gradually spread from her neck to her shoulders, upper back, lower back, and eventually to her legs. After several months she became aware of some sensation throughout her body and began to get fewer bruises.

Tension cannot be talked away. Recently I saw a new client who bragged that he was relaxed and in the best of health. "Just give me a nice, deep massage," he said.

The condition of his body, however, belied his words. The first thing I noticed was that the back of his neck was as hard as a tree trunk and quite painful under pressure.

"Do you get a lot of headaches?" I asked him.

"Maybe once in a while."

"About how often?"

"At least once a week," he replied.

It always surprises me that people can have a problem of constant tension and still consider themselves in perfect health.

"I'm used to it," he commented. "I swallow a few aspirin and it's usually gone in a few hours." Like hundreds of others, he was talking away tension as if it did not exist.

You can try to talk tension away but it won't make a difference—the tension will still be there. Understanding is the only answer. *Why* do you have that headache? Is it the result of the trauma of an accident or the angry words you did not say to your boss? Only when you understand your tension can you deal with it most effectively and attempt to relieve it.

Chapter 2 · MUSCULAR THERAPY

Muscular therapy is a system of treatment and education. It includes a series of techniques and exercises designed to break down muscular tension and prevent it from returning. It encompasses a body of knowledge and techniques that enables the individual to counter his own tension as it occurs. Thus, when the client has mastered the necessary techniques and exercises, further professional treatment is unnecessary.

Muscular therapy can be divided into four parts:

1. Deep Massage
2. Tension-Release Exercise
3. Body-Care Techniques
4. Postural Realignment

Deep Massage

The concept of massage is a part of everyone's experience. Most people are aware of some of the principles without realizing it. An automatic response to pain or tension is to press on the affected part of the body. When our eyes hurt, we rub them. When our necks feel tight, we want someone to massage them, or perhaps we rub them ourselves. These manipulations can be called a kind of superficial massage.

Unlike superficial massage, which can touch only the muscle surface, deep massage can reach into the muscles and release long-standing tension and pain. These movements literally go deep into the muscles. By the use of intricate finger and hand techniques, a muscle or muscle group can be effectively penetrated to relieve tension and can increase localized blood circulation.

There are two basic kinds of deep-massage techniques in this system: stroking/kneading and pressure. Stroking/kneading techniques increase general blood circulation, while pressure techniques break down the deep tension.

Tension-Release Exercises

These exercises release tension in specific muscles and parts of the body. Tension-release exercises can be done alone and are as important as the deep-massage work. For example, when working to reduce jaw tension in people who grind their teeth, a common exercise is towel biting. While holding a towel in the mouth, clamped in place by the back teeth, it is pulled forcefully while being resisted. This technique when repeated daily will dramatically reduce tension in the jaw area. Tension-release exercise is a simple and important way to reduce one's own tension.

Body-Care Techniques

These techniques help in the *maintenance* of lower levels of tension and help in the reduction of tension *in a gentle way*. These techniques generally are more gentle and less active than the tension-release exercises. For example, when working to maintain a status of reduced tension and prevent its buildup in the neck, it is helpful to employ the block technique, described in chapter 6.

Postural Realignment

Postural realignment is crucial to maintaining a relaxed body. For example, when someone suffers from lower-back pain, all the therapeutic treatments available cannot guarantee solution of the problem until the underlying postural deviation is corrected. In the later stages of muscular-therapy treatment, an individual program of postural-realignment exercises is designed for each person when necessary. These exercises, when done daily, help the individual remain free from chronic tension and the pain and injury that it causes.

Case Studies

The case studies described here will give a sense of what muscular-therapy treatment is like.

Four years ago, a tall, twenty-seven-year-old female film editor came to me complaining of headaches that had been plaguing her two or three times a week for about ten years. The headaches would start at the back of her head and, in an hour or two, work up to the top of her head. She said the pressure was so intense that her head felt as if it were in a vise. Reading and working were agony, and aspirin and other drugs gave little relief.

The muscles around her neck and jaw and under her scalp were tight. When I squeezed her neck, she raised her shoulders and moved away from me. She said her neck was unpleasantly ticklish. Her jaw was clamped and her neck and shoulders were like steel, but the general tightness decreased as I moved down her body.

She started treatments twice a week. At first I concentrated on the back, with gently increasing pressure to loosen the areas around the heart and in the chest in an effort to improve the general circulation. At the same time I worked lightly on the neck and head. The area where the shoulder and neck muscles connect to the head (the occiput) was tender and could withstand only limited treatment.

As the back and shoulders started to relax, I began working with increasing pressure on the back of the neck and skull. When the superficial neck tension, which she felt as ticklishness, disappeared, I ventured deeper into the neck until I encountered a muscle so afflicted by constant spasm it felt like a bone. For weeks her head and neck were sore to the touch because we were breaking down tensions that had existed for years. Treatment of her back had also been painful at first, but by the time I discovered the major spasm in the neck, the back work produced no discomfort. We concentrated on the deep spasm, and

I recommended exercises to break down neck tension in addition to taking frequent baths. She did all the exercises regularly, indicating that she was learning to tolerate relaxation and that she was serious in her desire to help herself. At this point the decrease in body tension made her headaches slightly less severe, but they were still debilitating. Soon after we broke down the deep neck spasm, the headaches began to occur less frequently.

After two months she started coming only once a week, but her tolerance had so increased that the original twenty- to twenty-five-minute treatments were lengthened to thirty to thirty-five minutes. I started to work directly on her face, above and below the eyes, and on the forehead and jaw. The head must be worked on as a total unit in order to have a lasting effect. After another six weeks she experienced only an occasional mild headache.

During the last month we entered the final phase of the treatment, exploring the causes of the tension and correcting postural habits. She began to realize that physically she regularly placed herself in tension-creating positions. She was tall, and in her work she stood leaning over a table; she also wore high-heeled shoes. I suggested that she sit on a stool of an appropriate height, rather than stand, so that she wouldn't have to lean over so much, and I recommended that she wear shoes with flat heels. These changes, which we discussed in the final stages of treatment, helped her to maintain a lower level of tension, and she has remained free of headaches for the past three and a half years.

Ten years ago I received an emergency call from a voice teacher who was in pain. He was giving a party and had suddenly collapsed to the floor in a fetal position, suffering the agonies of an involuntary spasm on his left side. A doctor was called, and he diagnosed the problem as a severe case of sciatica, an affliction that often runs the entire length of the sciatic nerve from the last three lumbar vertebrae and the first three sacral vertebrae through the center of each buttock, down the legs, and branching into the feet. He was given a pain-killer and advised to rest, but the spasms persisted.

When he came to see me, he could hardly walk, sitting was intolerable, and standing was painful. Whenever he dropped his head forward he experienced a shooting pain down his back and into one leg. He was a large-boned, tall man with big muscles. Working on him was like working on two people at once. He was so tense that I was surprised he hadn't had an injury sooner. It come out later that he'd had morning lower-back pain for years. I insisted on seeing him three times a week because his tension was so great that I had to work slowly.

First I concentrated on his neck and upper back, softening the muscles to allow blood to flow more freely. For the next few weeks I worked on his hip and bad leg, slowly increasing the pressure. I asked him to gradually stop taking the pain pills, since they make it difficult to gauge how much treatment an individual can tolerate, as well as give a false sense of well-being that may encourage too much activity. He agreed to stop using them except when in severe pain.

After the upper body had softened sufficiently, I concentrated on the lower back and on the left hip and left leg only, so that the blood would flow into his bad side. I then turned to specific points that would relieve pressure on the sciatic nerve, always careful not to cause pain when working around these areas. After three weeks he felt much better, and encountered pain only when sitting for too long. After two months most of the pain was gone, and I began deep work on residual tension. If I had not completed that last step, the spasms that caused the sciatica surely would have recurred.

Cutting the treatments to two a week, I then systematically broke down tension throughout the body, but held off giving him exercises for a while, because one should be cautious in giving exercises to persons suffering with sciatica.

After a year he no longer needed treatment, and since then I have seen him only rarely, when he was under tremendous pressure. After ten years, he has never had a recurrence of his original sciatica.

Some General Principles of Muscular Therapy

A Functional Approach

The approach in muscular therapy is functional rather than mechanical. The body is seen as a total organism, not an assortment of isolated parts, just as a car would be studied as a complete running unit rather than as a pile of components.

For example, one can approach a sprained ankle mechanically, with injections or massage to the ankle or lower leg. However, if the ankle is seen as part of the total body, a part in need of blood that is not forthcoming due to compensating tensions, then treatment of the muscles of the back, the hip, and the entire leg would be necessary to alleviate pain in the ankle. Thus, the functional approach takes into consideration the relationship of the part to the whole.

Initial Reaction to Treatment

The first important effect of treatment is that the subject gradually becomes aware of tension in specific places. Later, if there is an increase in tension, he becomes conscious of it immediately and considerable discomfort results. Another sign that the body is loosening up is that the neck and back begin to make spontaneous cracking sounds during normal everyday movement. The spine is aligning itself naturally.

Results of Treatment

When layers of tension have been removed through deep massage, clients report that they:

1. Are more aware of their bodies
2. Have improved blood circulation
3. Heal faster
4. Feel more energetic
5. Move with greater ease and freedom
6. Need less sleep
7. No longer feel pain when pressure is applied to muscles
8. Lose weight more easily
9. Generally feel better

Intolerance of Relaxation

People are not used to being relaxed, and even mild relaxation can make them uncomfortable. They must unconsciously assume a tense position, such as crossing their legs or raising their head while lying on the table.

When people have been tense for twenty or thirty years, they're used to it. The muscles are, in a sense, comfortable, and they resist change.

Our bodies change and mend as slowly as plants grow or the earth erodes. Unfortunately, humans are impatient. Anxious to relax, they take hot baths, drugs, and alcohol. They want a cure in minutes. The body must be respected. Most tension is accumulated over a long period of time and should not be dissolved too quickly.

Relaxation Is Achieved Slowly

There is a limit to the degree of relaxation a person can tolerate in a given time in any learning process, just as there is a limit to the amount of information one can learn in a given period of time. The average student cannot assimilate an entire course in French or chemistry in a few weeks; retention will be inadequate, and initially understood information will become confused. And so it is with the body.

When a muscle is relaxed too rapidly it will recontract within a short period of time. Moreover, this contraction often will be more severe. The body clamps down very hard to stop what was thrust upon it too quickly. I've seen this happen to people who come to see me after undergoing accelerated forms of treatment elsewhere. Frequently it takes a long time to undo the damage when the body is pushed too far too fast.

Occasionally the tension returns in a new place, although the individual will not recognize that it is the old tension. The location of a symptom does not tell the whole story, but the pattern in which the tension moves from muscle to muscle often does. To be lasting, relaxation must proceed at a cautious and deliberate pace.

Sometimes during treatment people feel strange itching or tingling sensations. The body is waking up. Often, this is the time to stop that treatment. In the early stages of treatment, work in five- to seven-minute segments, alternated with rest periods to permit assimilation, is the best schedule. During the intervals, a heat treatment with an infrared lamp and gentle breathing and relaxation exercises are advisable. After several weeks, when treatment begins to take effect, the client often falls asleep during the intervals.

Tension-breaking exercises should be done between deep massages. If these exercises are done consistently they permit greater toleration of relaxation.

Anyone who has a rudimentary understanding of the techniques can relax tensions, but constructive muscular therapy should proceed at a certain pace and in a specific order. Each case depends upon the individual and a functional understanding of his problems. Thus, although many of the skills of deep massage are easily mastered, the necessary sensitivity and understanding can be developed only through extensive training and experience. Muscular therapy is a powerful tool, and going slowly minimizes the dangers of that power.

Children and Young Adolescents

Muscular therapy is not advisable for children and young adolescents. Tension in children is primarily emotional in origin—it is armor. This is beyond the scope of muscular therapy. If you plan to learn the deep-massage methods in this book, do not practice them on children sixteen or younger. It is also important to realize, in dealing with young people or adults, that if you suspect they have any skin, muscle, or bone disease, deep massage is also not indicated. If you have any doubts, it is a good idea to ask the person to consult his or her doctor before you proceed.

Salt Baths

Occasionally add two cups of sea or rock salt to your bath. The salt facilitates relaxation by increasing the tension-drawing effect of the water. If you've swum both in oceans and in lakes, you may have noticed the effect of salt water. The ocean salt water makes you feel pleasantly tired. When you emerge from a fresh-water lake, usually you are invigorated.

Shower Massage

The shower massage is a showerhead pipe attachment that releases pulsating streams of water in speeds ranging from slow to fast. The pressure and the speed are regulated by faucet control. The apparatus functions as a regular shower and is easily attached.

The shower massage is an effective tool for relaxation. It is good for sore muscles and helps increase blood circulation.

Use it as hard as you can take it in the fast pulsating position. Direct it especially to the forehead, top and back of the head, neck, fingertips, hands, arms, down the full extent of the trunk, legs, feet, and even the toes, heels, and soles. Keep it on aching or fatigued areas for long periods of time.

Go Soak Your Head

Water has long been known for its therapeutic qualities. We have seen how a bath or a shower can be helpful, but when time is short, soaking your head in water can often have similar beneficial effects. To clear that foggy feeling in the head or a mild tension headache, or if you're tired but must keep going, fill a sink with cool to cold water and submerge your head. You can also stick your head under the faucet and allow the water to run over it with some force for three or four minutes. This procedure stimulates circulation in the head and scalp, makes the head feel clearer, and makes you more alert. Just remember to come up for air.

Sauna and Steam

Both the sauna and the steam room can help you relax. The sauna is slightly more effective, especially for those who tend to be claustrophobic. (However, if you have heart trouble, you should check with your doctor as a precautionary measure.) In a sauna, dry heat makes you perspire. Thus, the moisture comes from inside the body. In a steam room, the moisture is part perspiration and part condensed steam. In either case, you can sit, lie flat, or elevate your legs (see page 15). Be sure to breathe deeply. Your first exposures to sauna and steam should be brief. Begin with two-to-five-minute sessions and slowly increase exposure to a maximum of twenty to thirty minutes. Exposure to these types of heat is relaxing and beneficial, but build your tolerance for them slowly. A bucket of cold water and a face cloth to squeeze over your head can help prevent headache. If you're feeling claustrophobic, place the wet face cloth over your face and breathe through it. However, if the experience becomes too unpleasant, leave immediately and take a cool shower. You can go back and forth repeatedly between a cool shower and a sauna or steam room.

Deep Breathing

Breathing helps the body to relax. By introducing oxygen and removing carbon dioxide, it assists the body's repair process. Many people breathe shallowly, using less than twenty per cent of their actual lung capacity. Their ability to heal is thus greatly diminished.

In breathing the diaphragm moves down, the chest expands slightly to create a partial vacuum, and air rushes into the lungs. People often don't understand that when the chest cavity expands during inhalation, muscles contract. The relaxing of the chest muscles comes only during exhalation. Therefore, proper exhaling is especially important to relaxation.

Many people breathe abdominally. Breathing with the abdomen by moving it mechanically encourages chest tension and diaphragmatic weakness. During proper breathing, the abdominal area and the chest will move only slightly. Most movement takes place just below the chest in the area of the diaphragm.

Try deep breathing. If it causes dizziness, return

Chapter 3 · GENERAL BODY CARE

Deep massage is only one aspect of muscular therapy. Body care is another part of the treatment. In this chapter we will consider many aspects of daily body care that are essential but often neglected. Without critical evaluation of and re-education about how we routinely care for our bodies, the positive effects of muscular therapy cannot be maintained or maximized.

It is a common assumption that if a body does not function properly, it can be fixed. People look on their bodies as machines that science can alter and repair. The fallacy here is in assuming that the body is a mechanical system and that its malfunctions can be easily traced and fixed. The body is a living organism, not a machine. It has emotional as well as physical components. Once out of order, it will not necessarily respond to treatment. Don't take chances with your body. Sound daily maintenance is worth a score of dramatic treatments. Take care of your body now and you may not have to worry in the future.

Your body cries out for help in many ways. It sends out signals in the form of stiffness, pain, exhaustion, and colds, to name only a few. Listen to your body's messages and take action to find and correct the causes of these danger signals.

The following do-it-yourself body-care techniques are simple, brief, and inexpensive. Add as many as you can to your daily routine. They may save you a visit to your doctor or muscular therapist.

Baths

One of the most important, easiest, and most enjoyable body-care techniques is a nightly half-hour bath.* The water should be comfortably warm but

* If you have heart trouble, you should check with your doctor first.

not too hot, although tolerance to heat varies from person to person. The water should be pleasant to get into and not cause you to perspire while in the bath. Extreme heat perpetuates tension. A hot bath dilates the superficial vessels of the skin, thus diverting blood from the muscles to the skin surface, which can lower blood pressure. This makes the heart pump harder and faster and creates a slow, general counter-contraction in the muscles. The result is a depletion of energy, and the ensuing weakness often is interpreted as a relaxed state. A warm bath, on the other hand, draws tension from the body. The gentle

buoyancy of the water has a relaxing effect and clean skin breathes better with unclogged pores.

It is helpful to concentrate on relaxing the body while in the bath. Don't neglect the head. Submerge yourself several times so that only your eyes, nose, and mouth are above water. Rub the skin firmly with a stiff brush or Loofa sponge to stimulate circulation at the skin surface.

to normal breathing. Note how many deep breathes you can take before you become dizzy. Deep breaths and greater respiration will increase your ability to relax. You can practice deep breathing while sitting, lying down, or walking your dog. Do it once or twice a day, taking ten or twenty deep, long breaths. Don't strain or push, and concentrate on a full exhalation. (See chapter 6 for specific breathing exercises.)

How You Eat

How you eat can be as important as what you eat. Some people gulp their food, hardly chewing at all. There are many reasons for improper eating habits. Some people feel that eating is unimportant and rush through it. Others, who eat by themselves, hurry because they are lonely. Many eat fast out of nervousness or habit.

If you chew your food thoroughly until it is liquefied, the stomach and the intestines have less work in breaking down the food particles and digestion is more efficient. When you swallow a piece of food whole, the stomach has to work longer to break down the mass so that digestive enzymes can thoroughly permeate the food particles.

Chewing twenty-five to fifty times is advisable for each mouthful of food. If you follow this procedure you will eat more slowly, get full faster, and probably consume less. Thorough chewing is not easy, because after ten chews you may find that there is no food left in your mouth. You'll have to concentrate on using the back of your tongue to keep the food in your mouth, until it becomes a habit. One method is to put down your fork after each bite and actually count the number of times you chew.

Sleep

During the day the body uses energy. A good night's sleep is necessary to restore energy and repair cells. If you sleep a reasonable amount of time— five to seven hours, or eight if your daily work is strenuous or draining—and wake up feeling fatigued, you may have a medical problem about which you should consult your doctor, or you may be suffering from excess tension.

If you need much more than eight hours of sleep to feel rested, your body probably is tense and therefore needs the extra time to repair itself.

Tension can also prevent you from falling asleep in the five to fifteen minutes needed by most normal, healthy adults. To help sleep better:

1. Leave enough time for a full night's sleep.
2. Don't eat or drink before going to bed.
3. Take a warm bath to help you relax.
4. Do some of the eye exercises recommended in chapter 6.

Vacations

Taking a vacation at least once a year is a good idea, although two or three times a year is even better. Vacation as often as you possibly can. Try not to stay home when you take a vacation. If you live in the city, go where the air is clean. Even if you live in an environmentally clean place, you should give yourself a relaxing change of scene.

Tight Clothes

In an effort to appear stylish and thin, people often wear clothes that are too small. These garments create constant pressure on the abdomen, waist, lower back, and, indirectly, the diaphragm. If your belt is too tight, it causes the muscles of the abdomen to contract, and this results in tension. When you try to look like something you're not, by pulling your shoulders back or sucking your stomach in or forcing your body into positions that are unnatural, you further compound muscular tension.

Fortunately, the tension-causing girdle is not worn as commonly as it once was. Constant wearing of a girdle prevents the abdominal and buttock muscles from functioning properly and causes them to weaken and sag.

Shoes

The healthiest and most comfortable shoes are those that are shaped like the foot. They should be moderately squared off at the toes. If the shoes have pointed toes that squeeze the feet, the toes will be pushed together and the feet will become tense. If you observe people's feet at the beach, you'll see many sets of toes jammed together from too-narrow shoes or hammered down from shoes that are too short. Physically distorted feet frequently are the result of poorly fitting shoes.

The selection of children's shoes is important because their feet grow so quickly. Platform shoes are especially dangerous and totally unnatural. The Association of Podiatrists issued a statement on the frequency of accidents due to platform shoes. Shoes with very high heels are bad for both the feet and the legs, since they place them at unnatural angles. Similarly, the new popular shoes with the heel lower than the toe are also extremely destructive for most people. They shift the weight unnaturally back to the heel and place stress on the Achilles tendon, calf muscles, and lower back. If you try to run in negative-heel shoes, you probably will feel pain in your legs. A low heel, however, does no damage.

Sneakers and soft shoes are best, since man was meant to walk on the soft earth. Shoes shouldn't hold you up; muscles should do that job. A rule of thumb might be: the less and softer shoe, the better. Choose a shoe that allows the foot to bend in any direction and provides complete freedom of movement. As the hardness of the ground increases, so should the softness of our shoes. If the sole is too hard, try two Dr. Scholl's inner soles, sized to the length of your foot, in each shoe.

Beds

Sleep on a firm mattress, the harder the better. Soft beds giving little or no support can be destructive to the body, especially the back and neck.

Chairs

The best kind of chair provides a few inches of padding on a firm foundation and allows your feet to rest firmly on the ground. It should be of a height that permits your legs to slope down slightly from the hip to the knee, with the lower leg perpendicular to the floor. Different people require chairs of varying heights. The proper height is generally the distance from the bottom of your heel to the back of your knee when you are in a sitting position. A low chair is bad for the lower back; it tips the pelvis backward. A chair that is too high is not as dangerous, although it can hamper circulation from the knees down. Chair arms should be sufficiently low to permit the shoulders to relax and should not raise them artificially. The depth of the chair should match the distance from behind the knee to the back of the hip. A shallow chair is not harmful, but one that is too deep encourages you to lean back and slump the lower back.

Tables and Desks

Tables and desks that are too high force you to raise your shoulders. If they are too low, you'll lean over and strain your lower back. The proper height for a table or desk depends on the length of your

*Those with lower back problems should always place a little pillow in the small of their back. Special Posture Curve™ Lumbar Cushions are available from Relaxation Tools, Inc. Box 1045, New York, N.Y. 10025.

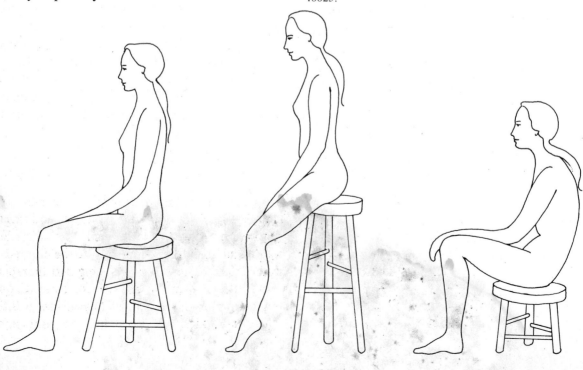

trunk and arms. If the table comes up to your elbow when you are sitting with arms bent, it is the proper height.

Propping your feet up when you sit at a desk may feel good, but it adds strain and pressure to your lower back. Keep your feet on the ground.

Before deciding upon your table or desk height, be sure your chair height is correct.

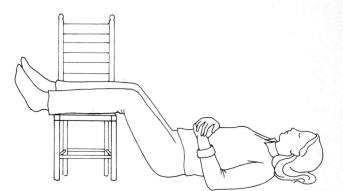

a chair for five to ten minutes once or twice a day. Be sure not to lock the knees and to keep them slightly bent.

When you are standing your blood must defy gravity to return to your heart. By elevating your legs, you help your blood circulate. This exercise is especially helpful if you spend a good deal of time on your feet, since it encourages blood circulation in the legs. While elevating your legs, you can read, talk on the phone, or do anything you like. If you have a heart condition, however, check with your doctor, since this exercise is recommended for some heart conditions but is dangerous for others.

Exercise and Health

Exercise enhances blood circulation, increases respiration, maintains strong muscles, and increases the strength of the heart. To be effective, exercise must be done regularly. Irregular exercise, particularly too much too quickly, can be harmful. Adherence to a schedule is important. The right exercises for you depend on your body's structure, needs, and problems. People with tense legs shouldn't run for exercise, although it might be an ideal sport for a loose-legged person. Everyone should find an activity he enjoys and do it regularly.

Swimming

Swimming is the best exercise because it uses almost every muscle in the body and increases respiration. Moreover, the body is weightless in water and therefore is unlikely to be injured. And water is, as we have seen, relaxing and therapeutic.

When I say swim to relax, I don't mean competitive swimming. Have a good time. Float a little, do a few laps, kick on your back, on your stomach,

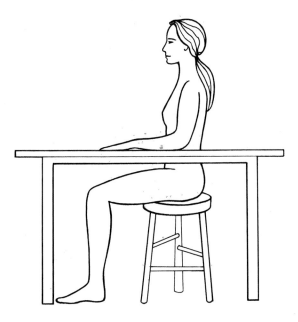

Elevating the Legs

Tension in the legs can be alleviated by lying on the back and resting the legs against a wall at a forty-five-degree angle, or resting the lower legs on

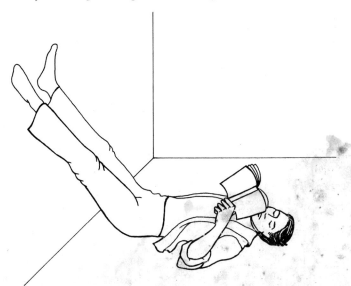

submerge your body in deep water and stretch in all directions. If you're feeling creative, do an underwater dance. The breast stroke is especially good exercise because it uses all muscles equally. Swimming daily or two or three times a week will do wonders, but if you have lower-back problems, avoid diving.

Exercises to Kill Yourself

Exercises that are too difficult and cause you to strain are harmful to your body. Similarly, excessive repetition of the same movement and exercises done too quickly are destructive. Many people think exercise isn't doing any good unless the sweat is dripping and they are dying with pain. Good exercise should be pleasurable.

Weight lifting is one of the worst forms of exercise for muscles. It strains, overworks, and develops big, bulging, tight muscles. The most unhealthy muscles I have seen were developed through weight lifting. A man in his early forties, who lifted weights weekly at his gym, came to me recently complaining of cramps in his arms and legs. After I worked with him for several weeks with no noticeable improvement, he admitted that he was not doing the recommended exercise and body-care techniques, but felt compelled to continue his weight lifting. He thought exercise had to be vigorous and painful in order to be good for him. He made it impossible for me to help him by perpetuating the unhealthy condition of his muscles.

Travel Care

The fatigue, tension, and possible pain of travel can be prevented. One of the main causes of these problems is lack of movement. As we've said before, muscle activity enhances circulation. When you sit for a long time, your legs and feet may fall asleep, cramp, or swell, as a result of insufficient circulation. Some people get headaches, others feel foggy. Lower-back pain and discomfort in the upper back and shoulders are also common.

Crossing time zones disturbs the body's sleeping, working, and eating habits. Readjusting takes time, but meanwhile, keeping relaxed can minimize problems caused by travel.

Travel-Care Kit

When traveling by car, keep a tennis ball and cork in the glove compartment. On an extended trip, take a block and pen flashlight to use when you stop for the night. The use of various-size balls, the cork, the block, and the penlight, are body-care techniques, which are fully detailed in the exercise chapter. These techniques are easy and can make travel a more relaxing experience. If you're traveling with a friend, you might want to learn the chair-massage techniques described in Lesson 13.

In a Car

Don't abuse your body just because you are on the go. Travel and discomfort are not synonymous. In a car the following suggestions can be helpful.

1. Stop frequently, at least once every hour. Get out of the car and walk around. Shake your arms and legs vigorously. Kick them in all directions. Do some shoulder rolls, described on page 35. Get your body moving after a period of enforced inactivity.

2. Try placing a small pillow behind your lower back. It can give extra support to prevent stress in that area.

3. If you are not the driver and the car has reclinable seats, push yours all the way back from time to time. Put your feet up if you can. Vary your position as often as possible.

4. Use the ball techniques for the sitting position in the upper, center, and lower back areas and in the backs of the hips as shown on pages 38–40. Work with the tightest areas.

5. If you are the driver, avoid holding your head and neck tightly. Without taking your eyes from the road, let your head drop slightly forward. Rock your head back and forth so that you sense a dynamic balance of your head on your neck rather than a tight position. If you are a passenger, you can do the full head-drop exercise as shown on page 33.

6. Do facial exercises to keep yourself alert. Raise and lower your eyebrows, flex your nose, stick your tongue out as far as it will go, stretch your mouth wide open and then close it tightly, push your chin forward and backward forcefully. Be inventive.

7. To encourage blood circulation in the shoulders and arms, raise, drop, and circle the shoulders. See chapter 6 for more-detailed instructions. If you are

a passenger, clench and unclench your fists. While driving, squeeze and release the wheel alternately.

8. To stimulate circulation in the lower back, tip your pelvis forward and back, allowing your trunk to follow. Do the pelvic-release exercise; squeeze and relax the buttock muscles. Keeping the rest of your body fairly stationary, move your rib cage from side to side. Alternately stretch up out of your seat and slump down.

9. A car is a great place to yell when the windows are rolled up. Yelling and singing increases breathing and releases tension in the upper body.

10. Do the cork technique shown on page 32.

11. If you're not at the wheel, remove your shoes and move your feet a lot. Stretch your toes and curl them, and rotate your ankles and flex them.

Never drive when you're tired. Not only is it dangerous, it can create enormous tension. Take along your favorite food, but go easy on junk food.

In a Plane, Bus, or Train

In a plane or train, take advantage of the greater freedom of movement. Don't sit like a vegetable. Explore. Keep active and interested, and you'll feel better. The following techniques and exercises may be helpful.

1. Remove your shoes.

2. Loosen your belt. (Don't wear tight garments when traveling.)

3. Try to take a short walk every half hour.

4. Use the chair-ball techniques in your seat.

5. Try heel raises while standing. Tighten your buttocks and straighten your knees before you raise your heels. Then come down and relax. Repeat a few times.

6. Try the metatarsal-lift exercise shown on page 43. Pull your toes back toward your head, then stretch them apart in the air, and repeat.

7. Do the squat exercise, holding on to a seat as you squat down and come back up.

8. If there is room, stretch out the whole length of the seat for a period of time and lie down.

9. Elevate your legs whenever possible.

10. If permitted, get off at every stop and walk around.

The various exercises and movements described in the car section are also helpful on planes, trains, and buses. Try facial, shoulder, and feet exercises. Use a pillow, and carry your favorite foods if possible. Keep moving as much as you can. You may feel funny doing these exercises, since people will look at you curiously, but when you see how much better you feel, you won't care.

Chapter 4 · DRUGS

We live in a drug culture. There is a drug for every ill and a taker for every drug. Sometimes drugs are necessary; many times they are not. Too often drugs are taken as a matter of course. People take pills to sleep, to wake up, to relieve a headache, to study, to relax, and even to have fun. While some drugs in appropriate circumstances can help, under other conditions they can interfere with the body's natural functions. Though harmful side effects of some drugs are well known, many people continue to take them. And beyond these recognized dangers are a host of subtle and cumulative side effects, some of which have not yet been discovered.

I am not against all drugs. Antibiotics, pain-killers, and anti-inflammatory drugs, to name only a few, have their rightful place. I am, however, against the use of drugs simply because they're available or acceptable.

Pills are not necessary for sleeping, waking, studying, or dispelling headaches. These ailments are often the results of problems that can be treated without drugs. Sometimes they are medical problems, but more often they are the results of muscular tension. Some drugs will release tension temporarily, some will diminish the intensity of the symptoms, but in most instances, drugs only camouflage the symptoms and encourage the body to build up a craving for drugs. They may also produce side effects. For instance, birth-control pills alter natural functions in a woman's body. They produce a state of pseudo-pregnancy, changing the natural hormonal cycle. In my experience of working with women who take birth-control pills, I have noticed that physical sensation is diminished or altered, the healing rate is decreased, and certain pain states such as headache are more persistent. There are many other known side effects.

Pill taking alters and to some extent deadens body feeling. Use drugs only as a last resort and only when prescribed by a doctor.

Alcohol

We live in a world in which an occasional social drink is hard to avoid. Although an occasional drink can sometimes help the body to relax temporarily, large amounts of alcohol are definitely unhealthy. Recent medical studies have shown that even very small amounts of alcohol can damage the liver, heart, and brain. These amounts vary from person to person, but they do have cumulative effects.

Alcohol can directly damage muscles. In experiments conducted with individuals consuming about a fifth of whiskey a day for four weeks and a nutritionally sound diet, muscle-tissue biopsies examined under an electron microscope revealed "profound damaging changes."* Dr. Leigh Segal, of the University of California at Davis, has found signs of

* Arthur Fisher, "Sober, Yet Driving Too Much," *New York Times Magazine*, May 18, 1975, p. 72.

abnormal heart-muscle tissue in rats that were on a relatively low alcohol dose.†

Abstinence from alcohol is best, but small amounts are not seriously detrimental. In terms of the effect on muscular tension, a little alcohol is preferable to marijuana, heroin, LSD, or tranquilizers.

Smoking

Smoking is often an effort to relieve tension in the mouth and jaw. In my work I have not found it to interfere with treatment of tension, but, since smoking is obviously detrimental to health, I always encourage people to stop. However, some people get a great deal of pleasure out of it and should stop only when they really want to. Many find that they do want to stop smoking and that it is easier after muscular-therapy treatment.

Hard Drugs

In this category I include heroin, opium, cocaine, and amphetamines (speed). Although these drugs differ in many respects, the damage they do, from a muscular point of view, is similar. All are toxic in that they destroy cells. The muscles contract severely and the entire body becomes rigid. Interest in sex disappears, especially when heroin or speed is used.

Heroin is disastrous for the body. It is obvious from the withdrawal process—physical tremors, vomiting, chills, fever, involuntary spasms, insomnia, weeping, anxiety, goose flesh, hot flashes, high blood pressure, anorexia (loss of appetite), and loss of body weight—that heroin affects the entire body and all its functions.

Many heroin users cannot stand to be touched. A young male singer came to me for treatment. He was tight from head to toe and laughed no matter what part of his body I touched. He said he had a peculiar, ticklish feeling. If I persisted in touching him, he would lift his shoulder, roll off the table, and even grab my hands to stop me. This peculiar ticklishness results from tremendous tension. In this case it took many months to get the client to the point where he could tolerate treatment. He was not a heavy heroin user, but he did indulge in it several times a month. Although I encouraged him to discontinue use of the drug, he did so only for short periods of

† *Ibid.*, p. 65.

time. As a result, his body remained tight and he was never able to attain good muscular health.

Although the body does become addicted to heroin, in most cases the dependence is more emotional than physical. Users who are jailed can kick the habit in a week or less, but frequently they return to the drug when released, whether after a period of months or of years.

A woman who was addicted to speed came to me complaining of shoulder, back, and leg pain. Her body was totally rigid. When I suggested she stop taking speed, she said she wasn't addicted to it and could quit easily. After four or five weeks of treatment and much improvement, she started to complain that her condition wasn't improving fast enough. She soon stopped the treatments and returned to the drug to which she thought she was not addicted.

Soft or Hallucinogenic Drugs

By soft or hallucinogenic drugs, I mean marijuana, hashish, and LSD. During the past fifteen years the use of these drugs in the United States has exploded into a cultural phenomenon. While appearing to offer freedom and valuable new insights, they have actually done much damage.

In my experience, the soft-drug user contracts muscles chiefly in the head, eyes, neck, and shoulders. It is as if all the energy were sucked out of the body and placed in the head and brain and held there. The eyes of the soft-drug user often have a faraway look, like eyes of stone. "Stoned" is an accurate description.

Marijuana, hashish, and LSD often produce reactions similar to the behavior of the schizoid person. Perceptions can be distorted so that the individual senses the opposite of what is actually happening in his body. I see this very often in my own practice. Because of this reaction, it is difficult to explain to the users the destructiveness of the drugs. For example, a client may come in high and tell me how relaxed he is, but when I touch him with half of the pressure I used the previous week, he reacts violently. He will tell me that the pain was intense and may ask if I was leaning on him with my elbows. The client thinks he is relaxed, but in reality his body is tighter than before. Soft drugs deaden body feeling.

Users of soft drugs get the opposite of what they

desire. In search of cosmic connection and freedom, they enslave themselves. They have less sensation rather than more, they increase their tension rather than reduce it, and they turn their energy off instead of on.

Marijuana stays in the bloodstream for at least eight days, and it takes months for the residual effects to disappear completely. "Marijuana contains substances . . . stored in body tissues, including the brain, for weeks and months, in the same manner as DDT. . . . Anyone using marijuana more than once a week cannot be drug free.* Thus, one joint every two weeks is heavy usage.

As I have said, marijuana causes the muscles of the face, head, neck, and shoulders to contract. It especially affects the muscles around the eyes and the occipital muscles, which are at the back of the head. This can be felt by the therapist when he applies pressure to those muscles. These parts of a marijuana user's body are usually extremely sensitive to pressure. The speed of pupillary contraction is also greatly reduced and sometimes the eyes become light-sensitive. It is impossible to release a significant amount of tension in the marijuana user unless he stops using the drug.

Some time ago an eighteen-year-old girl came to see me. She complained of severe headaches that lasted over a three-month period before subsiding for one month. This pattern had persisted for three years. I noticed that her body was fairly relaxed, but her head muscles were contracted, and her eyes were tight and moved slowly. According to my analysis, her condition could be caused by a severe accident, neurological disorder or brain tumor, or drug use.

She ruled out an accident and told me that EEGs and a complete neurological examination had been negative. When I questioned her extensively, she told me that she had used marijuana and LSD about three or four years ago, but had never connected them with her headaches. She now realized that her last LSD trip, a particularly bad one, occurred a month before the headaches began. She was able to understand that the drug had triggered the headache syn-

drome. After several months of treatment, muscular therapy was able to diminish the intensity and frequency of the headaches. After a year the problem was completely gone.

I once treated a female dancer who had suffered for many years with a variety of pains. Treatment alleviated the pains in her neck, back, and legs, but periodically she would come in with a new pain or a recurrence of an old one. I asked her about her leisure and work habits, and about drugs although her type of tension didn't fit into the drug-user mold. She said she didn't use drugs—"only pot." She smoked marijuana about once a week with friends. When she traced the history of her drug use and the appearance of pain in the previous weeks, the pattern became clear. Every time she smoked, a pain appeared the next day. When she stopped smoking, the backsliding stopped and the results of the treatment lasted.

In this case, drugs were not the cause of the problem, but they did interfere with maintaining the results of treatment. This girl was one of many who think of pot not as a dangerous drug but as a harmless substance.

A filmmaker came to see me with severe pains in the back of his head and right shoulder. He was moderately tense elsewhere, but the greatest tension was concentrated in his head and shoulder. I told him the marijuana he smoked two or three times a week would make the treatment very difficult, but he continued to smoke. Over a period of months he improved slowly from treatments three times a week. He was diligent in the exercises and body-care techniques I gave him, but was adamant about continuing to smoke pot. As his confidence in the treatment increased, I made a deal with him: if he stopped smoking for three months, I would complete the treatment in that time and thereby save him the cost of a longer course of treatment. This represented a challenge to him, and he stopped using drugs and progressed quickly.

One day after he had been free of pain in the head, neck, and shoulder for some time, he reported that for four days he had been in violent pain of the type he used to have. After examining his muscles, I asked him if he had begun smoking again. He laughed and said, "I wanted to see if you were right. I couldn't believe it was true." He said that as soon as he had

---

* Gabriel G. Nahas, M.D., Ph.D., "Effects of Marijuana Use in Man," *Private Practice* (January 1975): 59. For the most extensive scientific information on marijuana, see Gabriel G. Nahas, *Keep Off the Grass* (New York: Reader's Digest Press, 1976).

smoked, he had felt his head go into contraction, and the pain had continued for four days. He hasn't smoked for several years now, and his health has remained good. Marijuana users rarely feel the contraction he experienced, because that contraction usually happens gradually over a period of months. Only someone with a relaxed and sensitive body will perceive the contraction after usage, because the difference in a relaxed body is dramatic.

Research statistics can be used to uphold any point of view, but my own observations in fifteen years of work with tension problems have convinced me that drugs, both hard and soft, are harmful to the body and its natural functions.

Chapter 5 · DANCERS AND DANCING

Dancers have found muscular therapy particularly effective. They are extremely interested in their bodies, and do not hesitate to seek help when they need it. Dancing can be a wonderful profession. People begin dancing for their own pleasure because it is fun. But the road to becoming a professional dancer can be a very difficult one. Many of my clients are dancers and I feel a special affection for them and for their art.

Most dancers incur at least one serious injury before they reach the age of twenty-five. Knee pains, strained tendons, and pulled and spastic muscles are so common that dancers are forced to accept them as a normal part of their work.

In fact, I have found that dancers, generally, have more trouble with their bodies than any other professional group, with the exception of athletes. As time passes they take their injuries for granted. Unfortunately, many have learned little about their bodies and how to take care of them.

Most injuries are in some way related to chronic tension. Tense muscles are more likely to be injured, just as dry brittle twigs are more easily snapped than supple green ones. A soft pliable body tends to bend. It can suffer severe twists and blows without injury. In order for the dancer to protect her* body—her indispensable and irreplaceable asset—she must learn

---

* I have used the pronouns *her* and *she* in this section because the majority of dancers are women.

to remain free of excessive tension. If she works under constant stress and makes no effort to alleviate her tension, injury is unavoidable.

Some tension is residual. It existed in the dancer's body long before she started dancing. Much, however, is current—a function of poor training and sometimes self-destructive attitudes. I think some people take up dance in an effort to break out of tense bodies. I do know that many people study dance to relieve their tension. Instead, the training often increases tension. Beginning dancers are usually overenthusiastic and work without regard for the needs and signals of their own bodies. Often the importance of relaxation and gradual, methodical work is not understood in many dance schools, and beginners find themselves building more tension.

There are many sensitive and knowledgeable teachers in dance schools and universities across the country who are highly competent and do an excellent job of teaching, while many others train tension into their pupils because they lack a good teacher-training background. Many fine dancers just become teachers without realizing that teaching is a profession that requires separate skills.

Young dancers often work in pained silence, despite their injuries and fatigue, without realizing that it could be different. They learn the pain-school philosophy, the belief that it is necessary and profitable to work in pain. They come to believe that to work in pain builds strength and stamina. They see that many of the successful dancers whom they emulate regularly suffer debilitating injuries. The maxim "the show must go on" is taken into the class. There is a myth that a missed class can never be made up. Students feel guilty if they want to stop in the middle of a class, and force themselves to continue to the end.

Gentle exertion beyond your limit does build strength and endurance. More than that, however, results in damaged tissue and increased tension. Gross overwork is no more constructive than a good beating. Developing strength is a constructive process involving increased contractile ability and growth of the muscles. If we remember that the body uses pain to signal that something is wrong, there can be no justification for working long after the signal to stop.

A young dancer who was an adherent of the pain-school philosophy came to me for treatment. She complained of lower-back pain, shooting pains in her legs, and spasms in her calves and feet. The pains kept her awake at night, and when she finally got to sleep she would sometimes wake up screaming from cramps. She lay stiffly on my table, breathing shallowly.

She had been dancing just three years but was a hard worker, and she had already auditioned for a major company and understood that she had almost been accepted. Her training and discipline had paid off, but she failed to see that it was precisely her overambitious work that was causing her trouble.

"It's so horribly unfair," she complained to me. "The better I get as a dancer, the worse I feel. Maybe it's psychosomatic—a death wish or something." The only thing wrong with her mind was lack of sound judgment. "I don't know what to do," she continued. "One of my teachers suggested working harder, so I picked up another technique class."

"So now you are taking two technique classes," I said, "of different types, of course."

"No, now I'm taking four, all ballet. I injure so easily that I need to build my strength, but since my interest is ballet, I see no point in studying jazz or modern."

She was wincing so much that it was difficult to work on her legs and still continue the conversation. I sat down next to the table.

"I understand you very well," I said. "Two technique classes and you improve twice as fast. Four, and again you double your progress. Well, four classes take only six hours a day. Why don't you take eight classes a day, or twelve?"

She thought I was serious. "Well, there's a point of diminishing returns," she answered. "After four classes . . ."

"That's right," I said. "But the point of diminishing returns is after *one technique class per day!* More than that, and you start losing ground. Your tension increases and the spasms that wake you up at night are aggravated by too many hours of work and too much repetition of the same exercises. You have no business taking even two ballet-technique classes a day, especially when you're suffering so acutely. You injure easily not because you lack strength but because you're always tense. And technique classes are no aid to relaxation.

"You have to realize that dancing is hard work. In three hours of dancing you work more of your muscles harder than a waitress on an eight-hour shift or a baseball player in a day's practice. You can't dance all day as though you were working at an ordinary job.

"You're exceptionally strong. If you were able to relax your body you could eventually take two classes a day, but no more than one ballet or modern-technique class and one other class—character dance, adagio, or repertory, perhaps."

My client stopped dancing for two weeks and I worked every other day on her spastic muscles. At first it was grueling work for both of us, but gradually her muscles began to soften. Her discomfort subsided as the acute spasms did. Her muscles gradually became less contracted and it was easier for her to sleep. By the end of her layoff, the tension had been noticeably eased and she was surprised—and delighted—that her jumps and turns were better and she could lift her legs higher than before. "It blew my mind," she told me later. "I got more from a two-week vacation than I would have gotten from working every day." She also found, once her tension was reduced, that she was getting more pleasure from dancing.

She went back to work and scheduled only one technique class a day, but she found it hard to discard her old attitudes. If a class did not go perfectly, she took a second. "My pirouettes were off today," she would explain, and if it was not her pirouettes it was something else. One day she came to my office on crutches after her second technique class. She had severely strained the cruciate ligament in her knee. It set her back six months.

She should have stayed after class to work alone on her pirouettes, not taken an extra class. If she had gone to the studio early for warm-ups, and stayed late, the one-and-a-half-hour class would have been extended by an hour and she would have been satisfied with her day's work, without subjecting herself to too much damaging repetition. This is what I recommend to dancers who insist on more than one technique class a day.

It is a good habit to get to class early and warm up fully before class begins. In many dance classes, the beginning exercises are not gradual enough or they involve severe stretching. Since it is difficult for an instructor to give the exercises that are ideal for each member of the class, every dancer must learn what specific exercises are best for her body. It is essential to warm up fully before a class, and warm-up exercises should build on each other extremely gradually. I recommend working on the floor for at least twenty minutes before each class. Start by lying on the floor and breathing. Shake your feet with gradually increasing force, warming and loosening the joints without subjecting them to stress. Gently loosen all the joints by flexing and extending, paying particular attention to the ankles, knees, and hips. Do the exercises you have found best for your own body. There is a sample dance warm-up at the end of the exercise chapter, on pages 48–9. Be fully warmed up before putting pressure on your joints by standing up to exercise, and dress warmly enough for the studio you are working in.

Professional dancers, when performing or in rehearsal, often find little provision for adequate warm-ups. It is your own responsibility to be fully warmed up each time you work, even for a small part. Only you will be laid off if you are injured. When demonstrating movements, teachers should remember to mark sequences rather than do them full out if they have not warmed up thoroughly before class. Many dance teachers create problems for themselves by working too hard and giving more classes than they would ever ask their students to take. Even if you have a tiny part in a show or a single difficult step to demonstrate in class, you can hurt yourself if your body is cold. You can also pay for this mistake for a long time.

Some dance injuries occur suddenly and for no apparent reason. You land from a jump and your ankle gives a jolt of pain. Soon it swells, and you are forced to take a week off. Yet, the step was ordinary, and you can never figure out why it happened.

Perhaps one of your knees always hurts but you can't remember when it started. It is often painful in the morning, but sometimes the pain subsides after a few hours, while at other times it plagues you for days. Chronic injuries sometimes seem strange because their fluctuations have no apparent cause.

In the first instance, the jump only acted as the trigger for the injury; in the second, the problem developed gradually. Both injuries were caused by excessive tension and/or poor alignment, often compounded by inferior training. The dance instructor, especially one who works with beginners, must correct many subtle errors. This requires an expert eye and a deep instinctive understanding of the way the body works. In many cases, a mistake that is serious enough to cause injury may show itself only as an unnaturally tense muscle or a knee that is not quite centered over the foot.

It is worth emphasizing that most dance teachers are extremely honest and well meaning. They have a deep love for dance and a sincere desire to help their students. However, they often do not understand how the body is structured and how this structure can move most easily and without damage. If I am critical of dance teachers generally, it is because of my years of treating dancers who have subjected themselves to damaging training. I believe that dancers must understand that some teachers will not train them safely or correctly, and I hope that my work will help toward this end.

It is important for the dancer to develop effective methods of dealing with excess tension, to improve her breathing, and to maintain good body alignment. These can be decisive in preventing injuries. Of primary importance are the dancer's methods of relieving tension. Proper warm-up, nightly warm baths, elevating the legs, and other appropriate body-care techniques should be an essential part of the dancer's regime.

The beauty of dancing is to allow the impulses of movement to flow unimpeded through the body. Forcing movement stops the flow and creates tension. When you find yourself beginning to push and strain, stop.

Proper breathing while dancing is essential. It keeps the body relaxed, prevents you from tiring fast, and helps the flow of movement. Since dancing is hard work, the body requires more oxygen than it does for normal activity. A good teacher stresses the importance of breathing and relaxing while moving and often goes through combinations of movements to show the student when to breathe in and when to exhale, just as he might demonstrate the placement of the arms. Breathing can and should be analyzed, although it is important to note that breathing varies slightly according to lung capacity. Many dancers, instead of breathing more to increase their oxygen supply while dancing, hardly breathe at all. Unconsciously they take a breath, hold it through several steps, let it out, and then gasp for more air. Their movements are choppy, disconnected, and have no flow. Breathing deeply releases tension and is an important part of dance training.

Good body alignment places the greatest stress where the body can most easily absorb it. If the joints are out of alignment, effort is wasted and movements are jerky and forced. The body must be well centered. The chest should sit squarely over the pelvis, not be pushed forward or sunken. The head should be balanced directly over the trunk. Thus the center of gravity passes directly through the middle of the body. Similarly, the legs, hip joints, knees, and ankles must all be in line with one another so that the lines of force pass through the central axis of the legs and into the center of the feet. If this does not occur, stress is put on areas not designed to withstand it, like knee and ankle joints, and the likelihood of injury is increased. Tension often creates poor alignment, and poor alignment creates additional tension. Both waste energy.

Good alignment and balance can be maintained by keeping the eyes properly focused. You must know where you are in space. The drifting of eye focus often causes injuries by breaking the concentration on what the body is doing. People with this problem often have a vacant, faraway expression in their eyes. When you are dancing well, you are aware of the space around you and your relationship to it. Getting out of touch with your environment can be dangerous when landing from a difficult jump or catching your partner.*

Here are some common misconceptions about how to achieve good dance posture:

1. *Squeezing the buttocks*: This breaks the energy flow between the upper and lower parts of the body and causes unnecessary tension in the abdomen, hips,

* Of course, these things are easier said than done. Indeed, it is difficult just to stand in proper alignment. From Mabel Todd and Lulu Sweigard to Irmgard Bartenieff, Carol Boggs, and Irene Dowd today, there have been many people who have devoted their entire life's work to the study of alignment as it relates to the dancer. See, for instance, Mabel E. Todd, *The Thinking Body* (New York: Dance Horizons, 1968), and Lulu E. Sweigard, *Human Movement Potential* (New York: Dodd, Mead & Co., Inc., 1974).

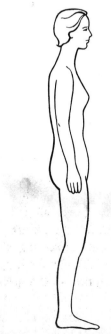

thighs, and lower back. When the buttocks are held in a contracted position for a long time, some of the circulation to the legs is cut off and pressure is put on the sciatic nerve. The expression "tuck it under" is often heard in dance classes, meaning to force the bottom of the pelvis forward. Forcing the pelvis under builds tension and is unnecessary. Tucking the pelvis under to force the back to be absolutely flat changes the natural curve of the spine, resulting in undue strain in the back. The pelvis is hinged to the spine, and if the buttocks and thighs are not tight, the lower spine swings freely with the pelvis. In order to achieve proper alignment of the pelvis and spine, tight muscles in the buttocks, thighs, and lower back must be relaxed first.

Try tensing the muscles either of your buttocks or of your thighs alone. It is difficult to do one without the other. In order to fully let go of contracted buttocks muscles, thighs trained to be held rigidly must be released as well.

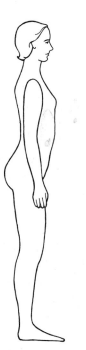

2. *Retracting the pelvis*: A retracted pelvis is commonly referred to as a swayback. When the top of the pelvis is tipped forward, the buttocks stick out and the abdomen protrudes. The head and chest may also be out of line, and the center of gravity is either in front of or behind the legs, making it impossible to maintain balance without excessive muscle tension. The lower back is particularly prone to excess tension. This makes it difficult if not impossible to execute proper jumping with a retracted pelvis. The upper body usually leans forward in preparation for the jump and then arches back in the jump itself, causing the lower back to absorb most of the shock from the impact of landing, sometimes with disastrous results. To avoid injuring the lower back, the pelvis should be aligned with the chest and legs.* This will allow the impulse for the jump to come from the floor through the feet and up through the entire body.

3. *Pulling the shoulders back and down*: If the shoulders are up and forward, it is because they are tense; pulling them back and down only results in a second set of tensions working against the first. Such tension constricts the muscles of the chest and back, restricts breathing, and contributes to tension throughout the body. This is a common cause of neck and shoulder injuries and of spasms in the middle and upper back. Tense shoulders must be relaxed and dropped. If they are not tense, gravity and the natural body structure will keep them down. Pulling them down is unnecessary. Some exercises that are helpful are the shoulder drop, shoulder rolls, and arm hitting.

4. *Pulling the head back*: When the head is too far forward because of unnatural tension, pulling it back results only in countertensions. The body fights itself, causing the neck muscles to contract, and it becomes difficult to rotate the head. People who pull their heads back develop a ramrod neck, spasms in the shoulders and upper back, and often severe chronic headaches. The head may be out of line in order to counterbalance other alignment problems, e.g., a retracted pelvis. The solution to an alignment problem often lies in another part of the body and can require professional help.

5. *Turning the feet out only from the ankles*: With this condition, the feet roll in and the arches fall. In a plié (knee bend), the knees go forward in front of the feet instead of out to the sides directly over them. This puts tremendous strain on the knee joint and the muscles surrounding it, especially on the inside. Tension is exaggerated in the ankles, calves, thighs, hips, and lower back in standing and walking and especially in landing from a jump. It is impossible to roll smoothly through the foot on landing from a jump, because the position of the leg eliminates

* An excellent article on pelvic alignment is Irene Dowd, "Finding Your Center," in *Eddy* magazine, 1977.

certain stages of the articulation through the arches of the foot.

When I see dancers with injured knees, I have them show me how they turn out and plié. Turning out from the ankles rather than the hip joints is often the cause of their injury.

A correct turnout starts at the hip joint, with the thighs and knees in line with the feet. In a properly turned-out plié, the first two toes should be visible inside the knee and the trunk should be vertical above the pelvis. If you have been turning out incorrectly, the proper position must be practiced daily with expert help.

The problem is further complicated by the fact that there are two kinds of turnout—stretch and strength turnout. *Stretch turnout* is the degree of turnout achieved in the hip joint while in a supported position, i.e., sitting or lying on the floor or being held in position by someone else. *Strength turnout* is the degree of turnout actually sustained in the hip joint while standing or moving. Muscle work and strength are required to maintain the latter position.

An individual's strength turnout is usually not as great as his stretch turnout. A muscle that is working while it is being stretched cannot lengthen as much as a muscle that is not working while being stretched. Too many dancers try to work with their stretch turnout rather than the turnout they can move with. When dancing, work with your strength turnout, increasing it only gradually.

To help increase your stretch turnout, refer to the turnout exercise on page 45. A good stretch turnout is the prerequisite for a good strength turnout. However, building the strength turnout requires correct exercises over an extended time period.

Every dancer should find a teacher who is aware of the correct principles of body alignment and the importance of avoiding tension and overwork.

Dancing correctly is pleasurable. Warm-ups at the bar or on the floor should be enjoyable rather than grueling. After class one should feel good, perhaps pleasantly tired, but not exhausted or in pain. In the body's language, a good feeling means we are doing things right.

While the *basic* cause of most dancing injuries is general body tension, there are a number of precautions you can take to avoid injury.

Stop when you feel yourself becoming overtired. Fatigue often precedes injury. A dancer must work to reduce fatigue-producing tension and avoid circumstances which increase it. A tired body is prone to contract suddenly under stress. The reflexes, the defenses, are eroded, and the body is more susceptible to injury.

Give yourself enough time to warm up. Proper warm-up is important since cold muscles are stiff and likely to tear, pull, or spasm. When muscles are properly warmed up, they are more pliable, stretch farther more quickly, and are less prone to strain and other injuries.

Avoid dancing on a concrete floor or a wooden one over a cement subfloor. Both are unyielding, which forces the legs to absorb too much shock. It strains the feet and calves particularly and often causes "shin splints." The ideal dancing surface is a wooden floor with open space beneath. If a character or ballet dancer must work on a cement floor, two soft, padded insoles in each shoe will help to some degree. A modern dancer who works in bare feet should avoid hard floors at all costs. If you have to work on a hard floor, make sure you plié with your heels coming down when landing from any kind of jump.

Take a class at your level of skill. Participation in a class which is too advanced forces the body to do things for which it is not ready. A dancer should not be ashamed to leave a class that is beyond her ability. To remain in the class can be a tragic mistake. Many schools have introduced a graded system so that no dancer can enter a class that is too advanced.

Avoid going on toe too soon. This is a common mistake in schools geared to young children. Parents and teachers are so eager to see results in the form of dance recitals that they put children on toe before their bodies are ready. Children's bones are flexible and can be twisted and bent by the strain and pressure of wearing toe shoes. No child should go on toe until she has had several years of training and, generally, not until she is twelve years old.

If you break your foot, don't dance. I once knew an excellent professional dancer who had developed pains in his foot during an all-day rehearsal for an evening performance. He went to the hospital to see if he could get a shot to kill the pain. The doctor insisted on giving him an X-ray and found that he had a slight fracture. When the doctor recommended that he rest for several weeks, he replied, "I have to dance tonight. This is a very important performance for my career."

"Well," the doctor told him, "your career won't be worth much if you don't respect your body."

The doctor refused to give him a shot of cortisone, so he took some pain-killers and performed anyway. In the middle of the performance they had to stop the show. He had broken his foot so badly that he couldn't dance for more than two years. Remember this story if you ever have doubts about dancing while injured.

It is sad that so many dancers think they must endure torture to realize their ambitions. You can learn to dance without pain, by working slowly and methodically and stopping when your body gives you fatigue or pain as a danger signal. Proper training in movement and relaxation techniques can enable most people to avoid building excess amounts of tension and to get rid of it when it does occur. Relaxed dancers are healthier and stand a better chance of becoming good performers, with long and productive careers, than dancers who endure constant discomfort without trying to understand what the body is saying and doing something about it.

I treated a leading soloist with the American Ballet Theater at Lincoln Center one Sunday night after a busy weekend. She had danced the leads that day in two full-length performances, two the day before, and one on Friday night. When she called me for a treatment, I expected to find her body at its most tense. Even a relaxed performer would be a little tense after such exertion.

To my surprise, her body was very soft. She was tired but relaxed. Fascinated, I questioned her in detail about her training, and I learned that her secret was simple. "I was always headstrong," she said, "and I never accepted any teacher as an expert on my body. I am the only expert. I work very slowly and do long warm-ups. I strictly limit the number of classes I take, and I'm not afraid to refuse to follow any teacher's instructions if they conflict with what I feel is right for my own body. Many times I get tired and stop before a class is over, rather than risk straining myself. I don't believe in too much repetition, and I'm very hesitant to learn unusual steps for special effect. At first it was hard for me, because they didn't like having their authority challenged, but I stuck to my guns and I've been quite successful."

A moment later she fell asleep on my table and I marveled at her independence and success. She has been relatively free of injuries, due to her good sense, her courage, and the care she gives himself. She profited immensely by knowing her body, trusting her own judgment, and taking responsibility for herself. Developing this attitude is my goal with clients who are dancers.

Chapter 6 · EXERCISE: AN AID TO RELIEF OF EXCESS TENSION

Exercise is an integral part of muscular therapy. Proper exercise helps to reduce tension and to maintain the gains made through treatment. Everyone should do some exercise regularly to help maintain good health. Most exercise increases respiration and circulation. By increasing the need for oxygen, exercise makes you breathe more deeply, and by contracting the muscles it helps push the blood back to the heart.

Exercise can have various functions:

1. Release tension
2. Building strength
3. Stretching
4. Coordination
5. Increase flexibility
6. Relaxation
7. Make one proficient at a skill
8. Reduce weight
9. Realign the body
10. Reshape the muscles
11. Warm up muscles before vigorous activity
12. Discharge excess energy
13. Fun

This book focuses on tension-release exercises, although I have also included some exercises for building strength, for stretching, and for therapeutic purposes.

Many of the tension-release techniques that are described in this section, such as hitting, kicking, towel twisting, the gagging technique, and others, were created by Dr. Wilhelm Reich. They are used in psychiatric orgone therapy as a means to break down armor and to elicit feelings. In that context, they are not mechanical exercises but are techniques specifically to elicit emotional response. In the context of my work, these techniques are used only to release mechanical tension.

Exercise can be destructive if it is not done properly. You don't have to exercise to the point of exhaustion or pain to reap benefit.

Being tense and being strong have virtually no relationship, although people often equate the two. You can be tense and strong, or tense and weak, or relaxed and strong, or relaxed and weak. In order to build strength, you have to increase your ability to control and sustain tension in a particular part of your body. This means a muscle tightens when you want it to; it's not tight all the time. Through proper exercise, your muscles develop and get stronger. This should be a slow process.

Another basic principle of exercise and strength building is that you should develop the amount of strength you need in the specific places you need it. For instance, if you are a stevedore, your muscle development will be different from that of a secretary or an acrobat. Muscles maintain strength only when used. Therefore, if you overdevelop unnecessary muscles, as in weight lifting, they will merely sag, deteriorate, and be ugly when you stop using them. If you have underdeveloped muscles, you will feel weak and will constantly strain yourself. Everybody's needs are different. Develop the kind of muscles that you need.

There is something wrong with a strenuous exercise program that does not account for individual body and tension differences. The same exercise might be excellent for one person and destructive for another. A yoga position called the cobra, in which the back is extremely arched, could be a fine exercise for a person with a relaxed back, but for someone with extreme back tension it could be terrible to the point of triggering a severe back injury. An intelligent approach to exercise is important.

In order to build strength, slowly increase the number of times you do an exercise. Rapidly increasing the number of repetitions might result in strain. Done properly, strength building is a painless and gradual process.

To build strength in a muscle, contract it, hold it, then release it. It's that simple. If you are unable to completely release the tension and rest the muscle, due to chronic tension, it is difficult to build strength efficiently.

If tension is never completely released in a muscle, the range of movement will be limited. Often, while exercising, people get hurt or go into spasm because they have increased tension in an already tense body, and the body, unable to tolerate more tension, goes into spasm.

Specific muscle groups are intended to be used for actions such as walking, bending, or lifting the arm. If other muscles are used in addition or instead, the result is bad muscular development or a poorly proportioned, inefficient body. For instance, the deltoid muscle is intended to raise the arm, but most people use the trapezius muscle excessively, raising the shoulders as well, and over the years they develop ugly, rounded shoulder muscles as a result.

The best way to safely, effectively, and permanently stretch a muscle is to stretch it while it is in a relaxed state; in other words, while the joint it crosses is neither extended nor bent.* When you stretch a muscle, you actually elongate its fibers. When the muscle is contracted, the fibers shorten, so if you try to stretch a muscle while it is in contraction, you're working against yourself. It is best to do most stretching while sitting or lying on the floor. Stretching should be approached gently and gradually. If your muscles are warmed up, you can stretch more easily, although you can use gentle stretching as a warm-up.

Never do exercises when you're tired. You need all your body faculties. Never strain when doing an exercise. If your body begins to tremble, it means you have had enough for the moment. Rest and try

* For a detailed elucidation of the differences between contracted, stretched, and relaxed states, see lesson 8, page 132.

again later. Don't measure the worth of your exercises by how much you sweat.

The following exercises are designed to be done at home by yourself. They are arranged roughly by body parts, starting with the head and working toward the feet. However, the effects of an exercise are not necessarily restricted to this classification. For example, an exercise requiring movement only of the legs can relax the hips, the lower back, and the chest area. These exercises are therefore arranged in a head-to-toe sequence for convenience of reference and not as a definition of their effects. They will be followed by warm-up procedures for use before athletics or dancing.

This chapter presents some of the exercises I use with my clients. There are, of course, other good exercises not listed here. When more extensive work is necessary, I often send clients to other people.

General points to remember about exercise:

1. Stay away from exercises that make your muscles hard or bulging.
2. Always breathe deeply when exercising.
3. Start slowly and build up gradually.

Eyes
Eyebrow Exercises

This exercise can be done anywhere, at any time, as often as you like. Begin, however, while looking in a mirror, to make sure you are doing it correctly.

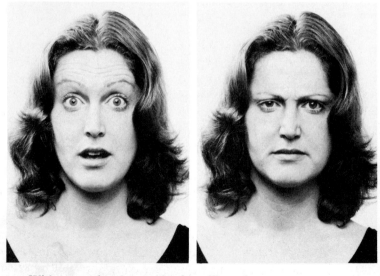

With your head completely still and your eyes focused straight ahead, raise and lower your eyebrows as far as you can. Do not move your head, jaw, or eyes.

There should be a great deal of movement of the eyebrows and the forehead. After you have mastered the technique, move the eyebrows up and down as fast as you can.

This exercise is good for relieving tension in the forehead, which can cause premature wrinkles, frown marks, and frontal headaches; and it can also help you concentrate when your mind begins drifting.

Eye Squeeze

Open your eyes as wide as you can, then squeeze them shut as tight as you can. Do this slowly and then rapidly.

This is a good exercise for releasing tension in the muscles around the eyes, for relieving headaches, and for people who drift off and do a lot of blank staring into space. You can do this several times a day, for a few minutes at a time. This exercise gets a great deal of blood moving around the eyes and is especially good when the eyes feel tired.

The "Light" Technique*

Use a penlight flashlight that stays on without your holding a button. The light should be bright, so keep extra batteries on hand. The exercise should be done in a completely or partially darkened room.

* The light technique was developed by Dr. Barbara Goldenberg Koopman. For further details on this technique, see Dr. Elsworth F. Baker, *Man in the Trap* (New York: Macmillan Co., 1967), pp. 50–52.

It can be done standing, sitting, or lying down on your back, although the latter is probably the most relaxed position.

The light should be shining directly into your eyes throughout the exercise and your head must remain completely still. Vary the distance from your eyes and the speed at which you move the penlight while you follow it with your eyes. At first move the light only at the speed at which your eyes can follow it, then increase the speed. Move the light in various patterns, i.e., figure 8s, Xs, Zs, and squiggles, or try the following patterns in random order.

a. A horizontal pattern from one side to the other as far as your eyes can see.

b. A vertical pattern to the extremes of your vision.

c. A diagonal pattern to the extremes of your vision.

d. Rotating your arm, move the light in the biggest circle you can make.

e. Extend your arm above the top of your head. Your eyes should be in the extreme upward-looking position. Move the light horizontally above the head in the extreme upward position.

f. Repeat the last pattern, with the penlight extended toward the legs.

g. Extend your arm to the side and move the light up and down vertically. Do this on each side, completing a square begun by (*e*) and (*f*). All these patterns can be done at any speed.

h. Hold the light directly in front of your eyes as far away as your arm will stretch. Slowly move the light toward one eye until it is two inches away or just comfortable, whichever comes first.

i. To rest the eyes periodically, make small, fast circles with the light about a foot in front of your eyes. Do this with your eyes open or closed.

These patterns can be interspersed with one another. You don't have to complete one before moving on to the next. Make up your own patterns, as long as the light is in your range of sight.

The light, with all its variations, is good for eye tension and fatigue. It can increase your ability to concentrate and has a positive effect on headaches and sleeplessness. It increases eye mobility, and is in general the best over-all eye technique that I know of. When you feel generally tense, it can help you to relax all over. The eyes are an extension of the brain, so in a sense the light technique stimulates the brain. Remember, the brain ultimately controls most of the tension in the body through nerve impulses.

The length of time you spend on the light technique will vary from day to day depending upon your tolerance. Stop if you begin to feel uncomfortable. Five to ten minutes, three or four times a week, should be the maximum. You can do it anytime, although bedtime is probably the most convenient. Try it prior to a test, or on a morning when you wake up feeling groggy.

Jaw

The Cork Technique

If you have any mouth or dental problems, give your dentist a call before doing this. If your jaw locks, spasms, or makes a cracking sound when you open your mouth wide, this technique is not for you.

This is one of the best exercises for jaw tension. You'll need some corks, which you can get at a hardware or five-and-ten-cents store. Buy a variety of thermos corks, approximately ¾ to 1¾ inches in length. Determine which cork to use by placing a cork vertically between your teeth. When you find one that you can place between your teeth and still open your mouth another ¼ inch, you have found the right size cork for you at this stage.

If it makes you uncomfortable, take it out sooner and try a smaller cork. You will drool a little while the cork is in place, so keep a tissue handy. Breathe normally during the exercise.

Place the cork between your teeth with the major portion of the cork outside your mouth, and leave it there for five to ten minutes.

After you get used to the exercise, slowly increase your time.

Once you become comfortable with this size cork, advance to a slightly larger one. The maximum size cork for most people is a 1¾ to 2 inches. It is good for the throat to talk while the cork is in your mouth, but telephone conversations are not recommended.

The cork exercise increases the jaw's range of movement, helps to break down tension in the jaw muscles, and can loosen a tight throat. Since breathing is improved and the voice is more relaxed and deeper, the exercise is especially good for those who sing or act. In general, it is beneficial to people with oral tensions, which are indicated by smoking, excessive eating, mouth twitching, and compulsive talking.

You can do this exercise anytime, but try to do it once or twice a day while you're doing something else—such as reading, driving, or watching television —so that you don't get bored.

Towel Biting

This exercise should not be done if you have caps, bridges, or root-canal work on your teeth. Towel biting is a prophylactic exercise, so don't do it when you have a headache or neck, shoulder, or back pain. This exercise should be done while lying on a bed. Begin gently, and gradually increase in vigor. You can do the exercise by yourself, but it is somewhat more effective when someone helps you.

Take a face towel and tightly roll one end of it, lengthwise. Make sure the towel is not too thick. It may rip, so don't use your best towel.

Place the tightly rolled end in one side of your mouth between your extreme back teeth and bite down hard. Don't let go of it.

Then, you or someone else should grab the other end of the towel and pull it gently at first and gradually with more firmness. Resist the pulling with your teeth. Pull against it slowly, quickly, front and back and side to side. Don't do the latter movement too fast at first—it may give you a headache. Think of it as a friendly tug-of-war.

After doing this on one side of your mouth for a few minutes, move to the other side for an equal amount of time. If it hurts or you find it unpleasant, don't do it.

If you start to gag when you place the towel in your mouth, stop the exercise. The throat is too tight and will not tolerate it. In this case, the gagging technique, page 36, should be done for several weeks before returning to towel biting.

Towel biting is effective in dealing with headaches that originate at the back of the head, and in alleviating mouth, neck, throat, and chronic jaw tension. Do the exercise two or three times a week, anytime that's convenient.

Neck

Head Drop

Do not do this exercise if you have a neck injury. Do this five or ten times. If you are working on

neck tension, do it several times a day. The head-drop exercise relaxes the muscles in the back of the neck.

The Block Technique

The block is one of the most effective tools for reducing head and neck tension.

In order to do this technique, you need a triangular piece of wood approximately three inches high by eight inches long.* Each edge of the triangle is constructed to exert different amounts of pressure. Make one rounded, one semirounded, and one sharp. Please read the instructions through completely before you begin this technique.

* Available from Relaxation Tools, Inc., P.O. Box 1045, New York, N.Y. 10025.

Lie on your back on the floor. Place the block on the floor directly under the back of your head, with the rounded edge facing up.

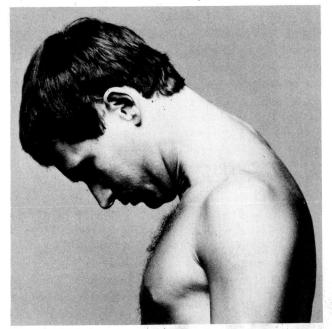

Sit or stand with your back straight and head erect. Suddenly let your head and neck muscles go and your head drop freely forward. Rest there for a moment, bring your head up, and repeat.

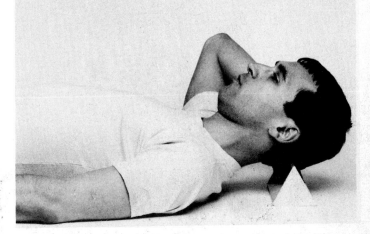

The rounded edge should be at the lower occipital line. The occipital region of the head is where the base of the skull meets the neck.

To find the occiput, place your hands at the back of your neck and move them up toward the skull. Try to relax the muscles of your neck. Don't tilt your head back or try to hold your head up off the block.

If using the block is painful, place a washcloth over the edge of it to blunt the intensity of the cutting edge. Later, discard the cloth.

Now, with your occiput on the rounded edge, roll your head very slowly, first to one side and then to the other. If you find a place that hurts, leave your head there for ten to fifteen seconds, but never keep your head in one place longer than thirty seconds. Continue to roll your head, finding all the painful spots that you can. If it's too painful to stop at these points, a continual slow, rolling motion is often easier to tolerate at first. When all the discomfort on the lower occipital line ceases, repeat on the upper occipital line, a half inch higher.

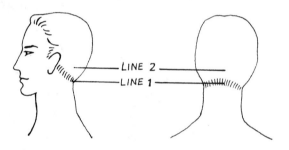

At first the block may slide or tip as you use it. If this occurs, *use one hand to stabilize it*. Placing the block on a rug may add further stability.

When the block no longer hurts on both lines, try the semirounded edge. When this no longer causes pain on both occipital lines, move to the sharpest edge, which exerts the most pressure.

Breathe and relax. While breathing, try to keep your jaw loose and slightly open to counteract any tendency to clench the teeth. Don't force your breathing. Just breathe gently and easily while you are using the block. If there is discomfort, you may tend to hold your breath—try not to.

In the beginning do not use the block more than four or five minutes at a time. As your discomfort decreases, gradually increase the amount of time you use the block.

Use the block twice daily until you no longer feel pain. Using the block at regular intervals is most effective. Five minutes each morning and evening is a good routine. Eventually the block will not hurt at all and its use will be pleasant. When the tension has been sufficiently reduced, you need use the block only as a tension detector. Place it under the occiput briefly several times a week to get a tension reading. If it hurts, you know you should use the block regularly again. If it feels fine, you still have a low level of tension.

If the block is used to excess, soreness may develop. If this occurs, discontinue use until the soreness is gone. Even after all discomfort is gone, it is very important not to leave your head on the block at one place longer than thirty seconds.

The block is not intended as a cure for anything, but it is an aid to breaking down tension in the head and neck. It can rid you of discomfort from physical tension in that area, but for those with severe neck tension, the block will probably not be effective.

Arm and Hand

Towel Twisting

If you have recently had a sprained or strained arm or wrist, do not do this exercise. Wait until you are stronger.

Twist a towel with both hands as if you were wringing water out of it. Once you have a firm grip and think you cannot twist any more, keep on twisting as hard as you can as if you're strangling it. Do towel twisting until your hands shake or you tire. Then relax your hands, get another good grip, and twist again.

This exercise is good for reducing arm, shoulder, and hand tension. It benefits people with cold hands or cramps in the arms or hands and those who suffer from pain in the joints caused by tension. It is also good for tension in the neck and throat, the sides of the chest, the breast muscles, and the muscles around the armpits. Do this exercise once or twice a day for two or three minutes at a time.

The Ice Technique

This procedure rapidly increases the blood circulation in the hands. It is especially good for pain in the finger joints or strain of any of the hand muscles, and it gives temporary relief from minor arthritic pain.

Put four or five ice cubes in a bowl of cold water. Place both hands in the water, take hold of an ice cube in each hand, and squeeze gently. Let the ice go for a moment and grasp it again. Repeat this process over a three- or four-minute period, removing your hands from the water from time to time. If your hands begin to cramp at any time, remove them immediately, rest a moment, and then continue. The ice technique should be done twice daily —morning and evening—until the hand problem is resolved.

Shoulder

Shoulder Drop

Raise your shoulders as high as you can, then let go suddenly, allowing gravity to take them down. Inhale when you raise your shoulders and exhale when you drop them. Do this ten or fifteen times whenever you feel tension creeping into your shoulders.

The shoulder drop is good for tension in the neck, shoulders, and upper-back areas. It is also a good warm-up exercise.

I had a client who found this exercise useful also as a barometer of tension. Every day she would do one or two shoulder drops in the morning. When it was painful, she knew she was tense, and by doing the exercise several times throughout the day she could prevent the discomfort that would otherwise occur by mid-afternoon. If it was not painful in the morning, she knew she could look forward to a relatively tension-free day without the exercise.

Shoulder Roll

Start by lifting one or both shoulders as high as you can, and roll them back, down, front, and up again in a continuous, circular motion.

Do one shoulder at a time, or both, simultaneously.

Do this about ten or fifteen times in one direction, then in the other direction. Be sure to breathe normally throughout this exercise.

The shoulder roll loosens your muscles and in-creases their flexibility. It can be done once or twice a day, or as needed.

Arm Circles

SINGLE ARM CIRCLES

Stand with your left foot about twelve inches in front of your right. Swing the right arm in a circle front to back as if you were winding up to pitch a softball. The elbow should be straight but not locked. Do this ten or twenty times. Reverse leg position and swing your left arm. Reverse your legs again and swing your right arm the other way, back-to-front. Reverse your legs and swing your left arm back-to-front. Rest for a moment between each of these four variations.

DOUBLE ARM CIRCLES

The forward double arm circle is more effective. Don't forget to breathe throughout.

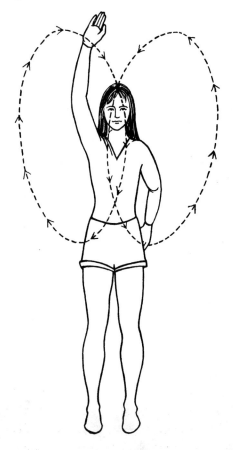

Stand with your feet parallel, about two feet apart, with your knees slightly bent. Making sure you don't lean backward, circle both arms, alternating in one continuous movement, first with both arms going in the baseball pitch direction, then in reverse.

These circles are good for mild pain or tightness in the shoulders and loosening up all the muscles surrounding the shoulder girdle. Through centrifugal force, they increase the blood circulation in the arms and hands.

Circles are also good as warm-ups in preparation for sports or more-strenuous physical activity. Do the entire series once a day.

General Upper-Body Techniques

The Gagging Technique

One of the most valuable techniques, this releases the jaw, tongue, throat, neck, chest, diaphragm, and abdominal muscles by causing an involuntary contraction and relaxation that shakes tension loose. It is most easily done before breakfast, but it can be done at any time of the day, although you should wait at least two hours after you've eaten to insure that no food will come up during the exercise. You may not find it pleasant at first, but the benefits far outweigh the initial discomfort. When you loosen up, you may even enjoy it.

This exercise can be done lying on your back with one knee raised and the sole of the foot on the surface on which you are lying, or while standing or sitting. Many people prefer to do it standing at the basin while they do their morning toothbrushing routine. If you have removable partial dentures, they should not be left in the mouth while doing this exercise.

Open your mouth and stick your tongue out over your lower lip. Put the index and middle fingers of one hand on your tongue and slide them all the way to the back of it. As you do this, exhale deeply through your mouth. You will experience an involuntary contraction and release throughout part or all of your upper body. You may not gag during the exhale at first. If this happens, keep breathing and try not to let your tongue pull back into your mouth.

When you begin to gag, leave your fingers in your mouth and keep on breathing and gagging until you've gagged three or four times. When you can gag easily, once or twice is sufficient.* Remove your

fingers, relax for a moment, and try the procedure again. People's bodies react differently to this exercise at first. Some people will not even be able to put their fingers in their mouth—the idea is too repugnant. If this is the case, the exercise isn't for you. Others will begin to gag as soon as their fingers touch the front of their tongue. These people can really benefit from this exercise. Gagging makes some people cough. With others, their heads or chests jerk forward. In some cases, the body will momentarily fold up on itself. These reactions reflect different stages of muscular blocking. They indicate where the gag impulse has been blocked in the body—the throat, jaw, neck, chest, diaphragm, or abdomen. For the relaxed, gagging causes a gentle rippling sensation through the body without violent reactions. Gagging opens the throat, relaxes the chest and diaphragm, and frees breathing. Often, the voice will drop in pitch and increase in resonance.

Do this exercise alone in a private place. It is especially helpful to singers, actors, and people prone to sore throats.

The Yelling Technique

An extremely powerful technique, this can relax tension in the forehead, throat, tongue, jaw, neck, chest, diaphragm, upper back, and abdominal muscles. It also improves breathing. Do not do this exercise while you have a sore or strep throat, bronchitis, or any other throat or chest malady. If you live in a place where you can make unlimited noise, you can yell out loud, but if noise must be restricted in your home, yell into a towel or pillow.

Open your mouth wide, take a deep breath, and yell as long and as loud as you possibly can on that one breath. If you must muffle the sound, press a pillow or a towel to your mouth. Keep yelling, trying to make each one louder than the last, until you get tired. It may take, five, ten, twenty, or even fifty yells, depending on what you need.

If this exercise makes you uncomfortable, don't do it. If it makes you cough, cough loudly and then try it again. If you are still coughing after five tries, forget it for now and try gagging. You can return to yelling later. Coughing often indicates tension in the throat. If you're a smoker and have a persistent coughing reaction, it will be difficult to succesfully execute the yelling technique.

---

* Once I treated a stockbroker who found that by gagging he was able to eliminate a tight band of tension around his chest. In order to function without tension, he would gag in the men's room several times throughout the day.

If you feel hoarse after the yelling technique and your voice is breathy, don't worry. You have begun to break down tension. The reaction will not persist when your throat loosens up. If after yelling you feel as if you have a sore throat, next time try the exercise with your tongue pushed out and down and your mouth opened wide. This keeps your throat more open. If the new position doesn't ease the soreness, don't do the exercise, but try gagging for three or four weeks, then try yelling again. If your throat is relaxed, yelling will not make it sore.

Yelling can be done daily at any time. It is recommended when you have difficulty breathing, feel a headache coming on or your throat contracting, or when you're angry, anxious, or scared. It is good for a spastic diaphragm, which can feel like a band around the chest or a pain in the solar plexus.

A good time to scream out loud is while driving in a car with the windows rolled up, provided you are alone. It is preferable to yell when alone.

Hitting Exercises

When doing a hitting exercise with any part of the body, use as much force as you can muster. Check to make sure you are not holding your breath during these exercises. Unless otherwise indicated because of an injury, do them until you feel completely exhausted. Never do an arm hitting exercise if you have recently had an injury above the hips, unless you are working under professional supervision. It is recommended that these exercises be done in private.

Arm Hitting

STANDING OR KNEELING

If your bed is of normal height, do the exercise standing next to it. If the bed is low or high, try kneeling on it.

Raise both arms above your head and clench your fists. Hit the bed as forcefully as possible with fists and forearms at the same time. If you are standing, allow your knees to bend.

Keep hitting as hard as you possibly can, increasing force as you go, until you feel exhausted. Remember to breathe regularly throughout the exercise. When you become tired, stop and rest for a few minutes, then repeat.

Do the exercise with your hands open if you find it easier. Hitting will tire you only for a few minutes, so you can do it anytime. After the exercise you will probably feel increased energy. If you feel a strain on your lower back during this exercise, try hitting in the lying position described below.

LYING DOWN

Lie on your back on the bed. Raise your arms, with clenched fists, straight above your body. Hit the bed along either side of you repeatedly with *all* the strength you have until you're exhausted. Rest, then repeat.

These two exercises break down tension in the lower neck, entire back, chest, shoulders, arms, and hands. They also increase breathing capacity. Do this exercise, in one of the two forms, once a day for a few months. After that, do it whenever you feel the need.

Elbow Hitting

Lie on your back on a bed, with your forearms raised, and hit the bed as hard as you can with your elbows. Hit with one at a time or both together. Take rest periods, but do the exercise for as long as you can.

This is excellent for releasing tension in the upper arms, shoulders, and particularly in the center back, chest, and diaphragm. If you have a lot of tension in any of these areas, do elbow hitting daily.

Deep Breathing

Deep breathing increases your breathing capacity, and your tolerance for relaxation. It also relaxes and slows you down when you feel tense. Deep breathing speeds the removal of carbon dioxide and other waste products from the blood and increases its oxygen content. The ability to breathe properly and deeply is probably the most valuable asset to a healthy body.

This exercise can be done standing or sitting, but lying is best. If you lie down, put a pillow under your knees. Lie on your back, with your arms at your sides, or your hands on your abdomen to see if you are belly breathing. Don't fold your arms behind your head, because it tightens your shoulders and upper chest. Drop your jaw slightly and breathe deeply through your mouth. Try not to move the lower abdomen or the upper chest while breathing to relax. The area of greatest movement should be just below the chest at the diaphragm and in the lower rib cage. Take five or ten breaths in this manner and then rest. Repeat this several times. If you get dizzy, stop. Remember that exhaling is the most important part of the exercise.

The Ball Techniques

The ball techniques are based on the principle that if you increase the tension in a muscle beyond its tolerance level, it will release some tension and increase circulation. The ball replaces the hands used

in deep-massage pressure techniques (see pages 57-9 for detailed discussion).

If you find any of the ball techniques very painful, your back is tense. Start slowly and build gradually. If you find the techniques too uncomfortable to do on the floor, do them on a bed until your muscles soften up enough to tolerate more pressure. If this is still too painful, try the chair-ball technique described below. In a chair you can moderate the pressure easily by leaning forward. This is a pressure technique you are in control of, and it is valuable in releasing tension. All you need is a small ball the size and firmness of a tennis ball.

Small-Ball Techniques

UPPER BACK

The three techniques that follow work on a muscle group called the erector spinae which runs from the back of the head through the neck and all the way down the back, flanking both sides of the spine to where it attaches at the tops of the hip bones.

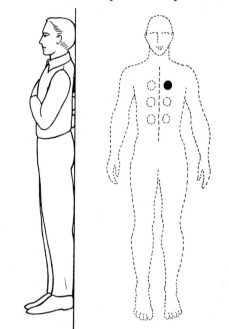

Place the ball on the floor. Lie on your back so that you are compressing the ball with the muscles between the spine and one shoulder blade.

Lie on the ball for a minute or so until you feel your back letting go. Slowly move the ball by slightly shifting your body in a zigzag fashion so that the ball moves toward and away from the spine alternately, covering a distance of about two inches. Stop at various points along the way when you feel a tight or painful spot. Then try it on the other side. Use the ball through the whole area between the shoulder blade and the spine from the top to the bottom of the shoulder blade, but never run the spine directly over the ball with pressure.

This technique releases tension in the shoulders and upper back. It can be used for general tension and also will help an injured or a spasmodic area. You can do it as often as needed. If you like, use two balls simultaneously, one on each side.

CENTER BACK

Place the ball under the middle back—from just below the shoulder blade to the lower end of the rib cage—and move it from side to side slowly on one side of the back, stopping at various places. Move over to the other side. Move up and down and cover the entire center-back area.

You need not limit the exercise to the muscles next to the spine. Move out farther to the sides. Make sure you are breathing regularly. In this section of the back, it is often helpful to use two balls at the same time.

This exercise is good for center-back and chest tension. It is especially helpful for those who have difficulty breathing deeply because of chest or diaphragm tension. Do it as often as you like.

LOWER BACK

Place the ball under your lower back and move it from side to side as in the preceding exercise. Leave the ball in one place for a minute or so, then move it to a new place, covering the whole lower-back area. *Be careful of the spine.* With the ball in these positions, raise one knee, then the other, toward your chest. This intensifies the pressure. The ball exercise done in this area breaks down tension in the lower back and increases flexibility and blood circulation. It's also good for menstrual cramps and for the lower-back tension that women often experience during pregnancy. Do it as often as needed, but be careful not to use too much pressure, since this is a sensitive area.

Place the ball behind your upper back and lean against the chair. Stay in that position about thirty seconds, then horizontally shift the ball over the long back muscles, alternating toward and away from the spine.

HIP

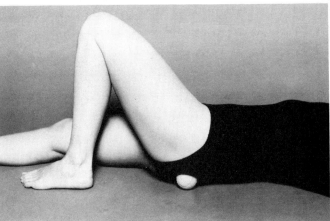

Lie on your back with one knee raised and the sole of your foot on the floor. Place the ball in various places under your hip and slowly drop your knee to the side.

Leave the ball in one position for thirty or forty seconds, then raise your leg, find a new place, and repeat.

This exercise relieves tension in the hip and is good for lower-back and sciatica pain. Do it as often as necessary.

Chair-Ball Techniques

Work on all parts of the back and hip can be done while sitting in a chair with a relatively firm back. It's an excellent technique to use on long trips by car, train, bus, or plane, or any other time when you have to sit for a long period of time.

Allow the ball to drop slowly down to the center back, working lower and lower in the same manner recommended in the floor techniques. It is often good to leave the ball in one place for several minutes at a time when using a chair, especially if it is not hard-backed.

Large-Ball Technique

THE CHEST RELEASE

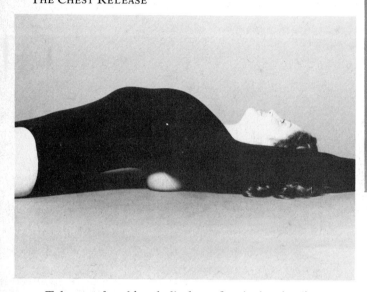

Take a soft rubber ball about five inches in diameter. Lie on the floor on your back and place the ball directly under your spine in the center back between your shoulder blades.

Place your hands out to the sides. Breathe and relax for a while. Then begin circling one arm to the side and above your head, slowly reaching as far as you can without effort. Circle with the other arm in the same way. Finally move both arms together.

This exercise breaks down tension in the center and upper back, chest, diaphragm, and upper abdomen. It is excellent for helping you breathe more deeply. Do it several times a week for five to ten minutes.

If your body is fairly relaxed, the ball techniques will feel pleasant and there will be no pain. Experiment with different-size balls of varying firmness. Keep one in your car, and carry one with you if convenient. If you travel a lot, it's a must in your carry-on luggage.

Lower Back and Waist

Waist Stretch

In this exercise move only from the waist up, keeping the body erect.

Stand with your feet parallel about twelve inches apart and extend your arms directly to the sides at shoulder height. Reach out toward the wall with your right hand, allowing the upper body to move with it.

When you've gone as far as you can, repeat with the left hand. Be sure not to bend to the side. When this exercise becomes easy, try it with your arms relaxed at your sides.

Repeat the movement twenty to thirty times, building slowly if you find it uncomfortable. This exercise is good for strengthening the lower back and stretching and strengthening the outer abdominal or waist muscles, and is a good warm-up.

The Waist Twist

This exercise loosens and stretches the muscles of the waist, abdomen, and lower back, but avoid it if you have lower-back pain.

When you've gone as far as you can to the right, swing your body to the left. Keep a brisk pace, with your body moving first and your arms following. Increase the twist gently and gradually. Repeat the exercise as many times as you like.

Stand straight with your feet parallel about eighteen inches apart and your knees slightly bent. Twist your upper body to the right as far as it will go, turning your head as you twist. Be careful not to move your feet. Your arms should be relaxed enough to swing freely and wrap around your body.

The Squat

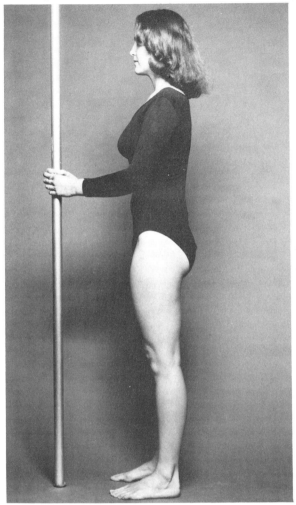

Stand facing something you can hold, such as a pole or two doorknobs on either side of the same door. Place your feet parallel, about eighteen inches apart. While standing about six inches away, take hold of the doorknobs and lean back slightly.

Keeping your back perfectly straight and your heels planted on the floor, squat all the way down. Make sure that your knees don't turn in but are directly over your feet. Exhale as you go down. Stay there for a second or two and inhale as you come up. Do this ten or fifteen times.

After several days, let go of the doorknobs while you're in the squat position and see if you can balance easily. Then regrasp and come up. When you are trying to balance, breathe normally. After you can do it easily, try the squat without holding on. Continue to do it both ways after that. The former accents stretching; the latter, strength.

The squat stretches and strengthens the muscles of the lower back and hips. While breaking down tension in the lower back, it builds strength in the legs and increases flexibility in the hip joints. It also helps to correct poorly aligned knees and ankles. Do this exercise every day.

Legs and Feet

Kicking Exercises

Kicking exercises are not for those who have active pains or injuries in the lower back or legs.

BACK LEG KICKING

Lie on a bed, face up. The bed should not have a frame, posts, or headboard to get in your way. Bend one knee, then straighten the leg up toward the ceiling and smash it down flat onto the bed. Do the movement slowly at first, gradually increasing speed and force, but keeping the foot relaxed. Kick with one leg for a while, or alternate one after the other. Try lifting your leg and thrusting it without bending the knee. Do what is most comfortable for as long as you can.

When you're exhausted, rest a moment and try again. This exercise is effective in reducing calf and thigh tension, especially the back of the thigh. It breaks down tension in the hips, abdomen, and lower back.

FRONT LEG KICKING

Lie face down on a bed and kick your legs fast and hard from the knee down. Your feet should be relaxed. Don't hold your breath. When you tire, rest a minute, then try again.

This exercise breaks down tension in the front of the entire leg, the hip, the lower back, and the abdominal muscles. It also increases blood circulation in the legs. Alternate this exercise with the back leg kicking, resting after each set.

Foot Shaking

Lie on your back, raise your feet in the air with your knees bent, and vigorously shake them. Keep your feet limp. Shake one foot at a time or both together. Remember not to hold your breath. Shake your feet until you begin to tire, then rest and repeat the procedure several times. Foot shaking is good for breaking down tension in the ankles, feet, and calves, and is a good beginning warm-up exercise.

Leg Swings

Sit on a table or any other object that will allow your lower legs to swing freely forward and back.

For freedom of movement, make sure there are four or five inches between the backs of your knees and the edge of the table. Begin by gently swinging one leg for almost a minute, slightly increasing the forward swing. Then, at the end of each forward swing, straighten the leg, hold it for a moment, and let it swing down. Do this three or four times; then, for a rest, swing without straightening two or three times. Repeat the straightening five or six times. Go through this process slowly, increasing the number of leg straightenings up to ten times. Stop sooner if your leg begins to tire. Repeat with the other leg.

Leg swings help to loosen the knee joints, and leg straightenings strengthen the muscles around the knees, especially in the front of the thighs. It is an excellent exercise to rebuild leg strength after a knee injury.

The Rolling Pin

The rolling-pin exercise improves knee-foot alignment. Proper knee-foot alignment means that the knees, when bent, line up with the center of the foot. Most people turn their feet out and knees in. This exercise reverses that position and breaks up the tension that holds the incorrect position. Do not try this with a soda bottle—you might cut your foot.

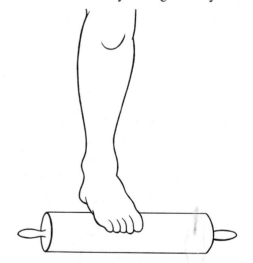

Place a rolling pin on a carpeted floor or on a towel on a wood floor. Hold on to a chair or some other object to help you keep your balance. Turn one foot in at a 45-degree angle to the rolling pin. Place the ball of this foot on the center of the rolling pin. Try not to change the angle of the foot throughout the exercise.

Metatarsal Lift

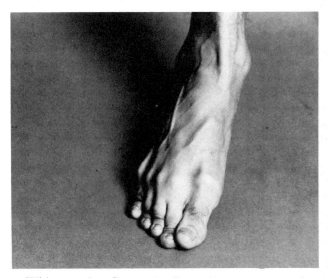

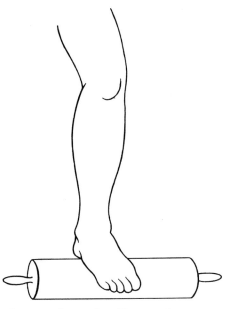

Bend your knee as far as it will go and press your heel toward the floor without touching it. Turn your knee out so that you can see your entire foot.

Maintain this position as you press down with your heel, and slowly roll forward until the rolling pin touches the front of your heel. Release the pressure and roll back to the starting position. Repeat with increasing amounts of weight on the foot, so that eventually all of your weight is on that foot. There may be discomfort or pain on the outside of the foot at first, so proceed gradually. It is essential to press down with the heel, turn the knee out, and keep the foot at the proper angle throughout the exercise.

In addition to improving alignment, this exercise breaks down tension in the feet and calves and stretches the calf muscles. Even if your problem is only in one leg, do the exercise with both feet. Don't do more than five or six rolls on each foot at first, then slowly increase the number. For this exercise to be effective it must be done frequently.

With your feet flat on the floor, lift the metatarsals by bringing the toes, without bending them, back toward the heel in a raking action.

If you have difficulty, hold the toes straight by pressing on them with your fingers.

Spread the toes apart, bring them up and out, and flatten them again.

Do four or five of these on each foot, alternating back and forth.

This exercise helps to straighten hammertoes and strengthens the muscles of the toes and feet. Do about ten sets of the metatarsal lift on each foot, daily.

Sickle Walk

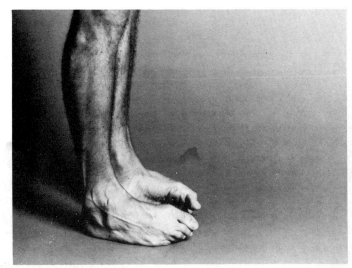

With the feet curled toward the inner ankle bone, stand on the outside edges of your feet. The soles of the feet should not be touching the ground but should face each other. The knees should be bent slightly. Take ten steps in this position, then rest. Repeat three or four times.

The sickle walk stretches the outside and strengthens the inside of the foot and ankle. It is helpful in correcting knee-foot alignment as well as in lifting fallen arches that are not congenital, and it is good for people who are constantly falling over on their ankles.

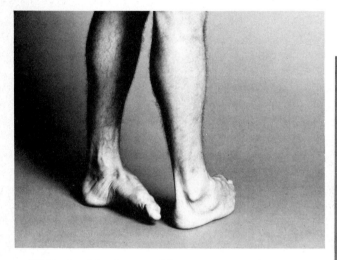

While in this foot position, turn your feet completely in so that your big toes are facing each other and your feet make a 160-degree angle. As you walk, one foot should be in front of the other. Step each foot over the other for ten steps.

Shakedown

Stand with your feet parallel, about a foot apart. Drop your head so that your chin rests on your chest, and very gradually bend forward, starting from the top, vertebra after vertebra, moving your head toward the floor. Let your knees bend slightly as you go down so that your fingertips just graze the floor and your head is in front of your knees. Completely relax your arms and hang. Take a few deep breaths and gently shake your shoulders. Then reverse the process, straightening vertebra by vertebra, beginning from the base of the spine, allowing the head to remain dropped until you are fully erect. Lift the head last. Do the exercise several times at varying speeds.

Take a few deep breaths, then lift only the head and look directly across the room. Suddenly drop the head and let it swing back and forth until it stops on its own. Roll back up slowly to a straight position, as in the first part of the exercise.

Once you're comfortable with the shakedown, try this variation: When the hands touch the ground, stay there.

During the drop, make sure your head is moving by the force of gravity alone.

Do about five or six sets of both variations of the shakedown. Alternate the two, if you like. The shakedown helps relax the neck, head muscles, and shoulders, and stretches the back muscles. Under proper supervision, it can also improve postural alignment.

Turnout Exercise

This exercise is designed especially for people who study dance, gymnastics, or other disciplines that require a turned-out position of the legs.

Find an empty wall about six feet wide that you can use regularly without moving a lot of furniture. Use masking tape or a pencil to mark your first try so that you can observe your progress.

In this exercise, gravity does the work for you. The normal weight of your legs gently and gradually pulls your legs down, stretching your inner-thigh muscles. The ideal time to stretch a muscle is when it is most relaxed. Lie there. You can read, talk on the phone, or breathe deeply and relax. Do this for at least five minutes a day, depending on how long you are comfortable. After a week, you should be up to ten minutes a day.

If your lower back is uncomfortable, place a pillow under it. If you feel an unpleasant pulling or pain in the backs of your knees, or near your hip joints, bend your knees a little. It means that you are stretching your tendons instead of your muscles. After doing this exercise faithfully for three or four weeks, your heels should be two to four inches farther down the wall.

Lie on the floor face up with your legs raised against the wall. Move in close to the wall so that your legs are at a 90-degree angle to your body and your buttocks are touching the wall. Now slowly open your legs as far as they will go without forcing.

This is your natural "stretch turnout" (for definition, see page 27), from the hip at this time. Mark the position on the wall just beside both heels.

This is one of the most effective exercises for permanently increasing the stretch turnout.

The Following Are Primarily Warm-Up Exercises

Knee Bounce

While lying on your back, bend the knees to the chest, and let the legs gently bounce from the knees down. Straighten both legs vertically, hold them a moment, then let them fall to your chest and bounce again. After doing this a while, straighten and let only one leg fall, alternating right and left legs.

The Bicycle

While lying on your back, place your hands under your hips. Raise the legs vertically and make believe you are riding a bicycle in the air. Try not to hold the abdominal muscles tightly.

Ankle Circles

With one leg lifted in the air, circle your ankle clockwise to its extreme range, then counterclockwise. You can do one leg at a time or both together. You can bend the knees and support the legs by clasping your hands together around your thighs.

Toe Flexing

While lying on the floor, bend your toes forward and back as far as they will go.

Knee Flexing

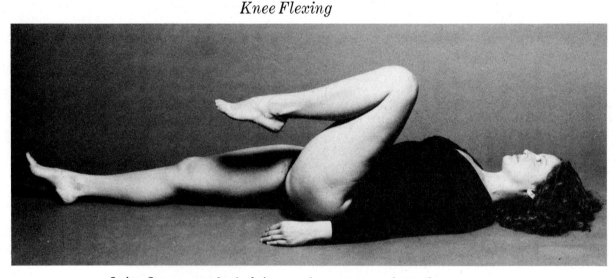

Lying flat on your back, bring one knee to your chest; then place the same leg back on the floor, straightening it out. Keep alternating legs.

Bent Leg Circles

Lying flat on your back, move your leg out along the floor, slowly bending the knee.

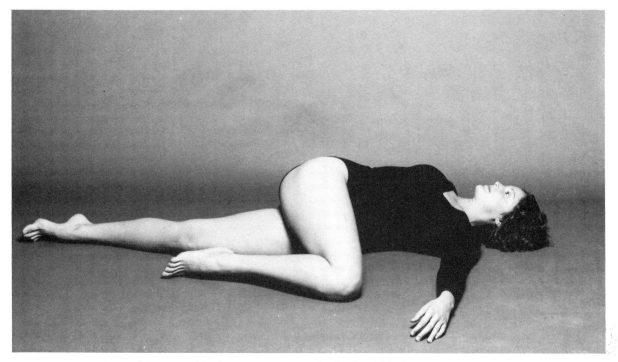

Reach with that knee across the body, 180 degrees over to the other side, allowing the hip of the rotating leg to come off the floor.

Straighten your leg as you bring it back to the starting position.

Do this several times. Switch legs and repeat. Now go back to the original leg and reverse the movement.

Straight Leg Circles

They are identical to bent leg circles, except that they are done with a straight leg. Both warm up the hip joint.

Descending Knees

This exercise is good for the lower back. Lying on your back, raise your knees and put your feet flat on the floor.

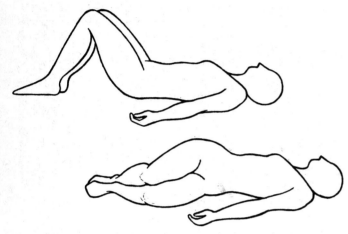

Lower your knees to the left side and try to keep your pelvis from retracting. Relax there for a moment and raise them once again. Allow them to fall to the right side.

You can do this exercise for some time since it doesn't require much exertion. Remember to breathe regularly throughout the exercise.

Small Jumps

Stand with your feet parallel or slightly turned out. Make very small jumps, barely leaving the floor. When you land from each jump, make sure that the knees are directly over the toes. When you look down, you should be able to see the first two toes on the inside of each foot. Your toes can remain in contact with the floor throughout, if that is easier. Each time you land, roll through the foot, making sure you don't come down with a thud. Your heels should not pop up at the end of a landing. If in landing you cannot place your knees over your toes, roll through your foot, or keep your heels down, discontinue the exercise until you find a professional who can teach you to do it properly.

Heel Raises

Stand with your feet parallel about one or two inches apart, squeeze the buttock muscles together, and simultaneously straighten both legs, using the thigh muscles. Inhale and rise up onto the balls of the feet. Hold this position for a few seconds and then slowly come down, exhaling. Keep your weight forward; don't rock back onto your heels. After every three or four heel raises, shake your legs out and relax. Rise only as high as you can with control, which could be as little as one inch off the floor.

Warm-Ups

In order to engage in strenuous activity without injury, the muscles must be warmed up. All warm-ups should be done gradually. Contrary to common belief, they should not be strenuous or straining, but easy, pleasant, and slowly building in vigor and effort. In general, warm-ups should begin with deep breathing. Exercises to warm up the legs should begin while lying with the legs in the air. In this way the muscles and joints in the legs are relieved of the pressure of standing. A warm-up should take at least five but not more than fifteen to twenty minutes.

Before you indulge in any sports activity, whether it be as calm as golf or as vigorous as basketball, do an appropriate warm-up. In the following pages are a sample dance warm-up, a general sports warm-up, and a runner's warm-up. Breathe through your mouth during every exercise, and for thirty seconds' rest between them.

Dance Warm-Up

LYING DOWN

1. Find a comfortable position and breathe for a few minutes
2. Foot Shaking
3. Knee Bounce
4. The Bicycle
5. Ankle Circles
6. Toe Flexing
7. Knee Flexing
8. Bent Leg Circles
9. Straight Leg Circles
10. Descending Knees

STANDING UP

11. Head Drop
12. Shoulder Drop
13. Shoulder Roll
14. Arm Circles, single and double
15. Shakedown

Sports or Athletic Warm-Up

LYING DOWN

1. Foot Shaking
2. Knee Bounce
3. The Bicycle
4. Ankle Circles
5. Knee Flexing
6. Straight Leg Circles

STANDING UP

7. Head Drop
8. Shoulder Drop
9. Shoulder Roll
10. Arm Circles
11. Chest Stretch
12. Waist Twists
13. Shakedown

14. Heel Raises
15. Run in Place
16. Small Jumps
17. Foot Shaking, while standing

Runner's Warm-Up

LYING DOWN

1. Foot Shaking
2. Knee Bounce
3. The Bicycle
4. Ankle Circles
5. Knee Flex
6. Straight Leg Circles
7. Bent Leg Circles
8. Toe Flexing

STANDING UP

9. Waist Stretch
10. Waist Twists
11. Heel Raises
12. Run in Place
13. Small Jumps
14. Deep Breathing

Chapter 7 · DEEP MASSAGE: MUSCULAR THERAPY THEORY AND TECHNIQUE

The image of massage in this country is poor. Many people associate it with prostitution, corruption, and the seedy side of life. In their business, many prostitutes utilize anything they can as a cover. They learn some simple massage techniques and call themselves masseuses and masseurs, to avoid prosecution. This has a decidedly bad effect on the image of massage and on the true professional who practices it. As a result, professional masseurs often encounter sneers or embarrassing remarks about their work.

The media exploit the sensational side of massage. Newspapers, magazines, books (even some so-called massage books), and films dwell on massage as a cover-up for the sale of sex, but rarely explore its importance in health and medicine. In England massage is highly respected and used in hospitals throughout the country. In France it is one of the most important facets of a physiotherapist's training. But in this country most physiotherapists receive only four to twelve weeks of superficial massage instruction. The Finns and the Japanese regard massage as seriously as the English and French do, and my own training course in muscular therapy and deep massage takes approximately two to three years.

In the past, true massage in this country was used only as medical treatment, never for the pleasure or increased well-being of healthy people. Now that the image of massage has deteriorated, the medical profession has moved away from the use of it. Doctors are reluctant to explore the possibilities of massage for posttrauma healing or tension states, and textbooks on these topics rarely mention massage. Twenty-five years ago, nurses were thoroughly trained in massage. The nurses I am training these days tell me that they learn almost nothing about massage in school, an unfortunate circumstance since they are in a position to use it effectively for large numbers of people. It is to be hoped that the medical world will rediscover the use of deep massage as an adjunct to standard medical treatment and physical therapy.

Getting Started

This chapter is intended as a beginner's manual to accompany private or classroom lessons in the basic techniques of deep massage and muscular therapy. These lessons will serve as an introduction to the subject.

You cannot, however, master massage from a

book. In the courses I teach, I demonstrate and explain each movement five or ten times. When members of the class first try to duplicate the movements just seen, they invariably do them incorrectly. The many subtleties of each movement cannot be explained in a book, but can be learned only by working with a good teacher.

People studying deep massage fall into four categories: (1) those who have a natural feel for the work and pick up the movements easily; (2) those who have difficulty in the initial stages, but, once they have picked up the basic skills, do very well; (3) those who are too tense and can master the movements only after they have received treatment to help them relax; (4) those who cannot do the work under any circumstances. The latter group, a small minority, includes people with tremendous tension in their arms, shoulders, or backs, people who have little sense of rhythm or movement, and people who tend to have cold, clammy, or sweaty hands while working.

Being Relaxed

In order to give a good massage, you must be relaxed yourself. If you are tense, you will transmit that tension to your subject. My students are required to undergo some treatment as part of the training. The number of treatments varies according to the degree of tension present. In addition to relaxing you, it is especially helpful to experience the movements on your own body in order to perfect them on someone else. It is important to know what the techniques feel like to gauge how much pressure should be applied and where.

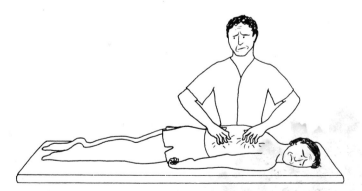

Brain-Hand Coordination

When you copy a movement, the brain sends signals to the hands, telling them what to do. Although everyone has some brain-hand coordination, it must be fully developed to master deep massage. As I mentioned before, beginners often see one movement but perform another.

About six years ago, a student who had completed one of my seminar-workshop courses requested private lessons. At the very first lesson she did *everything*, even the most subtle movements, correctly. I expressed amazement at her facility, and she explained that she had been involved for several years in Effort/Shape Training, a technique for studying the quality and shape of movement.* This previous experience had developed her hand coordination. Like this student, most people can strengthen their skill with practice and concentration.

Where the Tension Lies

The first thing I teach my students is to recognize and identify tension through visual observation. Then we proceed to identification by touch. It takes a great deal of study and practice to develop those visual and tactile skills. This is one of the most important skills, and one of the most difficult to acquire, for a muscular therapist.

Watching the Face

When working on someone's body, you have to know how much pressure to use. If you work too lightly, you are ineffective. If you apply too much pressure, you can hurt the subject. How do you judge how much pressure is proper for each individual? You can ask the person to tell you what hurts and what feels good, but some people feel foolish or weak if they say something hurts. Others are to shy to speak up. The best test for pressure is the subject's face. Often, people speak through their expressions more accurately than through their words. The face can tell you when the pressure is pleasurable and when you've gone too far. For this reason, watch the face constantly at first. If the subject falls asleep while you're working, you're using the right pressure.

* See Cecily Dell, *A Primer for Movement Description*, published by the Dance Notation Bureau, New York.

Pain Tolerance

Some people experience a deep-massage technique as painful, while others find the same technique pleasurable. The deciding factor is tension. A tense muscle will become more tense when pressure is applied to it, and beyond a certain point increased tension will be experienced as pain. A relaxed muscle will not tense in response to pressure and will usually experience the pressure as pleasurable.

Testing Your Pain

Testing your pain makes an injury worse. Often, after an injury, people will persistently test to see how their injury is healing, causing pain each time they do. Every time you do this you are straining and pinching the afflicted area, making it worse. If you must test the pain, do it once, and never again until the injury heals. Try to keep your movements within the limits of comfort, so that your pulled or strained muscle can rest to do the necessary repair work.

Don't Let a Friend Crack Your Back

Beware of letting someone who is not a trained professional do a chiropractic adjustment on your neck or back.

The spine can move out of line in a sideways direction or in a front-to-back direction, or there can be pressure. When this is chronic or severe, some professional help may be needed. But having a friend attempt to adjust the alignment of your back and neck vertebrae can be extremely dangerous. I know someone who couldn't turn his head for three or four weeks and someone else who had back trouble for more than a year, due to well-meaning friends. So when someone who is not a trained professional asks you if you would like him to crack your back or neck, just say, "No, thank you."

Problem-Solving Techniques

Certain techniques are helpful in learning to understand tension and what to do about it. I suggest investigating in the following manner:

1. Get a complete description of the problem:
   a. Where is the discomfort or pain? Have the subject indicate the specific area.
   b. How long ago did it start?
   c. What, in the subject's opinion, started it?
   d. How long does the pain last each time it occurs?
   e. How often does it occur?
2. Find out about past injuries, operations, or broken bones.
3. What kind of physical activity does the person engage in?
4. Locate the muscles, muscle groups, or body segments involved.
5. Try to determine the cause of the problem.
6. Why does it manifest itself in that particular way?

Talking During Massage

Talking during deep massage is not a good idea. If you are a beginner, it disturbs your concentration and at any stage can prevent the subject from concentrating on relaxing. Sometimes a client talks compulsively, a trait that indicates jaw, throat, and neck tension. In this case, suggest that he work at being quiet and concentrate on relaxing. You might have him use the cork technique as described on page 32. Let the subject do the cork exercise while you are working on him. If you know the movements well, conversation with the client is fine, when appropriate.

Supplies You Need

Both you and the subject should be comfortable. You can use a high, firm bed, a kitchen table, a mat on the floor, or the floor itself. Most people use the floor, with a few towels. If you are working on a professional table, the proper height of the table is usually equal to the distance from the floor to the bottom of your fist when your arm is at your side. If the table is lower it won't hurt you, but if the table is higher it will produce tension in your shoulders, neck, and back. A professional massage table is, of course, best. Portable ones run about $150, but if you become serious about the work, you'll want to buy or build a permanent one.

In preparation for work, place a couple of towels, or a piece of 1½-to-2-inch-thick foam rubber covered with towels, on the surface where the subject will lie. If the subject has a lower-back problem, a pillow under the abdomen is desirable. When working on the floor, place a large folded towel or a pillow under your knees for comfort.

Be sure to check your nails. Always have a nail clipper and a file with you. Your nails should be very short. To test them, point each finger, one at a time, into the palm of the other hand and press firmly. If you feel your nail at all, it's too long. It's not necessary to cut your nails this short at first, but if you get serious about the work, by the third or fourth lesson it's essential.

Creams and Alcohol

To eliminate friction, apply cream to the areas you are working on. Nivea Liquid and Albolene Cream are good. Baby oil is all right too, but mineral oil clogs the pores. Any cream that dries quickly, such as Nivea Cream, Vaseline Intensive Care, or Dermassage, is not good. I find organic coconut oil the best, because it has no smell, is not greasy, doesn't stain, is reasonably priced, and the thin quality lets you feel the body. A little more expensive, but also excellent, is the Edgar Cayce skin lotion Aura-Glow, a combination of peanut, olive, and almond oil, lanolin, and vitamin E.

Only experience will tell you how much cream to use. Too much makes the subject too slippery; too little creates too much friction. After the treatment is finished, alcohol can be used to clean the subject thoroughly, if he or she desires. Rubbing alcohol is good, but witch hazel does not cut through the grease as well. The more pleasant and effective alcohol is Superior 70 Alcoholado, a product of Puerto Rico. It can be found in groceries or drugstores in Spanish-speaking neighborhoods. When using alcohol, be careful not to splash it on the subject's face.

Attire

The worker should wear a smock to keep oil off his clothes. The subject should be in underwear or an open-back smock to provide maximum privacy while permitting access to the body. Allow the subject to change in private before and after the treatment.

When NOT to Massage

Under certain conditions precautions should be taken before deep massage is done. The following are contra-indications for doing deep massage:

1. Skin, muscle, or bone diseases
2. Infections underneath the skin
3. Pain or tension due to unhealed fracture of any bone
4. Presence of cancerous tumor, because of possible spread to bones
5. Severe arthritis, in which there is a danger of fracturing bones
6. Recently ruptured muscles and tendons
7. Generally poor health

In case of doubt regarding the presence of illness, a physician should be consulted prior to massage.

The Importance of Practice

There are no magic formulas to learn, and there are no shortcuts either. The only way to learn is to practice. Repeat each lesson many times, and have at least three or four separate practice sessions before proceeding to the next lesson. You can read all the lessons in one sitting, but go back to the beginning and take your time in learning them. *It is more important to learn a little bit thoroughly than a great deal superficially.* Getting the movements right—the difference between giving a treatment that does nothing and one that is successful—is possible only through work and practice. Practice sessions get longer as you learn more movements. Limit your lessons to two a day, though the ideal pace is one lesson and several days' practice before going on to the next.

The following lessons represent what I have found to be the most important and effective movements and techniques. There are hundreds more, but by mastering these you will gain the widest knowledge from the minimum number of techniques.

Follow the lessons in the order in which they are given. Since this sequence has evolved through years of experience, it is important that the techniques be learned, practiced, and applied in order.

Lesson One · THE GENERAL BACK

Leaning and Breathing

Two essential concepts in deep massage are leaning and breathing. Without a firm grasp of them, the work will be difficult.

Leaning means using your weight, not your strength. If you use your strength you will tire quickly and be unable to work for extended periods of time. Women often learn to use their weight faster than men do, because in most cases they are not as strong and must learn to apply the force behind the techniques by leaning.

Relax your arms and hands completely. Move your body so that it is leaning into your arms and

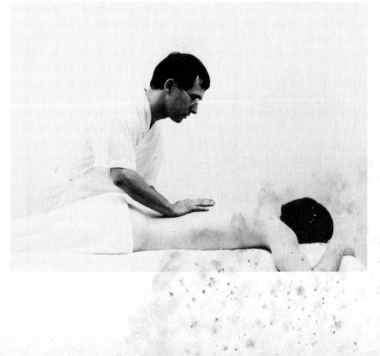

hands, with your elbows slightly bent. Do not squeeze or push with your fingers and hands. When you use your strength, you tighten your arms and hands, which only serves to make you and the subject tense. If you're not relaxed, the subject won't be helped by you effectively. For this reason, you must learn to breathe deeply as well as lean. Breathing is the key to keeping yourself relaxed.

The Firm Drag

Every movement has two parts—a lean and a drag. Pressure is generally exerted in one direction only. When returning to the starting position, the hands should almost always remain in contact with the body. Do not press too forcefully or lightly brush the hands on the body, but drag back firmly with only the weight of your hands. This is as important as leaning and breathing for a successful treatment.

Stroking/Kneading Techniques

There are two basic deep-massage techniques. The stroking/kneading technique begins with light movements and gradually increases until the pressure is strong. Movement is in the direction of the muscle fibers. This technique encourages the return of blood to the heart through the veins. It is primarily venous circulation that is disturbed by tension problems.

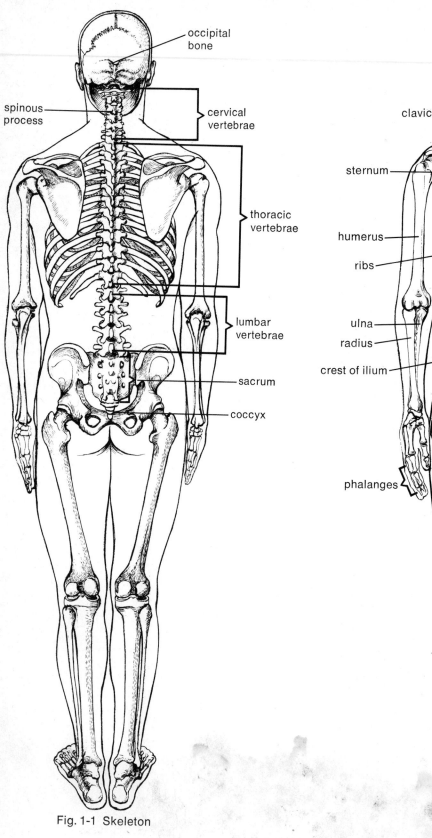

occipital
bone

spinous
process

cervical
vertebrae

thoracic
vertebrae

lumbar
vertebrae

sacrum

coccyx

Fig. 1-1 Skeleton

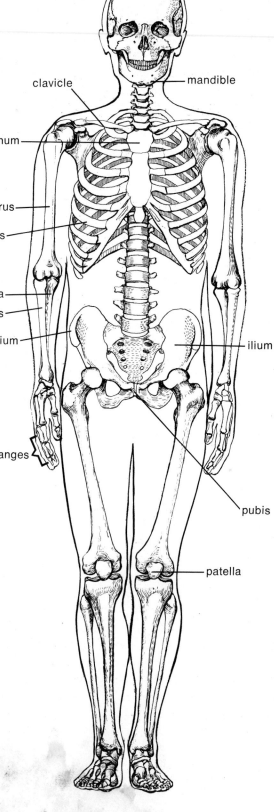

clavicle

mandible

sternum

humerus

ribs

ulna

radius

crest of ilium

ilium

phalanges

pubis

patella

Fig. 1-2 Skeleton

Pressure Techniques

Pressure techniques are the second type of deep-massage movement in the Benjamin System of Muscular Therapy. This method breaks tension quickly and sometimes causes slight momentary discomfort. Pressure movements are applied across rather than in the direction of the muscle fibers. They are effective for acute spasms, injuries, and serious tension problems.

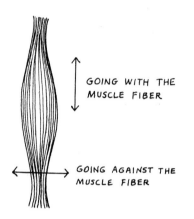

GOING WITH THE MUSCLE FIBER

GOING AGAINST THE MUSCLE FIBER

Muscles can accommodate only a certain amount of tension, although the actual amount varies from person to person. The pressure techniques increase the tension beyond the point of toleration. When this occurs, the muscle has no alternative but to yield, thereby releasing some tension. Thus, a client who tightens up in response to a pressure movement does not hinder the treatment and may even aid it by increasing the tension to the necessary degree. The general rule is to proceed as slowly as is necessary to enable the client to tolerate the treatment process. He should find it relaxing and enjoyable even when pressure techniques are employed.

Pressure movements go deeper and work faster than stroking/kneading ones, although both have the same objective. Stroking/kneading movements affect more superficial tension and encourage blood circulation at a much slower pace. For best results, deep-massage treatments should alternate pressure and stroking/kneading movements according to the client's needs.

Although in most cases alternating between heavy and light treatment achieves the best results, it is not always advisable.

If a client is sore from overexertion, a light treatment is indicated even if the previous one was light.

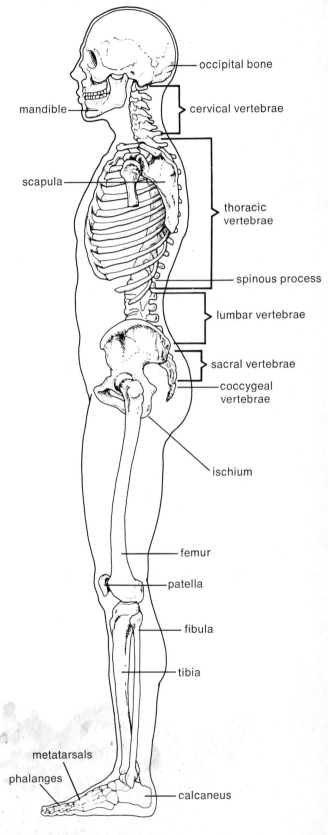

occipital bone

mandible

cervical vertebrae

scapula

thoracic vertebrae

spinous process

lumbar vertebrae

sacral vertebrae

coccygeal vertebrae

ischium

femur

patella

fibula

tibia

metatarsals

phalanges

calcaneus

Fig. 1-3 Skeleton

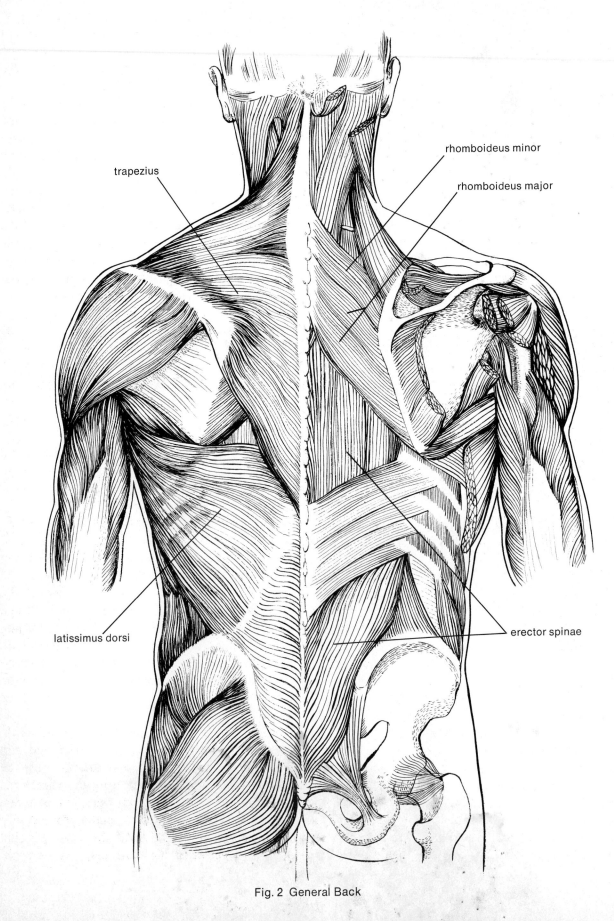

trapezius

rhomboideus minor

rhomboideus major

latissimus dorsi

erector spinae

Fig. 2 General Back

On the other hand, if a client comes in with a tension headache, a heavy treatment is called for regardless of the previous treatment.

Pressure movements, difficult to learn even with private instruction, can be dangerous when used by the unskilled. I have included instructions for a few pressure movements, and those described should be applied with great care. They should be executed lightly and only for short periods of time.

Muscles and Bone Structure

There are at least six hundred muscles in the body, or more, depending on how you wish to count. It is more important to understand the function of muscle groups than the names of every muscle in the body, since muscles always work in groups. In each lesson I will mention the largest and most important muscles for each body part.

In order to gain a sense of the muscles in relation to bone structure, study the diagram of the bones that make up the body. We will refer to some of the major ones throughout this section.

Joints

The point at which two bones meet is called a joint or an articulation. The contacting surfaces are covered with a layer of elastic tissue called cartilage. All freely movable joints also have a sac around them which produces a lubricant called synovial fluid to reduce friction and nourish the joints. The bones are held together with tough fibers called ligaments. These also help protect the joints. The movement of a joint is carried out by muscles that cross over it and usually attach to the bones on either side with cords called tendons.

Muscles of the Back

The main muscles in the back are:

1. *The trapezius,* which goes from the neck out to the shoulder and down to the center back, is a large, diamond-shaped muscle and one of the most important. The trapezius is involved in most actions of the shoulders and upper back, including raising, rotating, and pulling the shoulders down and back. It also draws the head back.

2. *The latissimus dorsi,* a large, triangular, flat muscle, extends over the center and lower back. It is attached to the spine from mid-back, to the top of the hip, and to the top of the arm. It pulls the arm sideways, helps extend it, and rotates the upper arm. It also helps in lifting and supporting weight.

3. *The rhomboideus major and minor* are muscles attaching to the spine and the inner border of the shoulder blades under the trapezius. These muscles rotate and lift the shoulder blades as well as draw them together.

4. *The erector spinae (paraspinal)* muscles are composed of more than nine hundred short muscles that run the length of the back on each side of the spine from the bottom of the skull to the tops of the hips. They are usually referred to as two muscles, one on each side of the spine. They bend the entire spinal column and are important in posture.

Why Work on the Back First?

In order for treatment to have a lasting effect, it must be given in a precise order, which usually but not always starts with the back. We work on the back first to encourage the circulation so necessary to relaxation.

1. Most of the muscles in the back are large and contain many muscle fibers. If they acquire and hold tension, they block blood circulation and energy flow to the rest of the body.

2. The lungs and breathing apparatus are located in the trunk. Deeper and freer respiration is essential to relaxation and can be encouraged by breaking down tension in the upper back.

3. The heart is located in this area. One of the essential purposes of deep massage is to encourage venous blood circulation. This is blood returning through the veins to the heart. Since all the blood in the body must eventually move toward and go through the heart, it is essential that this area be unblocked first.

We begin with the general-back-movement series, five gentle movements to warm up the back and prepare it for deeper work. These movements cover the entire back, the muscles right near the spine, the shoulders, the neck, and the lower back, in that order.

The movements in lessons 2, 3, and 4 proceed with gradually increasing depth into the more specific areas of the lower back, the shoulders, and the neck.

The intensity of the treatment thus builds and the deeper movements are given only when the body is ready for them. Lesson 5, on the deep back, is the beginning of intermediate techniques that go deeper and deeper into the entire back area.

How to See Tension in the Back

When someone has a humpback or a swayback, or stands hunched over or lopsided with all the weight on one hip, there is tension in the back. In general, any exhibition of stiffness while moving is a sign that the back is tense.

Causes of Tension in the Back

Mechanical Causes

1. Daily heavy work, such as that done by a landscaper, ditchdigger, mason, contractor, or longshoreman.
2. Poor posture habits.
3. Improper calisthenics or dance training.

Emotional Causes*

The primary emotional cause of tension in the back is pent-up anger. We've all heard the expressions "Get your back up," "My back is against the wall," and "Get off my back." These are various expressions of rage. They are used when someone is angry and the anger hasn't been released. These held-in feelings are reflected in tense back muscles.

How to Feel Tension in the Back

Touch the subject's back and notice both body temperature and tightness. If the skin is cold, there is probably a lot of tension in the area. Heat is distributed through the body by blood circulation. If one area is colder than the rest of the body, it usually means circulation in that area is diminished, and therefore the muscles are tense. If the skin is warm all over, it's usually a good sign.

While working, try to get a sense of where the body is contracted and where it is loose. This isn't easy at first. If you press gently and it hurts, it means there is tension. If the subject jumps or says it feels

* The ideas developed in this and all the sections entitled "Emotional Causes" are derived from the works of Wilhelm Reich.

strange or ticklish, it indicates more severe tension. The ticklish sensation often results when tense muscles become even tighter when touched. This response prevents penetration of the muscle because the body knows it would be very painful. The muscle tightening is the body's automatic defense mechanism.

Defining Terms

Movement unit or set: Throughout the lessons, a time count in seconds is given for each movement to indicate the proper timing. The movement is then referred to as a set or a movement unit. Both the stroke *and the return to the original position* comprise one set or movement unit. When two hands execute the movement one after the other rather than together, it may also comprise a set or movement unit.

Movement repetition: After each movement description is a suggestion of the number of times that movement should be performed. *This number applies only after you have fully mastered the movement.*

Corrections

Following the description of each movement is a section called Corrections. There are fifteen or twenty possible errors in each movement, depending on individual idiosyncrasies. The corrections sections list the most common errors. *Don't skip or skim these sections.* Study them carefully.

Your Position While Working

Stand to the left of your subject, facing in the direction of the head as on page 61. Your right hand is closest to the subject's body. If you are working on the floor, find and maintain a comfortable leg position. If you get cramps or pains in your legs or back, keep changing your position. Consistent discomfort means you are tense in general, or you're tightening your body in a certain position. You probably aren't leaning or breathing properly, but straining and using your strength instead.

Never straddle the body when working. You can do all the movements more efficiently from the side. Since we're aiming toward working on a table, your work habits should be applicable to table treatment.

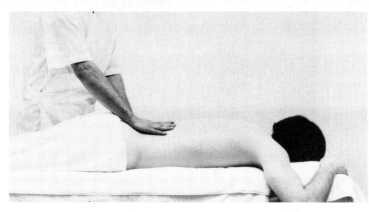

Left- and Right-Handedness

It is best to be ambidextrous. Always try to learn movements equally well with both hands, by practicing from both sides of the table. This increases your skill and sensitivity by balancing your muscular development.

If you are left-handed begin by learning all movements on the side opposite the one indicated in the instructions.

When the client is in the proper position, cover the legs with a towel and tuck it into the underwear, as shown below.

Remember to lean with your weight and to breathe to relax. It's important to learn these essential elements in the beginning.

General Back Movements

Read each movement description all the way through before attempting it. This applies to every lesson.

1. Heart Movement

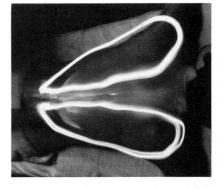

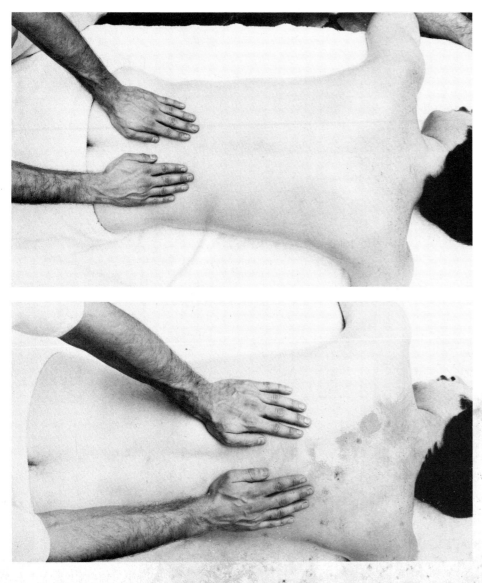

Stand to the left of the subject's lower back, with your feet parallel, the left one about a foot ahead of the right. Start with the hands in parallel position, with the heels of the hands on the crest of the ilium, which is the top of the hip bone. The weight is evenly distributed over the entire hand throughout the movement, and the elbows are slightly bent, never stiff.

Lean, letting your weight fall into the subject's body as your hands move straight up the back.

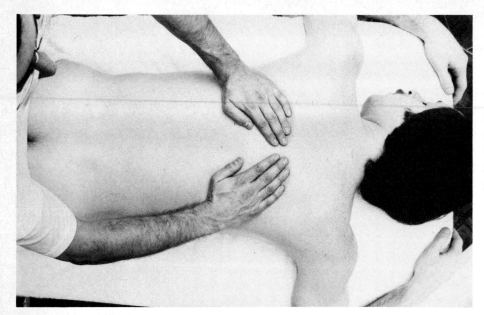

When your fingers reach the lower tip of the shoulder blade (the scapula), about two-thirds of the way up the back, turn the hands in to a 45-degree angle to the spine so that the movement takes in the shoulder area.

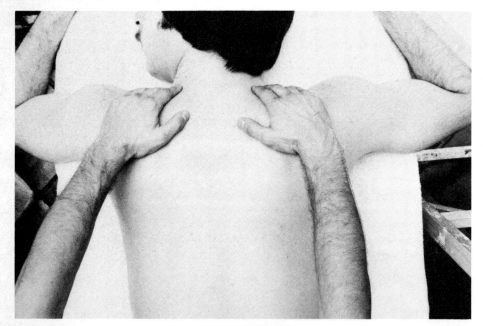

Continue the movement in this position to the top of the back, until the hands are on either side of the neck.

Come around the shoulders to the out-side of the back, straightening the hands to a parallel position once again.

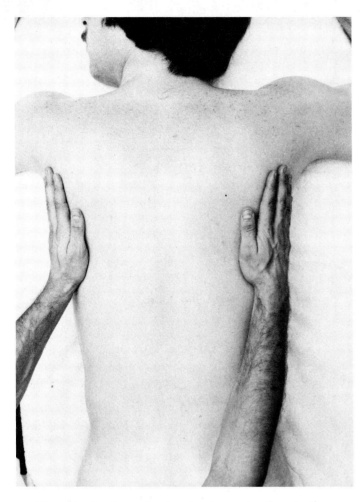

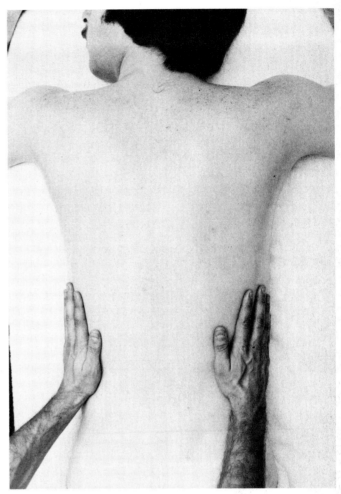

Now firmly drag the hands down to the starting position, being careful not to fall into the armpits with your fingers. Don't lean during the return part of the movement.

> *Timing:* EACH MOVEMENT UNIT SHOULD TAKE ABOUT FOUR SECONDS; TWO ON THE MOVEMENT UP, TWO ON THE DRAG BACK. AFTER YOU'VE MASTERED IT, DO THIS MOVEMENT SIX TO EIGHT TIMES. TOO MUCH REPETITION OF THE SAME MOVEMENT CAN BE IRRITATING TO THE SUBJECT.

CORRECTIONS

1. Begin your pressure at the very base of the back, not an inch higher.
2. Make sure you turn your hands in when your fingertips reach the bottom of the shoulder blades, not before or after.
3. Don't turn too much, only forty-five degrees, not ninety degrees.
4. Go all the way up to the very top of the shoulders, don't stop before.
5. Make sure your hands have equal pressure. Concentrate on the hand farthest from you, since that one will tend to be lighter.
6. Don't drag back too lightly or too heavily.
7. Don't go too fast.
8. Use the whole hand. Don't dig your fingertips into the back or raise your fingertips into the air.
9. Don't raise your shoulders.
10. Keep your elbows slightly bent, never stiff.
11. *Lean your weight, don't use your strength.*

2. The Basic Movement

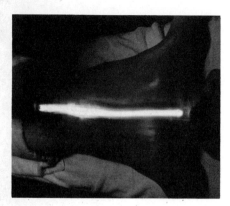

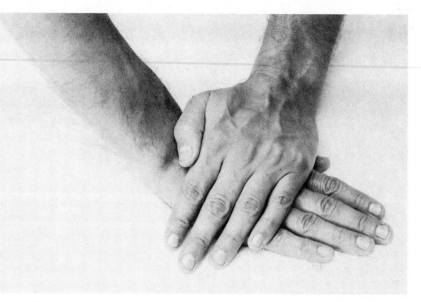

Place the left hand perpendicularly over the right hand, so the body weight is concentrated on one hand. This is called the basic position. It is used often, so make a mental note of it.

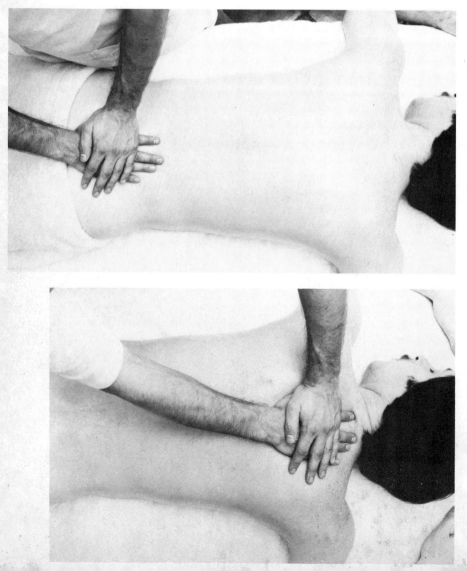

Stand to the left of the subject's lower back, facing slightly inward. The basic hand position is modified slightly by spreading the first two fingers of the right hand. Begin the movement by flanking the spine with these two fingers and placing the center of the palm on the sacrum.

Move up the back slowly, leaning your weight into the movement. The first two fingers, spread about an inch apart, should outline the spine. Your weight is over the entire hand; do not press either the fingers or the heel of the hand into the back. When your hand reaches the top of the back, drag firmly down to the starting position.

> *Timing:* EACH MOVEMENT UNIT SHOULD TAKE TWO SECONDS; ONE SECOND TO GO UP AND ONE TO DRAG BACK. ONCE YOU'VE MASTERED THIS MOVEMENT, DO IT EIGHT OR TEN TIMES.

CORRECTIONS

1. Make sure the index and middle fingers are about an inch apart, not together, and not two inches apart.

2. Use the whole hand; don't press into the heel.

3. Don't go too high and jam into the neck with your fingers.

4. Don't dig your fingers in.

5. Don't drag back too heavily. Both you and the subject rest on the drag back.

6. Don't push, lean.

7. Keep your right shoulder down.

8. Face into the body, not up toward the head.

9. Use the correct hand position; the right hand is on the bottom.

10. Don't wrap your thumb around your wrist.

11. Make sure the left hand is at a ninety-degree angle to the right.

12. Don't lock your elbows, keep them firm but loose.

3. Shoulder Circles

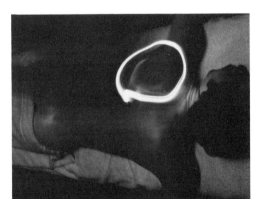

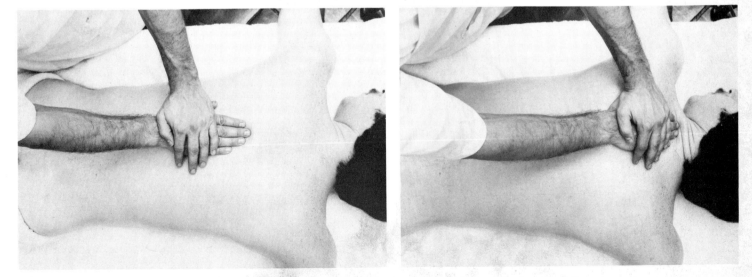

Start in the basic position on the left side of the spine, with the fingers of the right hand in line with the bottom of the shoulder blade.

Lean into your hand as you move up between the spine and shoulder blade.

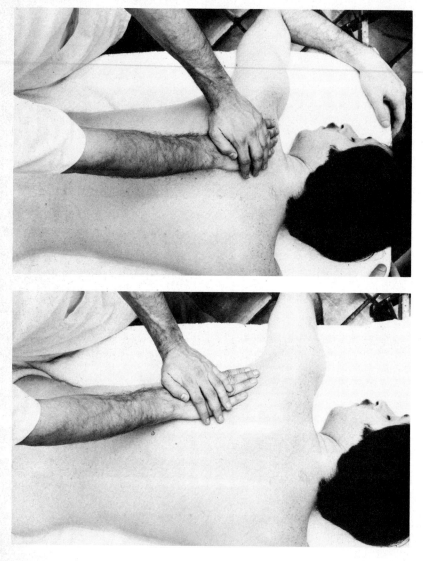

Keep leaning as you come around the shoulder.

Drag back on the outside of the shoulder blade to the starting position to form a complete circle. Half of the circle is a lean, half of it a drag.

Timing: EACH MOVEMENT TAKES ABOUT TWO SECONDS. DO SIX OR EIGHT CIRCLES.

After completing these movements on the left shoulder, *gently* move your hands across to the right of the spine in a figure-8 movement and repeat the movement on the other side approximately the same number of times, using the same hand. You will have to lean over somewhat.

CORRECTIONS

1. Don't hit the spine. Move up between the spine and the scapula.
2. Lean on the up-and-out movement only, not all the way around the shoulders.
3. Lean into your whole hand.
4. Don't do it small. Go around the scapula, not on it.
5. Don't slip into the armpit on the way back.
6. When doing the far shoulder, lean over the back so you use your weight.

4. Continuous Neck Movement

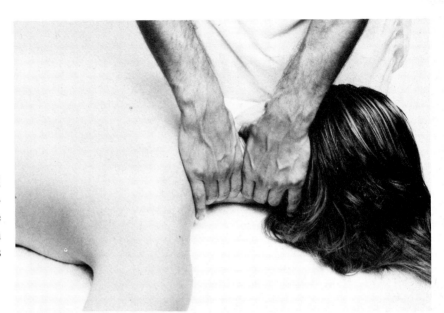

During this movement, the subject's head should be turned toward you. Stand directly to the side of the person and face his head. Grasping the neck, start with your hands side by side, with the thumbs touching.

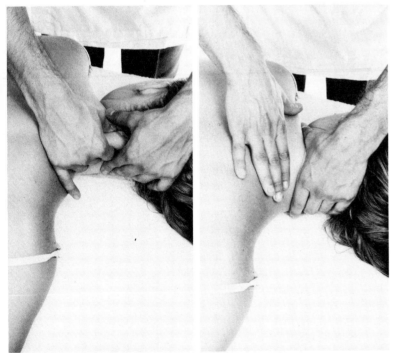

Knead the neck continuously, one hand after the other, touching the neck with the inner palm on each stroke. In order to do both sides of the neck equally, the hands must angle away from you, because the head is turned. If the movement hurts the subject, do it more gently.

Timing: EACH SET, CONSISTING OF A RIGHT—LEFT HAND COMBINATION, SHOULD TAKE ABOUT ONE SECOND. REPEAT EACH SET EIGHT TO TEN TIMES.

CORRECTIONS

1. Make sure the rhythm is even, not irregular or erratic.
2. Don't do it too lightly or too quickly.
3. Don't snap your fingers off the neck. Leave a half inch of skin between your fingers at the end of each move.
4. Make sure the thumb curve (see lesson 2, parts of the hand, p. 70) touches the neck with each movement. Really grasp it.
5. Come off at a 45-degree angle, so that both sides of the neck are worked on evenly. Don't come off with the hands straight up toward the ceiling.
6. Have a continuous flow.

5. Lower-Back Square

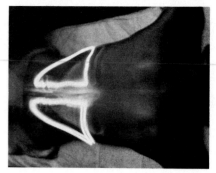

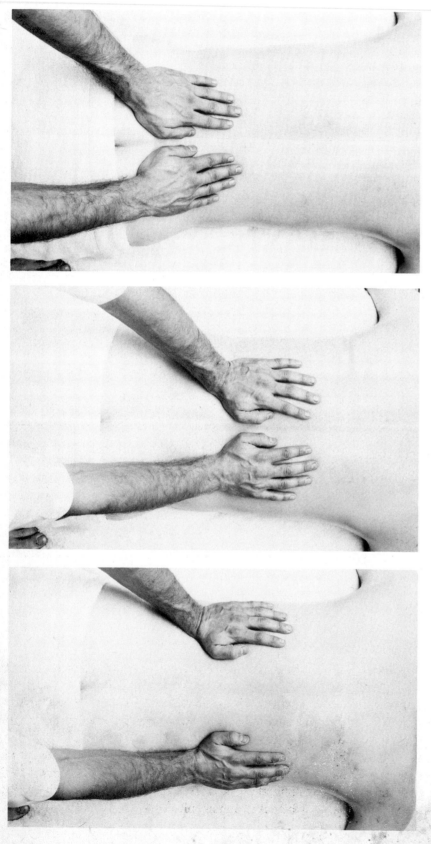

Start with the heels of the hands on the crest of the ilium (this beginning is the same as for the heart movement). The whole hand is used in the work, but slightly more pressure is on the heels of the hands.

Lean straight up to the lower edge of the ribs with the heels of your hands.

Keeping the heels at the edge of the ribs, continue to lean as the hands move straight to the sides.

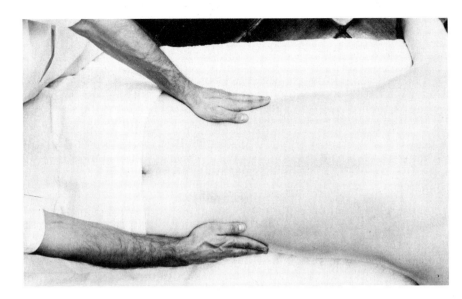

When the hands are on the sides of the ribs, drag back to the starting position.

Timing: THIS MOVEMENT UNIT SHOULD TAKE APPROXIMATELY THREE SECONDS AND SHOULD BE REPEATED SIX OR EIGHT TIMES.

CORRECTIONS

1. Don't lean into the top of the hip bone. Start just above it.
2. Lean especially into the heels of the hands, but be sure to use the whole hand.
3. Don't stiffen the fingers into the air.
4. Don't go too high and hit the ribs. It hurts the subject.
5. Make sure you press on the way out to the side, as well as when going up.
6. Try to scoop out the lower back.
7. Don't do it too small.
8. Stop just at the base of the rib cage.
9. Don't push, lean your weight.
10. Be sure to relax your shoulders.

Run through all the movements in sequence. Once you have mastered them, it should take you four to five minutes to run through the entire lesson's movements the suggested number of times. Now do all the movements from the other side to facilitate your ambidexterity.

Alcohol—Its Application After Treatment

When you have finished practicing these movements, pour a little rubbing alcohol in one hand and put it on the subject's back immediately while still holding the bottle in the other hand. Gently apply small amounts of alcohol three or four times until the back is lightly coated with it. Don't let it dribble on the subject. If you do drip some alcohol on the subject's back, immediately place your hand on the back and spread it around. Don't rub it in, just on.

Now put the bottle down. Throw the towel over the back, grip the shoulders through the towel, and firmly drag the towel down the back. Wrap the towel around one hand and wipe off the whole back again firmly.

The coldness of the alcohol may shock the subject, so complete the process quickly. One sure way to eliminate this discomfort is to use heated alcohol, which is extremely pleasant.

Lesson Two · THE LOWER BACK

When I speak of energy, I mean orgone energy,* a physical phenomenon that can be observed and demonstrated under scientific conditions. At the beach on a sunny day you may have observed energy as pinpoints of light dancing in front of you.

Put down this book for a moment and clap your hands together vigorously for about thirty seconds. Then rub them together for thirty seconds. Now rapidly shake your hands in the air for a minute. You may feel a buzzing or a tingling sensation in your fingers. Immediately after these activities, hold your hands with the corresponding fingers of both hands a half-inch apart for about a minute. You may feel a magnetism or pushing or pulling between the fingers, heat, or a pleasant tickling sensation. You are actually feeling the movement of energy between your hands.

When you do deep massage, if your hands get warm or tingly or you are conscious of a buzzing sensation in them, energy is moving into your hands. If your hands are cold, energy is withdrawing from your hands.

A great deal can be expressed with the palm of the hand and its use is important in deep massage. You must be able to move energy through the palms of your hands, which makes your hands warm. When you do deep massage, concentrate on your hands. If they become warm while you work, it means you are relaxing and allowing energy to move into your hands.

* Wilhelm Reich, *Function of the Orgasm* (New York: Farrar, Straus, and Giroux, 1973); *The Cancer Biopathy* (New York: Farrar, Straus & Giroux, 1973); "The Oranur Experiment," *Selected Writings of Wilhelm Reich* (New York: Farrar, Straus, & Giroux, 1973).

Parts of the Hand

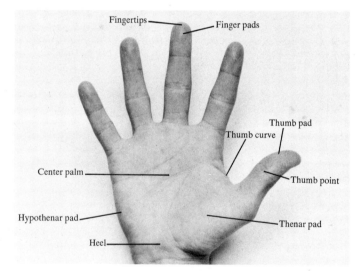

There are nine parts of the hand important to these lessons:

1. Center palm
2. Heel
3. Thenar pad
4. Thumb pad
5. Thumb point
6. Fingertips
7. Thumb curve
8. Hypothenar pad
9. Finger pads

Learn these names thoroughly. They will be referred to constantly throughout the lessons.

Dribbling the Hands

In deep massage, always touch the subject firmly. A light brushing or dribbling of the hands over the body makes the subject uncomfortable. It is at the least an unpleasant sensation that indicates you may not know what you're doing. A subject may not identify the specific feeling of that feathery touch as that which made him uncomfortable, but it still may prevent him from returning. The touch sometimes grows lighter just before you stop, so take care to finish up the work firmly, but gently.

Finding the Spinal Curve

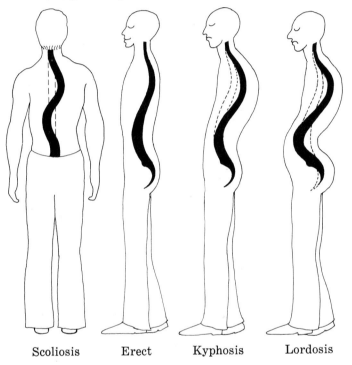

Scoliosis   Erect   Kyphosis   Lordosis

Get in the habit of running your fingers down both sides of the spine with medium pressure, to check its alignment. If the spine is curved to the side in a modified S, this indicates a condition of scoliosis. It generally means the muscles are tighter on the same side as the curves. Also check for the degree of kyphosis and lordosis. Kyphosis, or hunchback, as it is commonly termed, describes an accentuated backward curve in the upper part of the back. Lordosis, or a swayback condition, describes an accentuated forward curve in the lower back, and is generally associated with a retracted pelvis. If these are structural deformities, you cannot change these conditions with muscular therapy, but you can help eradicate pain associated with them. If tension or bad posture is the cause, then deep massage and therapeutic exercises can realign the spine.

Muscles of the Lower Back

The main muscles of the lower back are:

1. The lower part of the *latissimus dorsi*.
2. The lower segment of the *erector spinae*.
3. *The quadratus lumborum*, a thick muscle going from the lowest rib and the lower spine to the back of the pelvis. It bends the spine sideways, helps maintain the position of the pelvis, and functions in breathing. It is very deep and is important in posture.
4. *The iliopsoas*, which runs from the front of the lower spine through the pelvis to the front of the inner thigh. It pulls the bottom of the pelvis forward and up and flexes the thigh to the front.

How to See Tension in the Lower Back

The way someone moves can indicate tension in the lower back. Bending, turning, or straightening rigidly often means tension. If the subject's pelvis is chronically retracted (see page 74) there is tension in the lower back. When the subject is lying down, you may see an exaggerated lordosis (a big dip) in the lower back or an exaggerated kyphosis (a hump) above the lower back. Either condition is often associated with pelvic retraction and a tense lower back. When there is severe tension in the lower back, any pressure applied is painful.

Muscular-Pain Syndrome—A Functional Approach

It is often important to work first with the surrounding area rather than the area of pain. This breaks down the accompanying muscular blockage and brings blood and energy to the injured or tight part. Remember that the body functions as a unit. When a person has a pain on one or both sides of the lower back, it is generally accompanied by tension in the surrounding area. Specifically, the center back, one or both hips, and the outer thigh muscles will almost always be tight and pull against the lower-back area. Other common examples are neck pain accompanied by shoulder tension, forearm pain by upper arm tension, and foot pain by calf tension.

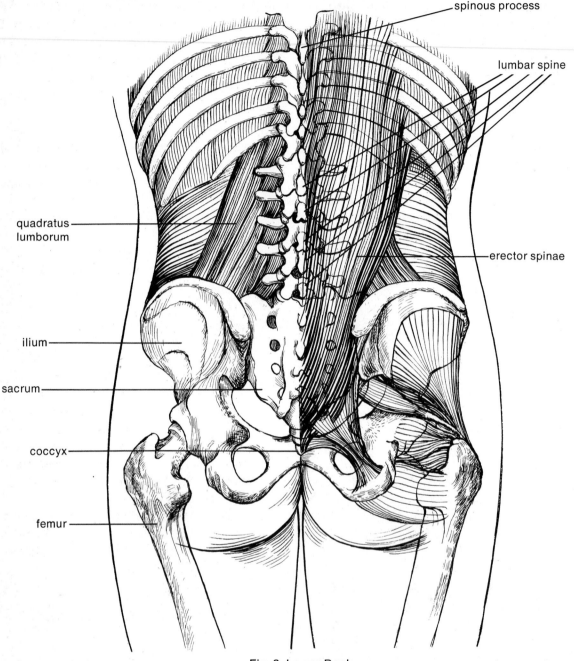

Fig. 3 Lower Back

For this reason it is often more important first to relieve tension in the surrounding region.

Spasms

A muscle spasm is a severe, involuntary muscular contraction that extends over time. There are two types of spasms: chronic and acute. Chronic spasm, which is often referred to as chronic tension, has usually been present in a muscle over a period ranging from several months to many years. It is usually emotional in origin, and is armor. It is not experienced as pain unless pressure is applied to the muscle. Chronic spasm is often not felt at all, but can be felt as stiffness, constant aching, or chronic fatigue. Acute spasm occurs when tension is pushed to its limit. It is extremely painful, usually occurs suddenly, and covers a broad muscular area. It can last for an hour, a week, or several months. Acute spasm often occurs when tension overwhelms the muscle already in a state of chronic spasm. The body crosses its tension threshold, and the resulting pain inhibits further activity until the muscle recovers. The triggering cause of an acute spasm can be mechanical or emotional.

A Case of Lower-Back Pain

A thirty-year-old dance instructor came to me with morning lower-back ache and occasional spasms of the lower back. The spasms extended across the entire lower back just above the hips. Her first visit indicated pressure on the sacrum, a fairly loose neck and upper back, and an extremely tense center and lower back. She had chronic spasms in the center back and acute ones in the lower back. Her hips were very tense, as were her outer thighs. She had had bad spasms for several days when I first saw her, and she told me that they occurred about every two months. Each spasm lasted about two weeks and they were becoming progressively worse. She could not remember when she last woke up without a lower-back pain. I explained that the pain was an indicator of a mass of tension in that part of the body. The situation was becoming worse because she had done nothing about the general tension in her body.

She was skeptical about muscular therapy. She had undergone other types of treatment in the past, but the spasms always returned.

Since the neck and upper back were soft, I began deep work on the center back, which responded quickly. Using considerable heat in conjunction with treatment, I worked only slightly on the lower back at first, and concentrated on the surrounding area. I traced the spasms to the hips and worked in that area, with special attention to the right hip and outer thigh, which were very tense. Hip and outer-thigh tension almost always accompanies lower-back pain. It soon became clear what was causing the lower-back spasms. She had a chronic spasm in her hip that she was unaware of. When there was an increase of tension in the thigh, hip, and center back, it became too much for her body to absorb, and her lower back would go into active spasm. As I dissolved the tension in the hip, the lower back also relaxed. As soon as she stood up, she realized the spasm had improved. I said that it would probably take another treatment or two for the relief to be

more lasting, and gave her instructions to take half-hour baths in the morning and at night. I warned her that she would be sore from the treatment because we had broken tension that had been there for a long time. When she came again, she informed me that the morning after the first treatment the spasm had disappeared completely, although she was a little sore from the treatment.

Later she underwent extensive treatment to relieve her morning lower-back pain, the forerunner of the spasm. After a month of treatments on her hips and legs, the morning pain appeared only occasionally, and then faded away after about five minutes.

As the treatment progressed, I gave her kicking and stamping exercises to do. Nearing the last phase of the treatment, we began to work on her physical habits. I had noticed during her first appointment that her feet turned out, her knees faced straight ahead, her weight was in her heels, and her pelvis tipped forward. I explained how this tipped-pelvic posture put damaging pressure on her lower back. As a dance teacher, she had an understanding of the body, and working together we corrected her posture in a few weeks, an unusually brief period.

After two and a half months her morning lower-back pain had completely vanished, due to the success in breaking the tension in her thighs, hips, lower back, and finally, at the insertion of the paraspinals, at the top back of the pelvis. I worked on this sensitive area slowly and gently.

Her warning of trouble was, of course, her morning lower-back pain, which was unheeded for many years and ended up in spasm. Now, after three years, her problem has not returned.

Causes of Tension in the Lower Back

Mechanical Causes

1. A ruptured or disintegrated disc. If the pain is of a long duration, fairly constant, or sharp, or caused by an accident, see an orthopedist. However, most lower-back pain is caused by tension, not by disc problems. And disc problems themselves are often the result of long-standing tension.

2. Incorrect dance, sports, or calisthenics training, which often include incorrect use of the pelvis.

3. Doing a great deal of lifting, improperly. Certain occupations demand constant lifting.

4. Poor posture habits.

a. Stand with your feet parallel, about eighteen inches apart. Place your fingers on your lower-back muscles just above the bone on either side of the spine. Now, tip only your pelvis forward by pushing your buttocks out, keeping your back straight. With this condition, the muscles of the lower back become tight and protrude. If you stay in this position and walk around coming down on your heels a little harder than usual, you'll feel each step jar the lower back and spine.

b. Stand and place your weight on one hip, sitting into that hip. With your hands still on your lower back, retract your pelvis. You should feel the lower back getting tight on the side you're sitting into. If you stand like this regularly, you are creating tension in your lower back.

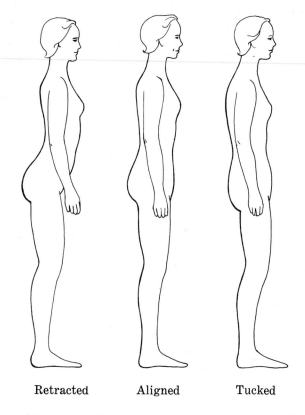

Retracted   Aligned   Tucked

Your weight should be evenly distributed between the two sides of your body. Stand on both legs, your feet pointing straight ahead, with your legs six to twelve inches apart, your hands dropped at your sides. Your head, rib cage, and pelvis should all be in line so that they are balanced and centered directly over one another.

c. Sit in a chair and tightly cross your legs. The effect is a tightening on one side of your lower back. It's best to sit with your feet flat on the floor, although if you don't have excess tension, crossing your legs won't hurt you. If you do have excess tension, it could trigger a spasm.

Emotional Causes

Because tension in the lower back may be emotional in origin, e.g., sexual fear and rage, it is important to work carefully in this area. It is also essential not to work too deeply into the pelvic area too quickly. This area includes the insertion of the lower-back muscles into the hip bones, the buttocks muscles, the inner thighs, the abdomen, and the pelvic floor.

Before practicing the movements in this lesson, warm up the back with the movements from lesson 1. Check yourself on leaning, breathing, and correct placement of the towel.

Lower-Back Movements

6. The Triple Heart Movement

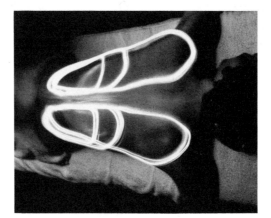

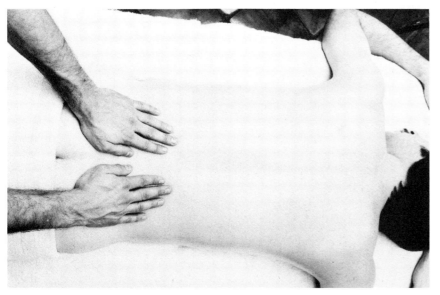

PHASE ONE
Stand next to the subject's left hip, with your left foot ahead of your right foot. Place one hand on each side of the spine just at the crest of the ilium, as in the heart movement. Your fingers are gently together and your weight is in the whole hand.

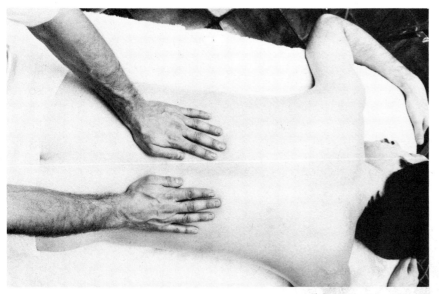

Keeping the hands parallel, lean and move up one third of the back, or about six inches. Release pressure as you move your hands to the side, and drag back to the starting position. The hands remain parallel throughout the entire movement.

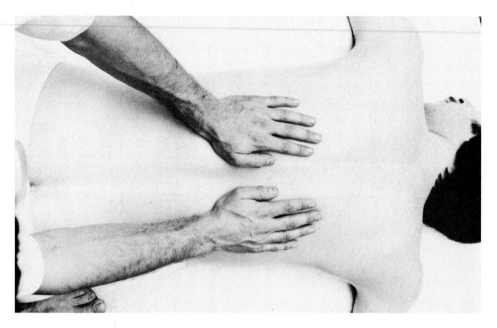

PHASE TWO

After doing this movement *once*, enlarge it to cover an area twice the size. This time the fingers go as far as the base of the shoulder blades. The hands are still parallel throughout. Each time you start a new phase, return to the original starting position.

PHASE THREE

The third movement is identical to the heart movement in lesson 1. Move your hands straight up, turning them in just below the bases of the shoulder blades so that the fingers are facing one another at a forty-five-degree angle. Continue up to the base of the neck. Then bring your hands back into parallel position as you move them slightly outward. Release pressure and drag firmly down the outer edge of the back.

This movement is a triple progression in which you cover one-third, then two-thirds, and finally the whole of the back.

> *Timing:* THE PHASES TAKE ONE, TWO, AND THREE SECONDS, RESPECTIVELY. DO ONLY FOUR OR FIVE COMPLETE SETS OF THIS MOVEMENT.

CORRECTIONS

1. Note the same corrections given for the heart movement in lesson 1.
2. Do not rush over the lower back when doing the second and third phases of this movement. This is the most common error.
3. Do not move too fast. The rhythm should be slow and even.
4. During the second phase, be careful not to let the fingertips hit the armpit.
5. Do not turn the hands in during the first and second phases, only during the last.
6. Do not turn the hands out.
7. In each phase, start your pressure at the bottom of the back.

7. The One-Two Lower Back

This is a complex and difficult movement because of its special rhythm. Rhythms, discussed in detail in lesson 5, have very different effects on the body. The movement here is similar to that of the lower-back square, but it has a slightly different shape and is done in an alternating rhythm. One of the more important rhythms to learn, it has four beats with a slowdown on the third beat:

1   2   3   4

Left, right, pause, drag back together.

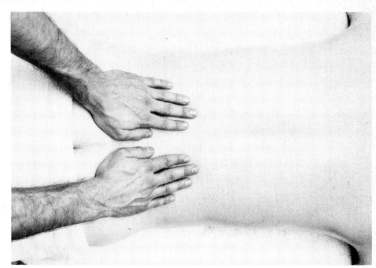

Standing just to the left side of the subject's hips, face toward the head. Place your hands at the base of the back, just below the crest of the ilium, as you did to begin the triple heart. The movement begins with your left hand at the base of the left side of the subject's back, just at the crest of the ilium (the top of the hip bone).

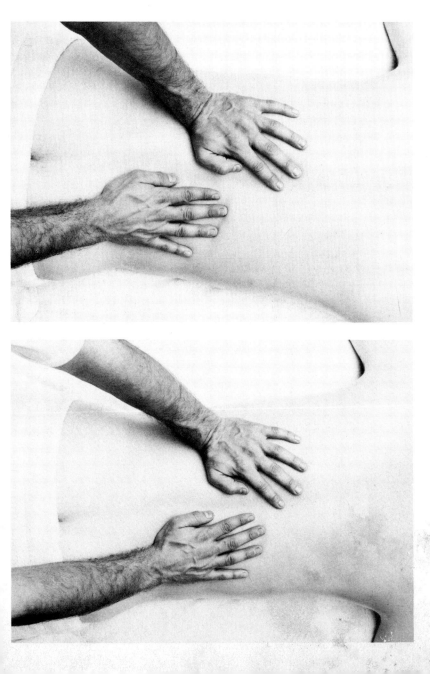

Using the whole left hand with the accent on the heel of the hand, move up the lower back until your heel reaches the base of the rib cage.

The right hand follows identically one beat later. As you move up, the hands turn slightly in toward the spine, about ten degrees.

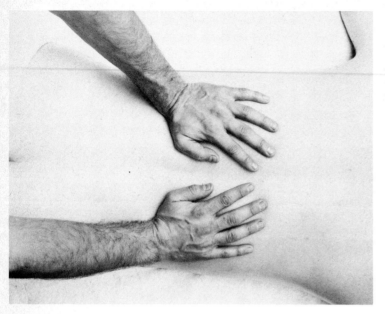

At the top of the movement, move the hands away from the spine, still using pressure. Then drag the hands together back down to the starting position.

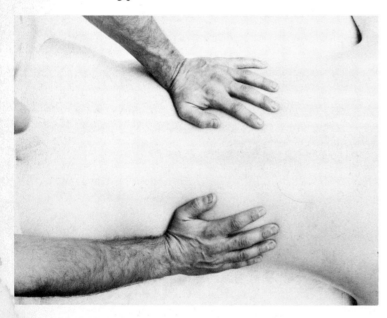

As the heel of each hand goes to the base of the ribs and back, it makes an oval on the lower back. The left hand leads and the right hand follows, starting one beat later. The left hand keeps moving but slows down at the top of the movement and waits for the right hand. Then, both hands drag back together. When the movement begins, the hands are parallel to the spine. By the time they reach the top of the movement, they have turned in about ten degrees. Imagine you are *scooping out the lower back* with the heels of your hands.

The hands should exert equal force. The hand on the far side of the back has a tendency to be lighter. Although there is slightly more weight placed on the heel of the hand, the entire hand is flat on the body during the whole movement. The rhythm is smooth, even, and very pleasant to both the subject and the practitioner. This movement takes a great deal of practice.

> *Timing:* EACH OF THE FIRST TWO BEATS TAKES SLIGHTLY LESS THAN HALF A SECOND. ONE, TWO, AND THE PAUSE USE UP ONLY A SECOND. THE DRAG BACK TAKES A FULL SECOND. THUS, EACH MOVEMENT UNIT TAKES TWO SECONDS. WHEN YOU HAVE THE PROPER RHYTHM, THE SPEED OF THIS MOVEMENT CAN BE VARIED, TO PRODUCE DIFFERENT EFFECTS ON THE BODY.
>
> DO THIS MOVEMENT TEN TO SIXTEEN TIMES.

CORRECTIONS

1. Make sure you are concentrating on the proper rhythm. It is easy to get it wrong.
2. Make sure your hands drag back together, not one after the other.
3. Do not have more pressure on one hand. The pressure should be equal.
4. Do not turn the hands in too much, only slightly.
5. Use your body weight.
6. Do not press in with your fingers.
7. Do not stiffen your fingers in the air.
8. Do not go too high and onto the ribs with the heels of your hands.
9. Do not go too low. The heels of your hands should meet the bottom of the rib cage.

8. Thumbs

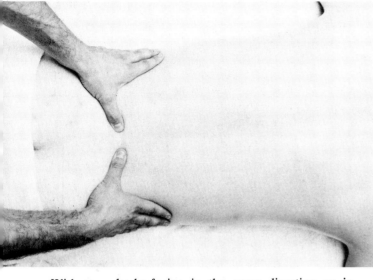

With your body facing in the same direction as in movement 7, place the hands at the base of the erector spinae muscles. Open the hands all the way so that the thumbs are an inch apart. Place the thumb pads so that they are flanking the spine in the *center* of these muscles.

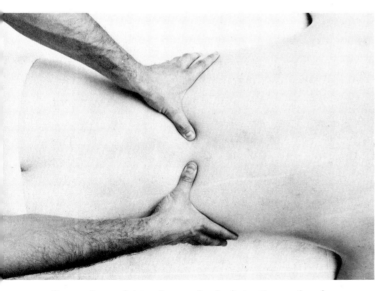

Lean the weight of your body into the pads of your thumbs, with your elbows slightly bent, as you move up about five inches.

Timing: IT SHOULD TAKE TWO SECONDS TO COMPLETE EACH UNIT. DO EIGHT OR TEN COMPLETE SETS.

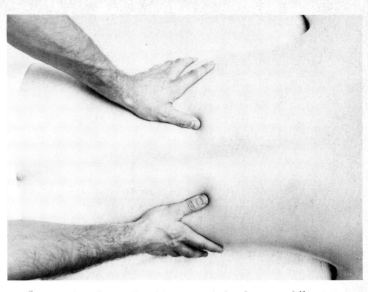

Draw the thumbs to the side toward the fingers while releasing the pressure.

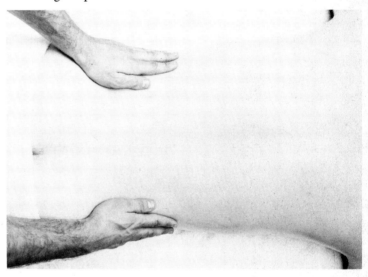

Relax your hands as you drag back to the starting position.

CORRECTIONS

1. Start right at the base of the paraspinal muscles, just to the side of the top of the hip bone, rather than on the hip bone or an inch above it.
2. Do not go too high, only about five inches.
3. Do not press in with the thumb tips or thumb points.
4. Lean, do not press, into the pad of the thumb.
5. Relax the rest of your fingers. Do not squeeze them into the sides of the back.
6. As the thumbs move out at the top of the movement, to join the hand, be sure to let up the pressure.
7. Keep elbows slightly bent and flexible.

9. The Stretch Movement

This one feels terrific to the subject when you get it right, but awful to you until you do.

FAR SIDE

Stand close to the table, facing directly in toward the lower back, with your feet parallel, about a foot apart.

Cross your hands left over right with the outside parts of your hands together, and place them on the lower back just to the right of the spine. As you do this movement, the pressure is in the whole hand, with special emphasis on the outer edge.

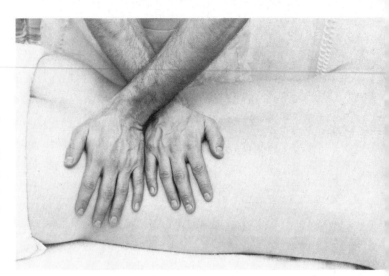

The right hand moves up the back while the left hand moves down the back and into the hip. The first three or four inches should be very deep.

Without lifting the hands, drag them back to the starting position.

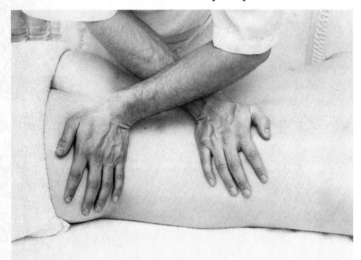

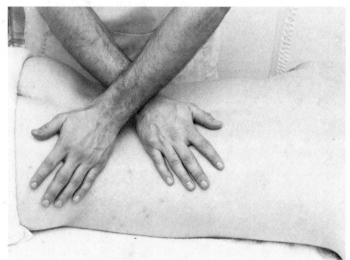

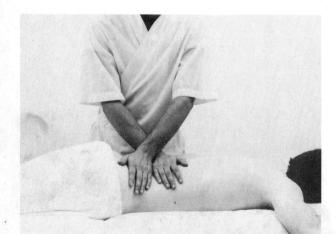

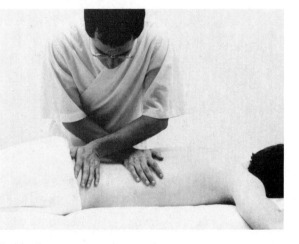

To use your weight efficiently and create strong pressure, your chest folds over the subject's back in a pumping action.

Timing: EACH UNIT SHOULD TAKE ONE SECOND, BUT TRY IT SLOWER AT FIRST.

NEAR SIDE

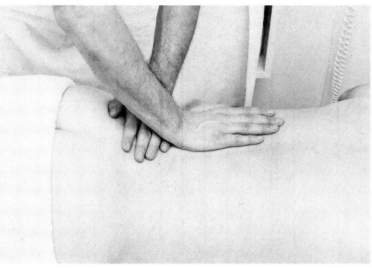

To do the other side of the lower back, reverse the position of the hands so that the right is crossed over the left, then turn your right hand at a ninety-degree angle to the left hand, with the fingers facing the subject's head, as shown above. The position on this side is altered to use your energy more economically.

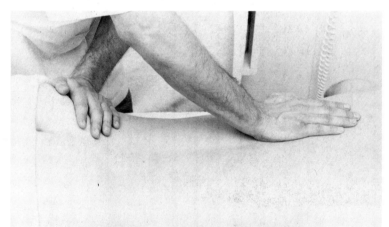

Do the same movement on this side using the new hand position. The only difference is that on the near side, greater pressure is on the heel of the right hand, just to the left of the spine, rather than on the outside of the hand, as on the far side. Remember to drag your hands directly back to the starting position without lifting them off the body.

Timing: THIS MOVEMENT SHOULD TAKE ONE SECOND PER MOVEMENT UNIT AND SHOULD BE DONE EIGHT OR TEN TIMES ON EACH SIDE.

CORRECTIONS

FAR SIDE

1. Make sure the left hand is over the right.
2. Do not use equal pressure throughout the movement. Press into the body with more force through the first three or four inches.
3. Do not hit the sacrum or the hip bone with the lower hand. Glide your hand to the side.
4. Do not hit the spine with the heels of your hands.
5. After you have learned the movement, do not do it too slowly. One second per movement is best.
6. Do not stand erect. Lean over and pump with your chest.

NEAR SIDE

1. Make sure your right hand is crossed over the left at a ninety-degree angle, not the reverse.
2. Make sure the pressure is on the heel of the right hand on this side.
3. Do not stiffen the fingers of the right hand so that they come off the body.
4. All the corrections for the far side apply here, except correction 1. Of course, if you are working left-handed, the hands are reversed.

10. The Sacrum Oval

The sacrum is a large bone at the base of the spine. Many nerves from the spinal cord run out of it, so do this movement gently.

Pressure is primarily in the *center of the palm*. Try to concentrate on the palm throughout the move-

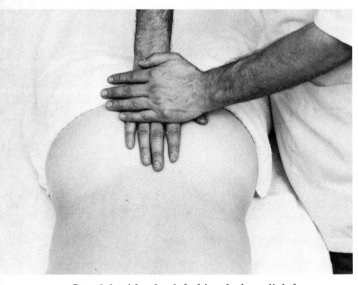

Stand beside the left hip, facing slightly in. Your hands are in the basic position with the right hand on the bottom. The right hand is relaxed, allowing the fingers to spread naturally. Place the right hand on the lower part of the sacrum so that the upper edge of the palm is at the very bottom of the sacrum.

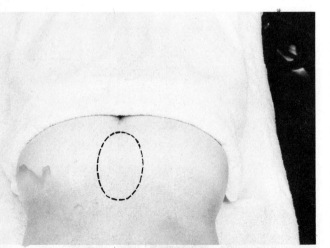

This movement is done in an oval shape, covering the whole sacral area in a clockwise direction. Lean on the up half of the movement and relax on the way back.

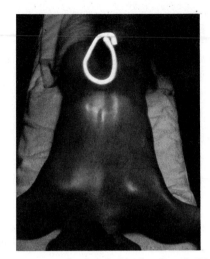

ment. *Do not use the heel of the hand.* Your hands should get warm.

> *Timing:* EACH MOVEMENT TAKES TWO SECONDS. DO FIVE OR SIX UNITS.

When you've concluded the movement, reverse it so that it is done in a counterclockwise direction. If hair in that region of the back should get knotted or matted, this is a sign that you are doing the movement incorrectly. It means that you are doing it too small, and in a circle instead of in an oval.

CORRECTIONS

1. Do not put pressure on the heels of the hands.
2. Do not make the oval too small.
3. Do not jam into the spine at the top of the movement.
4. Make sure your hands are at the bottom of the sacrum, not on the lower back.
5. Use the center of the palm, not the fingers.
6. Move in an oval, not a circle.

> Once you have mastered lessons 1 and 2, it should take you about ten minutes to run through all ten movements the suggested number of times. Try all these movements from the other side so that you balance your muscular development.

Lesson Three · THE SHOULDERS

Up to this point we have been using stroking/kneading movements exclusively. These are gentle movements done at various rhythms and speeds to relax the subject. They follow the muscle fibers and directly improve venous blood circulation.

Both stroking/kneading and pressure techniques encourage circulation by breaking down tension and freeing blood vessels from external muscular pressure. Pressure techniques, however, go deeper and work more quickly. In contrast to the stroking/kneading techniques, pressure movements usually go horizontally across the muscle fibers. Some are rather vigorous and therefore painful to those who are very tense. For this reason, a pressure movement is generally followed by a "smooth-out." This is a gentle stroking action that counteracts the soreness often induced by the harsher technique.

In this lesson we will introduce one pressure technique called the scapula movement. All the movements in these lessons are designed for people with little or no skill. There is no danger in using them, but be careful not to cause pain while working.

The Shoulder Joint

The shoulder girdle, consisting of the scapula (shoulder blade) and the clavicle (collar bone), has only one bony attachment to the trunk, where the

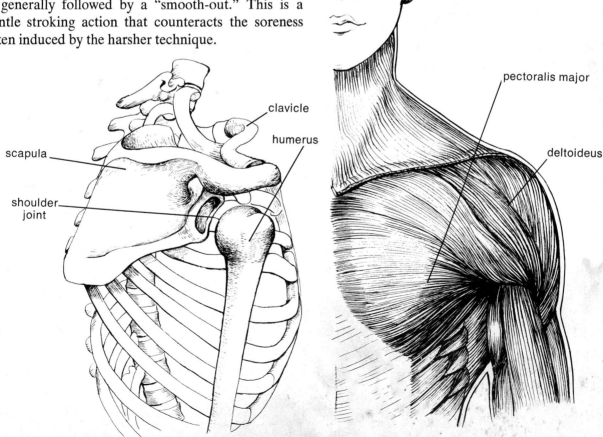

Fig. 4-1 Shoulder

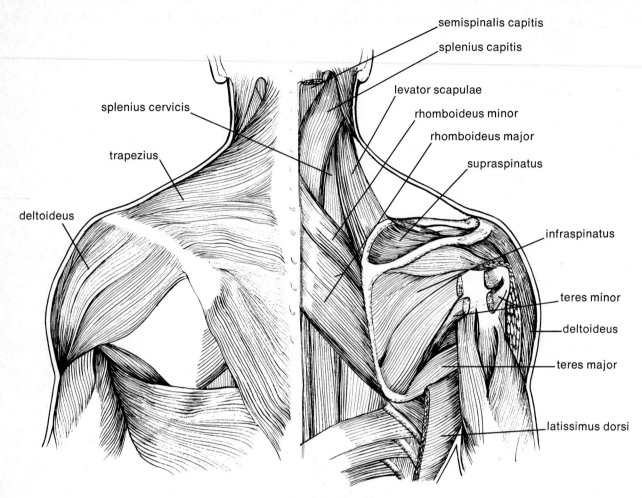

splenius cervicis

trapezius

deltoideus

semispinalis capitis

splenius capitis

levator scapulae

rhomboideus minor

rhomboideus major

supraspinatus

infraspinatus

teres minor

deltoideus

teres major

latissimus dorsi

Fig. 4-2 Shoulder

inner end of the clavicle attaches to the top of the sternum (breast bone). The shoulder joint is probably the most unusual in the body. It consists of a socket formed by the outer end of the scapula and a ball formed by the top of the humerus, or upper arm bone. The ball is large compared with the size of the socket, and is it not deeply imbedded in the socket. The joint has an almost unlimited range of movement because of this construction. It also makes the joint fairly unstable. For this reason, muscles play a large part in reinforcing the joint. The flexibility of the joint varies in direct relation to the degree of muscle development and the amount of tension in the area.

Muscles of the Shoulder

1. *The infraspinatus* covers the lower part of the scapula bone (shoulder blade). It helps in arm movement and holds the shoulder joint together.

2. *The supraspinatus* covers the top of the scapula bone and functions along with the infraspinatus.

3. *The deltoideus* covers the top of the shoulder and is composed of three segments capable of acting separately or as a unit.

4. *The rhomboideus major and minor* are described in lesson 1.

5. *The levator scapulae* goes from the top of the shoulder blade to the top of the spine. It lifts the shoulder blade and functions in arm movements along with the rhomboids.

6. *The teres major and minor* cover the scapula. The teres major aids in carrying out arm and shoulder movements. The teres minor works along with the infraspinatus and supraspinatus in holding the shoulder joint together.

7. *The trapezius* covers the whole shoulder complex and is interwoven with many of the above muscles. Muscles are not separate entities, but interlaced groupings and units. This is why the functional ap-

proach is, again, the best way to view the body and its problems.

How to See Tension in the Shoulders

Shoulders are an easy place to spot tension. The most common manifestations of tension in this area are:

1. Shoulders constantly raised.

2. Shoulders rounded or pushed forward. Young girls with developing breasts often round their shoulders to sink their chest in. Tall girls, self-conscious about their height, have the same tendency, as do some people who are shy.

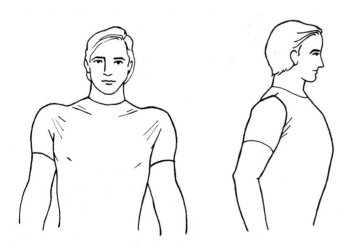

3. Shoulders pulled back and down sharply in a military stance are another indication of tension. This posture can be developed through poor dance and exercise classes as well as military training.

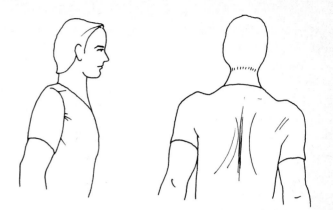

4. Retracted shoulders occur when the shoulder blades are pulled in toward the spine. This is a sign of tension, but it's a difficult one to recognize. One indication is a round protrusion between each shoulder blade and the spine.

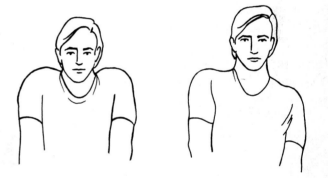

5. One shoulder higher than the other indicates tension. There are a variety of causes for this condition, but a common one is when a person uses one side of his body more than the other. For a balanced muscle structure, both sides of the body must be used equally.

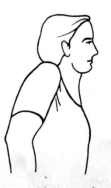

6. Shoulders pulled back and up, usually accompanied by a puffing of the chest, indicates tension in the shoulders as well as in the chest and diaphragm.

Causes of Tension in the Shoulders

Mechanical Causes

1. Occupational causes: The pianist, conductor, dentist, secretary, weight lifter, gymnast, dancer, or laboratory worker may all have tension problems in the shoulders.
2. Poor posture.
3. Shallow respiration.
4. Shoulder-bag or attaché-case syndrome. Always carrying either on one side may produce problems.
5. Accidents.

Emotional Causes

Tension created by withholding rage, fear, and sadness is often held in the shoulders. Therefore, approach this area gently at first, especially when practicing the scapula movement in this lesson.

Fear of Pressure

If your body is tense in a certain area, you may fear applying pressure to the subject in that area. This is particularly true of the shoulder-area movements. For example, in the demonstration of the scapula movement, some students gasp when the thumb is pressed firmly underneath the shoulder blade. They sense it would be painful if done to them, so they are overly cautious and find it difficult to apply pressure to someone else.

Apprehension usually can be overcome by relaxing your own shoulders through deep massage or tension-release exercises over a period of time. Relaxation of the practitioner becomes more important in advanced and deeper-massage movements.

Before you begin to learn the movements in this lesson, run through the movements for lessons 1 and 2. It is best to know them well before proceeding. They also act as a warm-up for the subject.

Shoulder Movements

The movements are done on the shoulder closest to you. When you finish the four movements, walk to the other side and repeat the movements on that side. In this entire series, the client's head is *facing away* from the side you are working on. I call this the "no punch in the mouth" rule. If the head is toward you, the subject might inadvertently get a punch in the mouth if your hand slips.

11. Combing

In this movement you're stretching the trapezius and pulling the blood down from the shoulder toward the heart. Use only four fingers, not the thumb; the fingers should be slightly curled and together.

Facing the subject's head, with your feet parallel, one ahead of the other, start by placing the left hand over the top of the shoulder and pulling straight down onto the back.

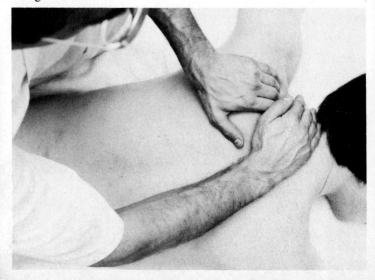

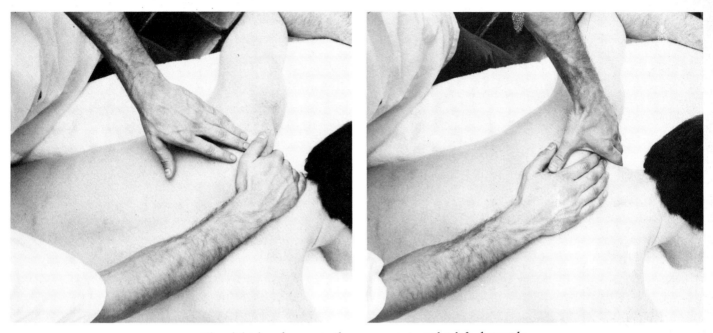

The right hand repeats the movement as the left descends to the bottom of the shoulder blade. The movements are done continuously, alternating the right and left hands; as one hand finishes, the other begins, so that there is no break in the flow of the movement. Try to visualize yourself combing the muscles of the shoulder down onto the back.

Timing: THE RHYTHM IS EVEN AND MODERATELY FAST, APPROXIMATELY ONE SET OF LEFT-RIGHT MOVEMENTS PER SECOND. DO TEN TO FIFTEEN SETS.

CORRECTIONS

1. Do not raise your own shoulders while doing the combing movement.
2. Be sure the subject's head is facing *away* from you.
3. Use the fingertips, or it will feel like nothing.
4. Don't squeeze the top of the shoulder with your thumb when you finish a movement.
5. Keep the rhythm even.
6. Keep constant contact. One hand is always on the body.
7. Don't hit the neck. Stay down on the shoulder.

12. The Deltoid Movement

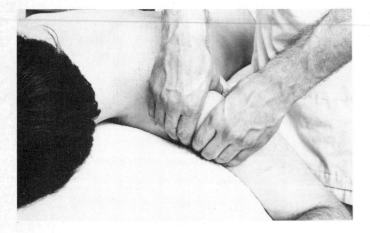

Your body faces the subject's head, as in the combing movement. Grip the deltoid muscle with both hands, as in the continuous neck movement. The hands should be at a 45-degree angle to the table in order to grasp the entire muscle.

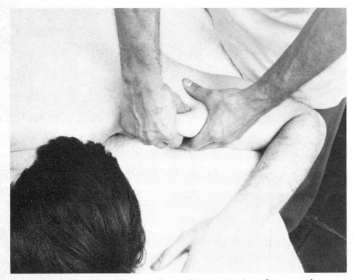

Begin a kneading action with your thumb opposing your four fingers. Each time you repeat the movement, make sure the thumb curve is touching the deltoid. Use your whole hand in this movement.

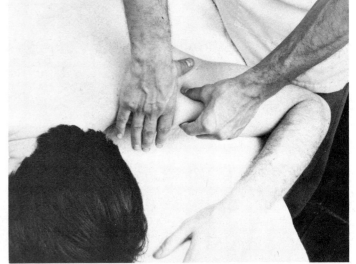

The movement ends when you have about one-half to one inch of skin remaining between your thumb and four fingers.

Be careful not to get your thumbs in the subject's armpits. Squeeze firmly and evenly and keep the rhythm of the movement moderately fast and even. Don't snap or pinch your hands off the body.

Timing: EACH COMPLETE SET SHOULD TAKE APPROXIMATELY A HALF SECOND, OR TWO SETS PER SECOND. DO EACH SET EIGHT OR TEN TIMES.

CORRECTIONS

1. Get the thumb curve onto the body. Don't apply only the fingertips.
2. Don't pinch off the body.
3. Don't come off perpendicular. Keep the hands at a forty-five-degree angle.
4. Keep your thumbs out of the subject's armpit.
5. Don't do the movement too fast.
6. Keep the rhythm even.

13. Scapula Movement

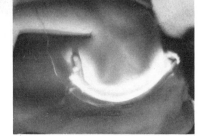

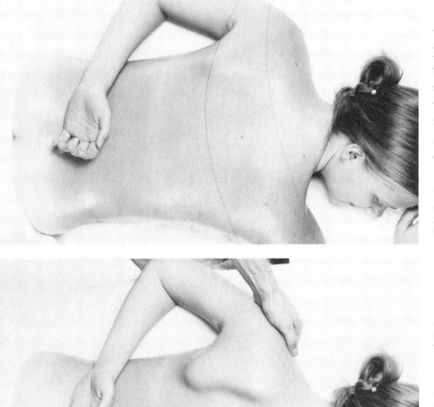

Your body is again facing the subject's head. Stand with the outside foot about two feet ahead of the inside. The outside foot should be in an even line with the scapula. Take the subject's arm by the wrist on the side you're working on, and place the hand on the lower back. Check to make sure that the elbow is relaxed. If the hand doesn't stay there easily and tends to slip off, or if it seems tense, place it by the subject's side, with the hand near the hip, the elbow facing out.

Place your left hand on top of the subject's shoulder. Gently slip around the top to the front of the subject's shoulder tip, so that your hand is between the table and the front shoulder tip. Each time you do this movement, lift the shoulder girdle as shown above and then gently release it. This enables you to penetrate the area underneath the shoulder blade.

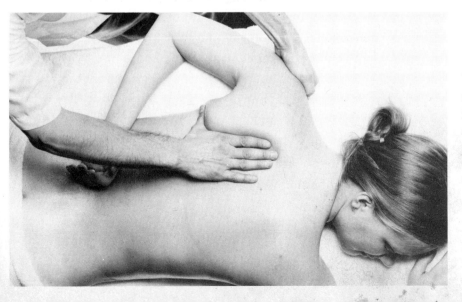

With your thumb at a right angle to your other four fingers, place your right hand in an open position, hugging the bottom of the scapula. This is the starting position. The thumb curve is firmly pressed against the bottom of the scapula bone. This movement is done mainly with the inside of the thumb.

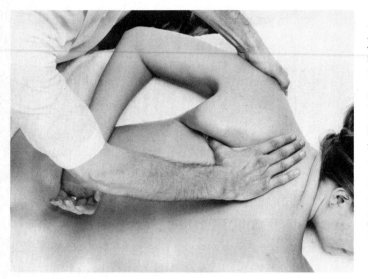

As you move, lean your body weight into your thumb and push up and under the shoulder blade with it. Your body will bend, as you see in the photograph at center left. As you begin the movement, lift the shoulder girdle with your left hand so that you can more easily go up and under the shoulder blade with your right thumb. As you go up, push gently underneath the scapula, and outline the bone all the way to the top. With a relaxed subject, the thumb should disappear under the scapula bone when outlining it.

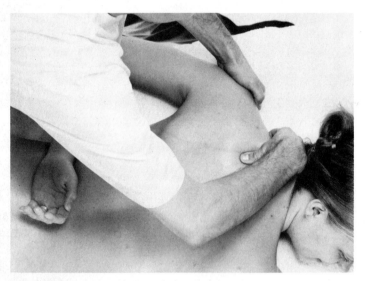

When you reach the top, squeeze your thumb and four fingers together until you have a half inch of skin between your fingers. *Don't* pinch off at the end.

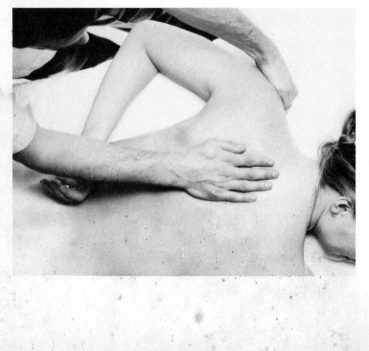

Release the pressure of the right hand and drop the shoulder with the left. Follow through with the thumb of the right hand so that it is parallel to the other fingers, and drag the entire hand back to the starting position.

As you do this movement, your shoulder rotates inward, your elbow moves out to the side, and your torso turns slightly away from the subject.

Be sure to watch the subject's face while doing this movement, since it is a pressure technique and may cause discomfort. If you see pain in the subject's face, lighten the pressure. If the subject is tense, you may not be able to get under the scapula.

Timing: ONE COMPLETE SCAPULA MOVEMENT SHOULD TAKE THREE SECONDS, TWO ON THE WAY UP, AND ONE ON THE DRAG BACK. YOU SHOULD DO FOUR TO EIGHT MOVEMENTS, DEPENDING ON THE SUBJECT.

This is a very difficult movement to learn. Be patient.

CORRECTIONS

1. Don't forget to lift the shoulder girdle gently with the outside hand, but don't dig the fingers in underneath the shoulder.
2. Be sure to release the shoulder when you ease the pressure and drag the hand back.
3. Don't try to outline the scapula with all the fingers, only the thumb.
4. Don't start too low, and don't jam the thumb into the subject's armpit.
5. Don't start too high and miss the bottom of the movement.
6. Don't be afraid to push underneath the scapula bone.
7. Check your nails. You'll scratch your subject if your nails are not *very short*.
8. Don't pinch off at the end of the movement.
9. After bringing the thumb through, drop the shoulder and drag the hand back simultaneously.
10. Don't forget to rotate your elbow out from your body to give the leverage you need.

14. *Scapula Circle*

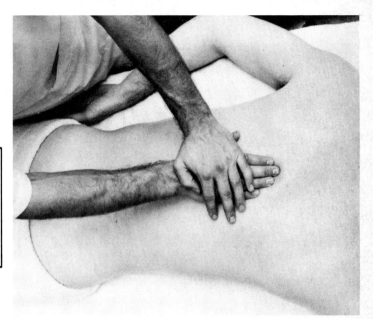

Place the subject's hand at his side on the table. With your body facing his head, place your hand in the basic position on the left side of the spine with the fingertips in an even line with the bottom of the scapula.

Circle the shoulder as in lesson 1, leaning up between the scapula and the spine, going around the scapula to the top of the shoulder, and then dragging back around the other side of the scapula. This movement is identical with the shoulder circle, except that the arm is in a different position. The movement reaches more of the muscles between the spine and the scapula in this position because the scapula moves out from the spine to expose more muscles. This movement smooths out the area, which may be sore from the previous pressure movement.

Timing: DO ONE CIRCLE PER SECOND. DO IT A LITTLE BIT SLOWER IF THE SUBJECT WAS RESISTANT IN THE SCAPULA MOVEMENT. CIRCLE FIVE OR SIX TIMES.

When you finish all the movements, go to the other side and repeat them. Make sure the subject turns his head away from you. When you reach the scapula circle, you will be standing to the right of the subject's body, and your left hand should be on the bottom in the basic position.

CORRECTIONS

1. Bring the subject's hand down to his side.
2. Don't go too high and hit the subject's neck.
3. Don't drop into the armpit on the way around.
4. Stay between the scapula and spine, without hitting either.
5. Keep your fingers together.
6. When changing sides, remember to have the subject turn his head.
7. Keep the left hand on the bottom in the basic position when working on the other side.

Combine the movements of the general back, lower back, and shoulders. The entire process should take fifteen minutes.

Lesson Four · THE NECK

Breathing

The only involuntary system in your body of which you have conscious control without extensive training is the respiratory system. When breathing, it is important to exhale freely and deeply, as the energy moves through the body primarily with exhalation. In this way, breathing creates and maintains relaxation. Exhale quietly but fully while working on someone.

Healthy versus Unhealthy Muscles

Healthy muscles don't hurt when touched with gentle, moderate, or even strong pressure. They are taut and firm when we stand and supple and loose when we are prone. A healthy body has muscles that are supple in movement and skin that is warm and may have a pinkish cast.

When the muscles are unhealthy they look and feel hard or lumpy. Pressure usually causes pain or ticklish and weird sensations. The skin is often pale, prone to hives, acne, or rashes, and may feel cold in areas where tension exists. In rare instances, the skin is cold all over, indicating not only poor blood circulation but a total energy withdrawal from the skin. If the muscles are unhealthy, movement is often awkward and lacks natural grace.

Muscles of the Neck

1. *The splenius cervicis and splenius capitis* are deeply imbedded in the back of the neck. They draw the head back and rotate it.

2. *The trapezius* overlays these muscles.

3. *The sternocleidomastoideus* attaches to the mastoid process at the back of the head and the top of the sternum (the breast bone). It is used to turn the head from side to side, move the chin forward and up, and raise the head when lying down.

4. *The scalenus muscles* are deep muscles of the neck. There are three of them on either side of the neck going from the upper two ribs to the side of each neck vertebra. These muscles aid in bending the neck sideways and help to lift the top of the rib cage in breathing.

All these muscles are involved in controlling the movement of the head.

Neck Tension Test

Sit or stand in a comfortable position. Starting with your head dropped so that your chin rests on your chest, gently roll your head around as far to the sides, back, and front as you can.* If you have pain while rolling your head, your neck is tight. Some people cannot look up even slightly without pain because the neck is so contracted.

Take the back of your neck and squeeze it as hard as you can. If it hurts, or if your reflex is to raise your shoulders, you are tense. If it takes a lot of pressure before you feel pain, the tension is not great.

---

* Though commonly recommended for general exercise programs, I do not find this movement constructive. Due to the difficulty of executing the exercise properly, I recommend it only to test for tension.

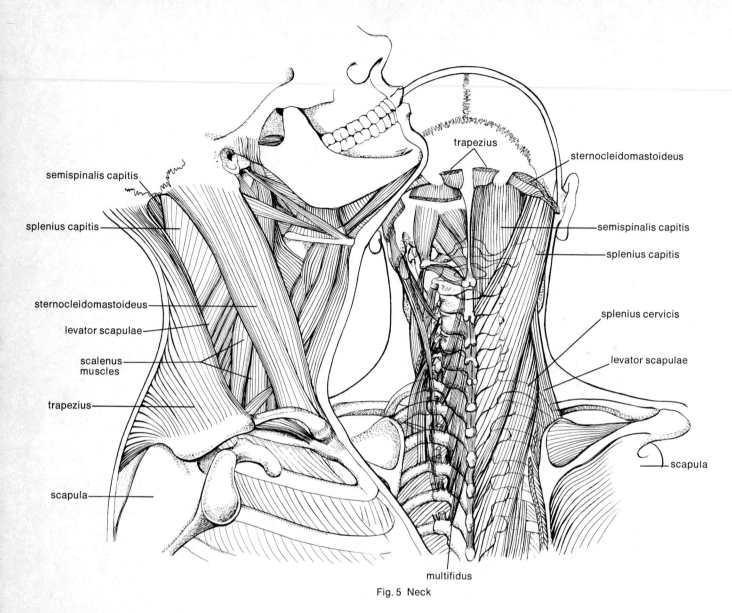

semispinalis capitis

splenius capitis

sternocleidomastoideus

levator scapulae

scalenus
muscles

trapezius

scapula

trapezius

sternocleidomastoideus

semispinalis capitis

splenius capitis

splenius cervicis

levator scapulae

scapula

multifidus

Fig. 5 Neck

How to See Tension in the Neck

1. There is tension if the head juts forward. The head is heavy and should be balanced at the top of the spine. When it is held forward and out of alignment, the muscles have to strain to support it. Only the slightest tension is necessary to hold the head properly.

2. Bulging muscles or veins in the neck are signs of tension.

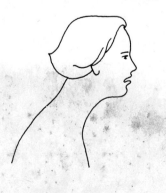

3. A "bull neck," in which the head is pulled down into the body, indicates tension. In combination with raised shoulders, a person with this problem appears to have no neck at all.

4. Difficulty in head rotation or looking up is an indication of tension in the neck.

5. People who clamp their jaws or grind their teeth, either awake or asleep, usually have neck as well as jaw tension.

6. A high, squeaky voice usually indicates neck and throat tension. So do gravelly, piercing loud, or breathy weak voices, and those lacking in projection or resonance.

7. A head constantly tilted to one side indicates a serious contraction caused by tension in the neck.

It is important to view neck tension as occurring in a segmental ring. The neck is a unit whose muscles function together. When chronic contraction exists, the whole neck contracts. The outer muscles will be referred to as the neck and the deeper muscles inside the center of the neck will be referred to as the throat. The deeper a person's tension is, the deeper the chronic spasms go into the neck.

Causes of Tension in the Neck

Mechanical Causes

1. Poor posture with the neck held in a forward position.
2. Whiplash or other injury to the head and neck.
3. An operation in the neck area.
4. Occupations such as:
   a. Models who hold awkward poses for prolonged time periods.
   b. Tunnel-stationed traffic officers whose natural hesitation to breathe creates neck and throat tension.
   c. Dentists who bend over patients in a crouched, uncomfortable position for hours.

   d. Singers who were trained incorrectly. Good singing is relaxing and therapeutic for the throat.

Emotional Causes

Repressed emotion can also cause tension in the neck and throat. Every emotion is expressed through our throat via our voices; repression of any emotion causes tension in the neck and throat.

Neck Movements

Before working on the neck itself, it is important to do the movements from lessons 1, 2, and 3 in preparation. Many muscles of the neck are continuations of muscles of the upper back and shoulders. You can often get the neck to relax by working exclusively at its outer limits. For that reason, many of the movements start at the base of the neck and move away from it. It is preferable to approach the neck in this manner before working more deeply and directly on it. Work on the neck must proceed gently, as it is generally a tense area. For the most part, when working on the neck, we push the blood down and away from the neck toward the heart.

Take a tissue, face cloth, or small towel and place it over the subject's head. Stand directly above his head. If it is facing the left, place your right hand on his head behind his left ear as in the center photograph on page 96, and work on the right side of the neck with your right hand. Be sure not to lean on the hand that's on the head. The function of that hand is to keep the head still. Do all five neck movements in this section on one side, then have the subject turn his head, and repeat them on the other side. If the subject's neck should get stiff on one side, alternate sides after each movement. Remember to use your resting hand to steady the head in all five movements.

15. Downstroke Side

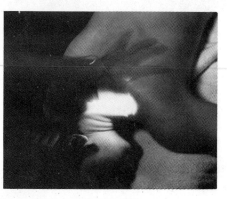

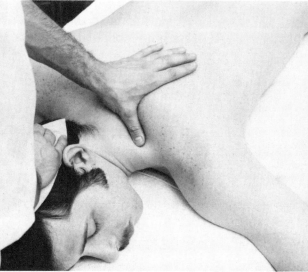

Standing in the position shown above, with the hand completely open, place the left thumb at the nape of the neck, just to the right of the spine. This movement is done exclusively with the entire thumb. The other fingers rest on the back.

Lean into the thumb, keeping it open and relaxed. Don't push with it or your hand will tire quickly.

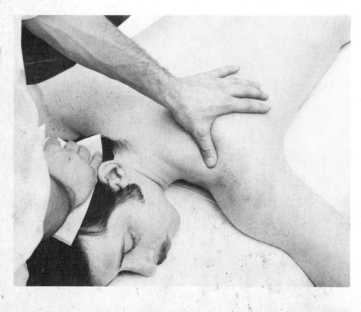

The movement finishes just before the juncture of the collar bone and the scapula. Don't jam into it. Lean on the way out to the shoulder, and, without breaking contact, relax on the drag back to the neck.

Timing: DO ONE MOVEMENT UNIT PER SECOND, SIX OR EIGHT TIMES.

CORRECTIONS

1. Put the correct hand on the subject's head.
2. Don't put the hand over or in the subject's ear.
3. Don't press down on the subject's head during the movement.
4. Remember to use a tissue or a small towel.
5. Make sure the working hand is always open.
6. Don't push with the tip of the thumb. Lean into the whole thumb.
7. Don't go too far and jam into the bone.
8. Use pressure from the very beginning of the movement. Don't start it in the middle of the movement.
9. Lean, don't use your finger strength.

Move your thumb out along the top of the trapezius, pressing the trapezius against the upper border of the shoulder blade.

16. The Downstroke Diagonal

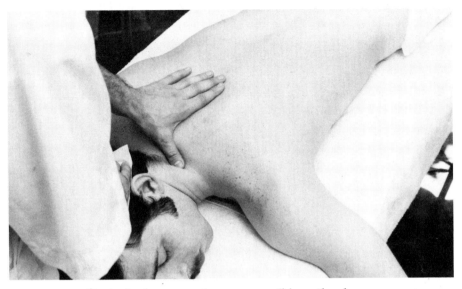

Begin in the same place as you did on the downstroke side, but now the inside of the thumb is pointed diagonally in line with the inner edge of the scapula.

This movement is done with a slight pressure on the thumb point. Open your hand, lean into the thumb point, and trace a forty-five-degree angle to the spine. This is the angle the scapula naturally assumes when we lie down. Be sure to run your thumb just the the side of the scapula, not onto it. The movement is finished when your thumb snaps over the edge of the trapezius muscle running perpendicular to the movement. When you get to the end of the movement, relax your hand without lifting it, and drag back to the starting position.

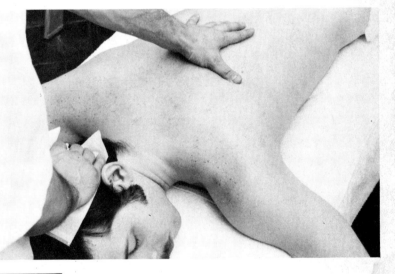

Timing: DO ONE MOVEMENT PER SECOND.
REPEAT THE MOVEMENT SIX OR EIGHT TIMES.

CORRECTIONS

1. Get the right angle. Don't go onto the scapula.
2. Don't make the movement too short or too long. Stop after snapping over the edge of the trapezius.
3. Lean into the thumb point. Don't just graze the subject's back.
4. Don't use your strength, lean.
5. Make sure you start high enough.
6. Don't lift your hand at the end of the movement. Drag it back.

17. The Downstroke Spine

This movement works on the erector spinae, the muscle that goes from the neck all the way down the sides of the spine to the top of the pelvis.

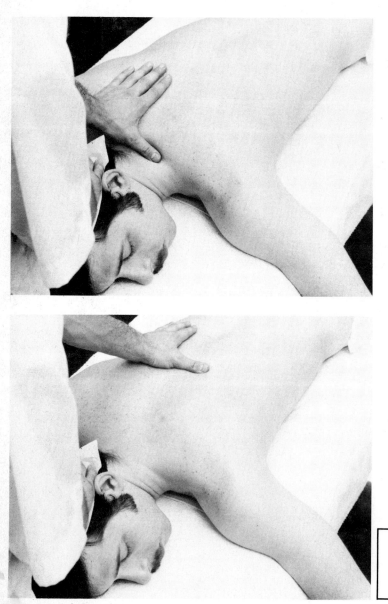

Standing in the same position, place your hand with the four fingers facing straight down toward the lower back, with the thumb perpendicular and just to the right of the spine. Be sure to start at the nape of the neck.

Lean into the center of the erector spinae muscle with your thumb point and stretch it away from the neck as you stroke downward to the center of the back. Now relax your hand and drag back to the starting position. All pressure should be on the thumb point.

Timing: EACH MOVEMENT UNIT TAKES ONE SECOND. DO SIX TO EIGHT OF THEM.

CORRECTIONS

1. Make sure you start high enough.
2. Don't hit the spine.
3. Be sure to do the movement on the correct side of the spine. All the movements are done on one side before going to the other.
4. Don't go down the entire back, only halfway.
5. Put pressure in the thumb point.
6. Don't lift your hand at the end of the movement. Drag it back.
7. Don't lean on the subject's head.

18. The Bridge

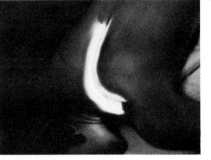

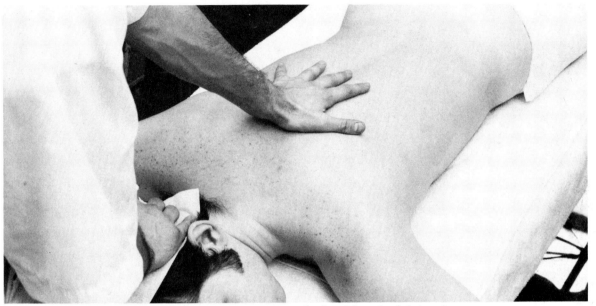

The right hand is in the same position on the head but the left hand assumes an entirely new position. To find the position, place your left hand flat over the spine on the center back. The fingers are spread wide and point toward the feet.

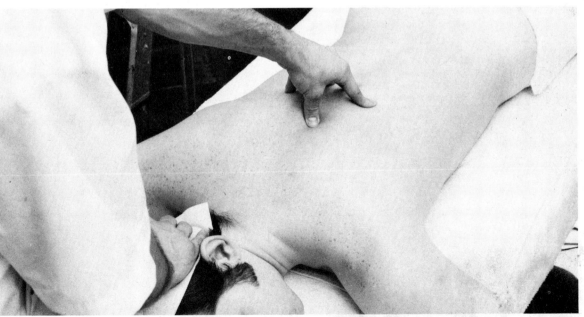

Keeping the fingers straight and the pads of the fingers on the back, draw the center palm into the air about three inches. The thumb should be at the edge of the trapezius muscle just to the right of the spine. Do this once to find your position.

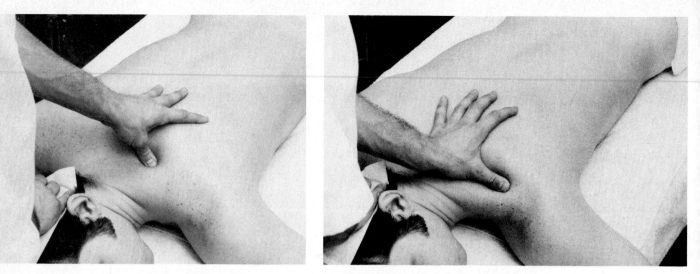

From this starting position, make a half circle, gradually curving out from the spine, around the scapula, and ending where the clavicle and shoulder blade meet. Do not jam into the junction of these bones. The pressure in this movement is all in the pad of the thumb. As you come to the last 1½ inches of the movement, lighten your pressure. As each movement progresses, the bridge you have begun with slowly collapses until your hand is almost flat as you finish at the top of the shoulder.

Drag the hand back to the starting position, reversing the movement exactly, but without pressure. This time rise directly into the bridge position. Because this is a pressure technique that can be done lightly or deeply, depending on the subject's tension, be sure to watch his face during the movement. This technique works intensely on the levator scapulae, an important muscle that raises the shoulder blade. As you come down, your bridge collapses and your hand turns slightly away from your body. If you don't use your body weight, you'll wear yourself out and your thumb will hurt after a short while.

> *Timing:* EACH MOVEMENT UNIT SHOULD TAKE TWO SECONDS, ONE ON THE STROKE AND ONE ON THE DRAG BACK. DO EIGHT OR TEN.

CORRECTIONS

1. Make sure the hand position is correct.
2. Don't press down on the subject's head with the bracing hand.
3. Be sure the fingers are facing down and the thumb is facing up.
4. The pads of the fingers should be on the body.
5. Make sure the fingers are spread far enough apart.
6. Lean into the thumb pad.
7. Don't hit the spine or the scapula during the movement.
8. Don't jam into the bone at the end of the movement.
9. Make sure you're curving out properly in a half circle.
10. Remember to turn your hand out in the last part of the movement.
11. Don't forget to collapse your hand toward the end.
12. Don't lift your hand at the end of the movement. Drag it back.

19. Neck Circles

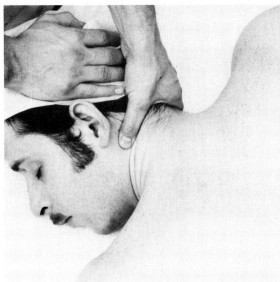 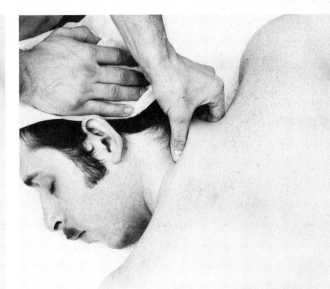

Stand in the same position above the head. With the left hand, gently grip the extreme top of the subject's neck at the edge of the hairline. The thumb is on the top of the neck, the thumb curve is touching the neck, and the four fingers are underneath it.

Release pressure and drag back gently to the starting position. Be careful to watch the subject's face. If it registers pain, lighten the pressure immediately. Some subjects cannot tolerate this movement. Be sure not to hit the back of the head with the heel of your working hand. Don't use your fingertips.

Don't pull the hair, and don't catch the underside of the subject's neck with your fingers and pinch it into the table. As you do this movement it turns into a circular clockwise motion on this side.

> *Timing:* A COMPLETE MOVEMENT TAKES ONE SECOND. DO ONLY SIX OR EIGHT.

After the neck circles, have the subject turn his head, then reverse your hands and go through all the movements on the other side.

Exerting moderate pressure evenly on both sides of the neck, stroke downward to the base of the neck. As you go down, move toward the back of the neck so that the thumb and fingers come closer together, breaking the thumb-curve contact.

CORRECTIONS

1. Be gentle. Don't squeeze too hard.
2. Rest the supporting hand behind the subject's ear, not on it.
3. Do not lean on the subject's head with the stationary hand. Hold the head still with moderate pressure.
4. Be sure the thumb curve is touching the back of the neck when you begin.
5. Try not to hit the back of the head with the heel of the working hand.
6. Don't pull the hair.
7. Move in a clockwise direction.
8. Use pressure only on the downward stroke.
9. Be careful not to pinch the neck into the table. Ask the subject to tell you if this should happen.

> Now put lessons 1 to 4 all together. The whole sequence should take about twenty minutes.

Lesson Five · THE DEEP BACK

The movements in this lesson go more deeply into areas we have already worked on. It is best to begin work on each new section of the body gently and slowly. As you do the movements, increase the pressure and speed slightly, and then level off. You can vary your speed within a movement depending on the needs of the subject.

Keep in mind that the time count is not a rigid, static rule, but an indication of the tempo of each movement. By following the suggested number of repetitions of each of the movements, you will have a broader picture of the total rhythm dynamic of each treatment. This dynamic may vary with each treatment depending on how the subject feels that day, and on how you feel. An intuitive sense of timing is an asset, but since most people don't possess that quality, this training is designed to develop it.

Rhythms

Rhythm, in the broad sense, is the organization of pulse. Rhythms have a profound effect on the body. For example, rhythm can play an important part in natural childbirth. In deep massage, work rhythms must be adjusted to each subject. If a subject is speedy and tense, establish a slow rhythm to counter this. If the subject is sluggish, use quicker rhythms. If there is a lot of soreness from strain or fatigue, try a slow rhythm in conjunction with heat.

Alternating rhythms, as in the one-two lower-back movement in lesson 2, have the effect of catching the muscle by surprise. You can alternate rhythms at different speeds. Sometimes alternating or irregular rhythms that enable you to penetrate muscles by surprise are necessary.

Some people work with irregular rhythms without realizing it. Their movements are disconnected and

jerky, and there is an unevenness in the number of movements and in the flow from one movement to another. This abruptness often makes the subject tense. Improper pressure, sloppy hand drags, constant slipping, cold, or dribbling hands, or a tense practitioner can produce an unpleasant treatment. Often the rhythm is simply inappropriate for the subject. Expertise in rhythms comes only with advanced study, but now is the time to start thinking about it.

Breathing

The importance of breathing has been detailed in various sections of this book. A common error while working on a subject is to hold your breath. When concentrating on the movements, people often forget to breathe. When you work, concentrate on breathing. After you've mastered the first five lessons, go through the movements thinking only of your breathing. Breathe evenly, through your nose and mouth, and take a deep breath occasionally. Exhale on the long upward strokes. Proper breathing will increase your endurance and energy.

Transition Movements

Now that you are reasonably accomplished at some beginning techniques, it's important to look at the movements as they relate to one another. Techniques that link one movement to another are called transition movements. When working on a section of the body, one movement should flow into another easily and continuously. The subject should not be aware of the changes, although when moving from the back to the legs or from one leg to another, a momentary break is fine.

The following are transition movements from one part of the body to another. To change from the basic movement to the shoulder circle, lead into the shoulder circle by doing the first half of a basic movement. When you finish the continuous neck movement, lead into the lower-back square with the second half of a heart movement. After the sacrum oval on the lower back, do half of a basic movement to get to the shoulder for the combing-action movement. When you go from the thumbs technique on the lower back to the stretch movement, don't lift your hands, but drag them firmly through the starting position into the first movement. Mastery of the firm drag as a transitional movement is especially important, for it is used often. If transitions are not smooth, the treatment will seem choppy and disturbing rather than relaxing to the subject.

If you forget the next movement, continue the present one until you recall it. Don't hesitate. The following run-through exercise is a good way to learn the sequence of movements. Unlike the techniques of the previous lessons, those in this section can be done as a unit or sandwiched between other movements where their placement will be indicated.

The Run-Through Exercise

The run-through exercise makes the proper sequence of movements second-nature, thus enabling you to move from one movement to another without hesitation. At this point, sticking to the given order is essential, although as lessons progress some flexibility will emerge.

When you run through a lesson, do only one of each movement. Then repeat the sequence ten or fifteen times. After it becomes easy with each of the first four or five lessons, run through all the lessons linked together. Again, do only one of each movement and repeat the entire sequence ten or fifteen times. If you make a mistake, go back to the beginning and start over again. Run through perfectly at least five times.

Greater Mobility Increases Recovery Rate

When a person's muscles begin to relax, he enjoys an increased physical mobility. He can move more freely and recovery from injury is more rapid. Some find this rapid recovery the most amazing benefit of losing excess tension.

A young actress came to see me several years ago. She was suffering from a severe back spasm. She told me that it normally took her two to three months to recover each time she hurt her back. After six months of treatment she rarely had back pains, but one day she was shooting a movie on location in New England during the winter and nearly froze. As a result, she had a recurrence of violent pains in her back. She tried the techniques I had recommended, such as baths, hitting, and the ball techniques, but they did not help. Discouraged, she returned to New York for treatment. After one deep treatment she recovered almost immediately because of her increased mobility from previous treatments and her diligent practice of exercises and body-care techniques.

Deep-Back Movements

20. Pressure Circles at the Occiput

This movement stimulates circulation in the head and neck and breaks tension at the occiput. Done with the tips of the three middle fingers, pressed firmly together, it is a circular action about a half inch in diameter. The circles are done in eight sections, four on each side of the back of the head. They move across the entire occipital area, where the neck muscles attach to the skull at the back of the head, from ear to ear.

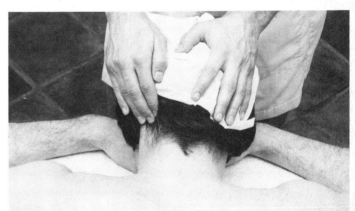

Stand in the same position at the head of the table as in the neck lesson. Have the subject place one of his hands on top of the other, palms up or down, and place his head straight down with the forehead on the hands. Some people are more comfortable in this position with one hand under the forehead and one hand under the chin, palms face down. Place your left hand on the subject's head to hold it still. Use a tissue to keep the hair clean.

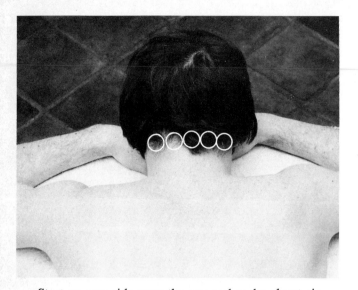

Start on one side near the ear and make about six to eight small circles, pressing the muscles at the occiput into the skull. The circles are purposely small, so that you don't pull the subject's hair. The skin should move with you as you do the movement. If you're moving over it or pulling the hair, you are doing it wrong.

Take your time on each circle. You can do this movement with either hand or switch hands in the middle.

> *Timing:* EACH OF THE EIGHT SEGMENTS SHOULD TAKE TWO TO THREE SECONDS. GO THROUGH THE ENTIRE SERIES TWO OR THREE TIMES.

CORRECTIONS

1. Don't pull the subject's hair.
2. Be sure to hold the subject's head still with your other hand.
3. Don't make the circles bigger than a half inch in diameter.
4. Don't do the movement too lightly or with too much force.
5. Make sure you are directly at the occiput.

21. The Deep Neck

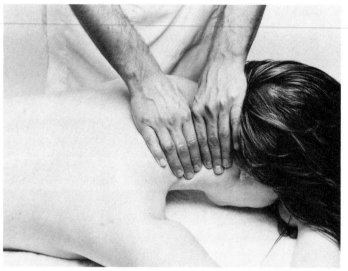

The subject's head is face down in the same position as in pressure circles, but now you are standing at the left side, facing the neck. Grip the neck with your thumb and four fingers, as in the continuous neck position (lesson 1).

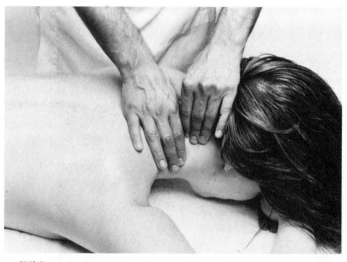

With your hands on the neck, one following the other, begin a kneading action identical with that in the continuous neck movements. The hands come straight off the neck toward the ceiling. Work at the center of the neck lightly, then deeply, then lightly again, using your fingers and thumb.

Don't snap off the neck. The movements should end with about a half inch of skin between the fingers. If the subject has a short neck, use only the first two or three fingers and the thumb to get into the area.

only twice, because it goes very deep. Finish with eight or ten gentle movements in the center of the neck, to smooth it out.

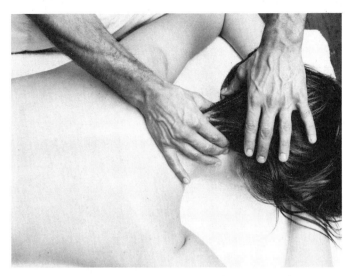

Move the entire movement up about an inch and a half so that you are just below the skull. Using the fingertips, go deeper and deeper into the muscles at the base of the head. The right hand works with slightly more force than the left.

As you knead, move back to the center neck, lightening your pressure to allow you and the subject to relax.

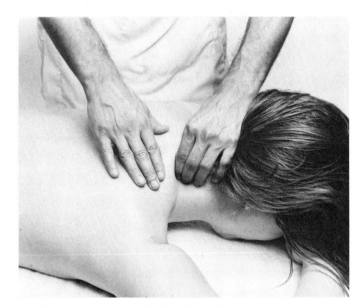

Pressing deeply with the fingertips, move down an inch or so to the junction of the neck and the shoulder. In this phase use the left hand a little more forcefully than the right.

Move back to the center of the neck and repeat the entire sequence. Do the deep-neck movement

---

Timing: EACH MOVEMENT—A RIGHT-LEFT HAND COMBINATION—TAKES ABOUT ONE SECOND.

1. DO ABOUT SIX MOVEMENTS LIGHTLY, SIX GETTING DEEPER, AND SIX LIGHTLY AGAIN IN THE CENTER OF THE NECK.

2. WHEN YOU MOVE UP TO JUST BELOW THE SKULL, TRY FOUR TO EIGHT DEEP MOVEMENTS, DEPENDING ON THE SUBJECT'S TENSION. DO ONLY WHAT HE CAN TOLERATE WITHOUT DISCOMFORT.

3. WHEN YOU MOVE BACK TO THE CENTER, DO THREE OR FOUR MOVEMENTS LIGHTLY.

4. AT THE BASE OF THE NECK, DO FOUR TO EIGHT MOVEMENTS FORCEFULLY.

5. DO EIGHT OR TEN MOVEMENTS BACK AT THE CENTER.

At the occiput, at the top of the neck, you are working on the tendons and muscle fibers that attach the muscles to the head. On the center and lower neck you are stimulating the nerves of the head that pass through the neck and breaking down tension deep in the neck muscles. The deep-neck movement is a pressure technique. The pressure circles and the deep-neck movements should be done only after the basic neck movements.

CORRECTIONS

1. Make sure your hands come off evenly.
2. Don't apply too little pressure.
3. Make sure you go deeply at the bottom part of the movement, although it is difficult.
4. Be sure to grip the subject's neck so there is contact at the thumb curve.

22. Thumb Combing

The purpose of this movement is to break down deep tension in the trapezius and other muscles of the shoulders through a combination of deep and gentle techniques. It contains part of the combing action in lesson 3, but goes deeper, especially into the top of the shoulders. Stand on the left side of the subject's body, facing the head.

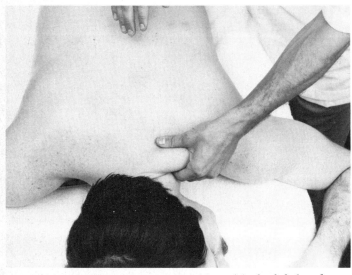

Squeeze the top of the shoulder with the left hand, thumb opposing the first three fingers. As you squeeze, pull your hand off in the direction of the subject's head, rather than up toward the ceiling.

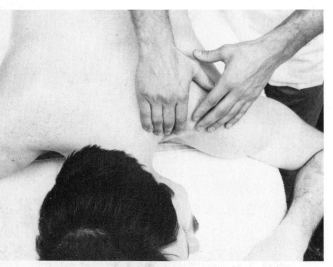

As your thumb finishes, immediately begin a combing action with your right hand, identical with that in lesson 3.

Don't snap the fingers off the shoulder. You are primarily squeezing the trapezius muscle. This is a combination technique—a severe movement followed immediately by a gentle, smoothing-out motion. Remember to watch the subject's face during this pressure technique.

> *Timing:* THIS COMBINATION TAKES ABOUT ONE SECOND. DO THE MOVEMENT ABOUT EIGHT OR TEN TIMES, AND FINISH OFF WITH REGULAR COMBING.

After the finish, go to the other side of the body and repeat the sequence. This movement can be done now or can be inserted after regular combing in the shoulder series. You can also alternate regular combing and thumb combing.

CORRECTIONS

1. Don't snap your fingers off the shoulder.
2. Remember to do regular combing afterward to smooth out the area.
3. Use a regular rhythm. Don't comb unevenly.
4. Be aware of the person's threshold of pain, and don't exceed it.
5. Be sure your hand comes off toward the subject's head, not toward the ceiling.
6. The squeezing hand is the outside hand.

24. The Oval

A pleasant movement to apply and to receive, this technique can be administered anytime in this sequence or in any of the previous lessons. The oval acts as a bridge between other movements. It distributes energy throughout the back and smoothes out areas worked on vigorously. The oval improves blood circulation especially in the erector spinae, the quadratus lumborum, the latissimus dorsi, and the trapezius muscles, and stimulates circulation in all the muscles of the back.

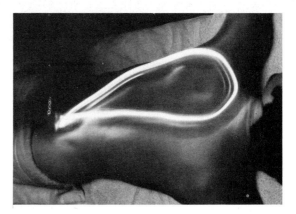

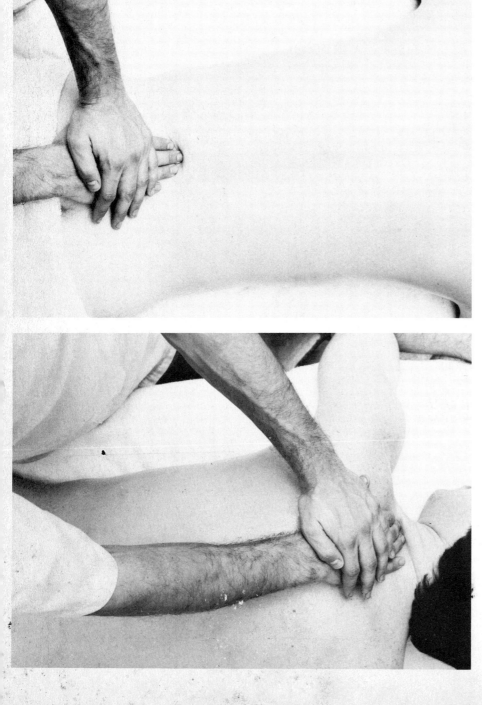

With your feet parallel, about eighteen inches apart, continuously rock your weight from the left foot to the right. In the basic position, with the right hand on the bottom, place the right hand at the base of the back on the left side of the spine. The heel of the hand should be resting gently on the upper part of the hip bone, the four fingers together, and the thumb in an open, relaxed position.

As you begin the movement, assume a minimum amount of tension in the fingers by curling the fingertips slightly into the body. With your weight on the entire hand, but especially the center of the palm, move up the left side of the back along the spine to the top of the shoulder beside the neck.

23. The Hook

This movement, which breaks down tension in the erector spinae, quadratus lumborum, and latissimus dorsi muscles, can be done here or inserted after the stretch movement on the lower back.

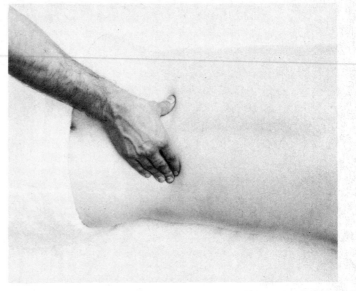

Facing the left side of the subject's lower back, start at the base of the back, right above the hip bones. With your hand in a hooked position, as if you were making a **C** with it, place the thumb on one side of the spine and the four fingers on the other side. The pads of all the fingers should press the respective outer edges of the erector spinae muscles. Press down and in as if to grip them. Your hand will be more or less open depending on the width of the subject's back muscles.

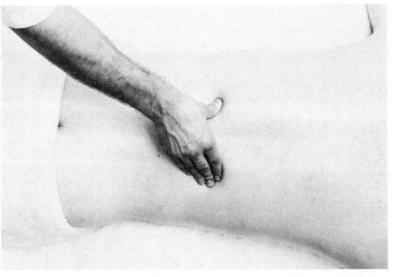

Maintaining this position, move your hand firmly and quickly up the back about five inches. This movement is done in a pulsating rhythm. Push up with pressure and drag back lightly to the starting position.

Timing: EACH MOVEMENT UNIT SHOULD TAKE APPROXIMATELY ONE SECOND. THE RHYTHM OF THIS MOVEMENT IS DIFFERENT FROM ANY WE HAVE DONE THUS FAR. THE DRAG BACK IS DONE ABOUT TWO OR THREE TIMES FASTER THAN THE UPWARD STROKE. WHEN YOU'VE MASTERED THIS MOVEMENT, INCREASE THE SPEED SLIGHTLY. DO THE HOOK SIX OR EIGHT TIMES, THEN INTERRUPT WITH ANOTHER MOVEMENT SUCH AS THE OVAL, WHICH FOLLOWS, OR THE LOWER-BACK SQUARE, OR THE ONE-TWO LOWER BACK IF YOU WANT TO DO IT FOR A LONGER PERIOD.

If you have mastered the hook, and if you have extremely short fingernails, try using the tips of the fingers instead of the pads. This method is even more intense, so remember to watch the person's face.

CORRECTIONS

1. Don't apply pressure to the center of the erector spinae muscles, only to the outer edges.
2. Don't hit the hip bone. Start the technique a half inch above it.
3. Don't go up more than five inches; this is a lower-back movement.
4. Drag back without pressure.
5. Don't move too sharply or abruptly.

CORRECTIONS

1. Don't forget to apply finger pressure.
2. Don't make the finger pressure too deep, and watch your nails.
3. Be sure to start at the bottom of the back.
4. Press in with the whole hand, not just the heel.
5. Be careful not to hit the spine during the movement.
6. Be sure you go up to the shoulder, but don't jam into the subject's neck with your fingertips.
7. Release the pressure when coming down.
8. Be sure to alternate sides. Don't do too many sets of movements on one side at one time.

Do the last four movements in this section from the other side to balance strength and dexterity. At this point, you will probably be moving more efficiently. All the upper-body movements, including the ones you've just learned, should now take approximately twenty minutes.

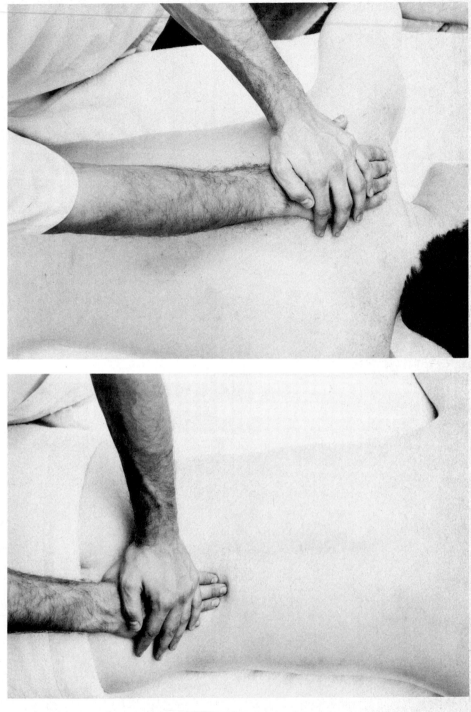

Still using pressure, move out to the side, as in the shoulder circle in lesson 3. Relax the pressure from the fingers and hand and drag firmly down the outer border of the back to complete an oval movement.

Repeat this movement two or three times on one side. Then, standing in the same position and using the same hand, gently cross over at the base of the spine and repeat the movement on the other side of the back. Alternating from one side to the other, do the movement on each side two or three times.

Timing: THE UNIT SHOULD TAKE 1½ TO 2 SECONDS. YOU CAN KEEP REPEATING THIS SIDE-TO-SIDE ALTERNATION, BUT DO NOT DO MORE THAN THREE MOVEMENTS ON EITHER SIDE OF THE BACK WITHOUT CHANGING SIDES. ONE MOVEMENT ON EACH SIDE IS ALSO A GOOD WAY TO DO IT. YOU MAY REPEAT THIS MOVEMENT UP TO FIFTEEN OR TWENTY TIMES. IF THERE ISN'T A PROPER RIGHT-LEFT BALANCE, THE MOVEMENT CAN BE IRRITATING.

Lesson Six · THE BACK THIGHS

Muscles of the Back Thighs

Hamstring Muscles

If you put your hand under your thigh just above the knee, with your thigh perpendicular to your body, you'll feel three taut strings. These are the tendons of the three muscles called hamstrings. They run from three points behind the knee and join to form a single attachment at the bottom of the pelvis. The two that attach at the inside of the knee are the *semitendinosus* and *semimembranosus*; the one at the outside is the *biceps femoris*. These muscles bend the knee and extend the thigh backward. They are often severely strained at the junction with the base of the hip, but are often painful all the way to the knee. The deeper the pain in this area, the longer it takes to heal.

Adductors and Abductors

When you move the leg in or out, two sets of muscles are used. The muscles that spread the legs are the abductors and those that bring them together are the adductors.

The gracilis, located in the inner thigh, is one of the adductor muscles. It also flexes and rotates the thigh and helps to steady the thigh bone in the hip socket in erect posture. The gracilis is sensitive to touch and is easily strained.

The tensor fasciae latae, on the outside upper third of the thigh, is an abductor muscle. It spreads the legs and helps hold the thigh in the hip socket. It is used in standing and walking. This muscle tends to be tight in people who stand a great deal, especially if they sink their weight onto one leg. It should be given special attention, particularly in cases of lower-back pain.

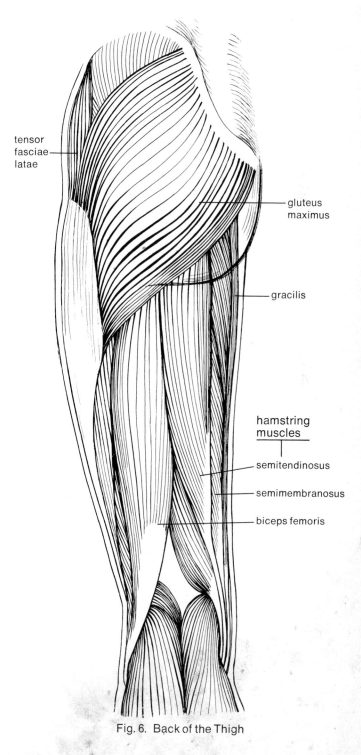

Fig. 6. Back of the Thigh

How to See Tension in the Back Thighs

The way a person walks can tell you a lot about his thighs.

1. A tough-guy, bouncy walk puts a lot of pressure on the thighs.

2. Feet turned out is a sign of tension in the entire leg; this condition puts strain on the ankle, knee, and hip joints.

3. A heavy walk is also often a sign of tension in the thighs. If the knees kick out and the feet slam down when a person walks, he has tension in the legs.

4. Bulging muscles in the backs of the thighs also indicate tension.

5. Tense muscles in this area tend to be puffy, swollen, hard, or cold to the touch. They may be unpleasantly ticklish or hurt a great deal under pressure.

Causes of Tension in the Back Thighs

Mechanical Causes

1. Poor alignment such as hip sitting, retracted pelvis, and turned-in knees.

2. Incorrect exercise, either too strenuous, causing strain, or too repetitive, causing muscle fatigue.

3. Strenuous exercise without a proper warm-up is often a problem for dancers or athletes.

4. Standing for long hours without rest, which is an occupational hazard to waiters, traffic officers, sales personnel, cooks, and others.

Emotional Causes

The legs are a place to which most people don't connect repressed emotions, but rage and fear, particularly sexual fear, can be held and trapped in the legs.

Work on the thighs often makes people nervous or uncomfortable. Unless there is an injury there that must be treated, leave the inner thighs alone. If you must work on that area, be aware of what your hands are doing.

Thigh Movements

Towel Technique

When you drape the towel properly, it outlines the area to be worked on. Not only does the towel act as a guide for several movements, but it gives the subject a sense of protection of the genital area. Even the slightest thing you do, such as placing the towel, reflects your confidence and ability. Awkwardness is easily transmitted to the subject.

Hold the towel lengthwise at its corners and place it over the subject's back, with the upper edge at the shoulder line and the lower edge covering the backs of the knees.

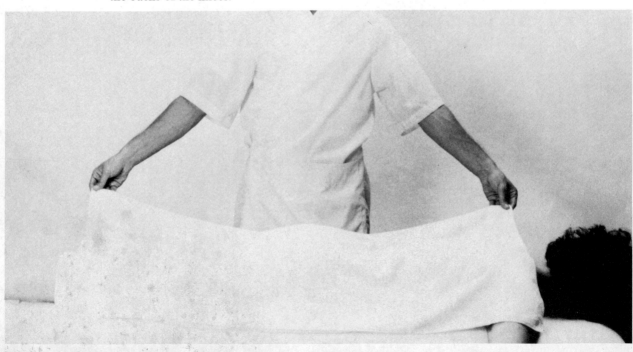

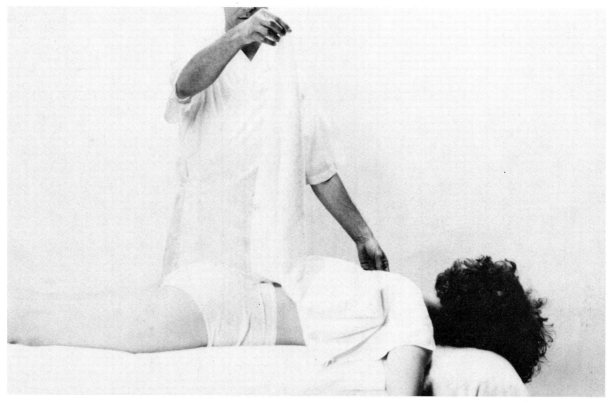

Release the upper edge of the towel, and, holding the lower corner,
lift it about a foot in the air above the lower back.

Gently place it between the legs, about four inches from the groin.

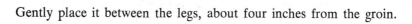

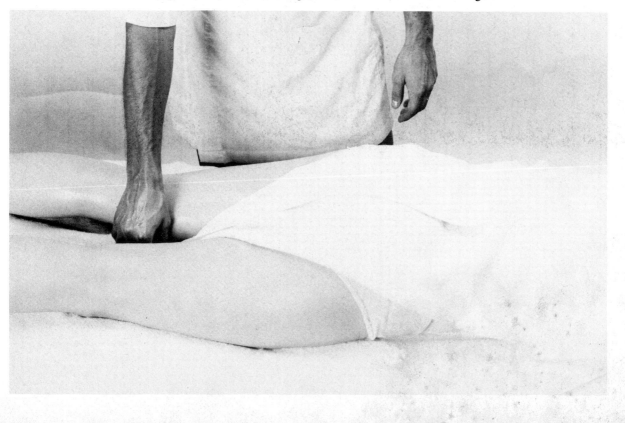

25. Basic Back Thigh

When working on the left leg, your hands are in a slightly altered basic position. The right hand is on the bottom, the left on the top. The fingers of the right hand are facing away from the subject's body, and the left hand adjusts its position as in the top photograph below. In this position the elbows are always bent and the body leans over.

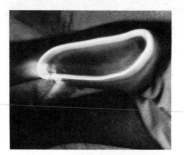

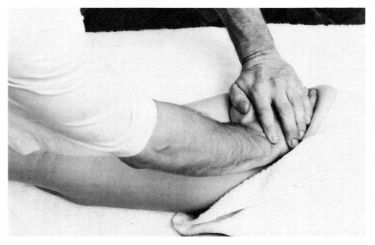

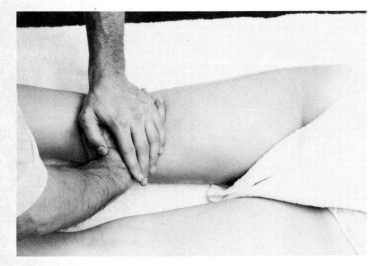

Standing to the left of the subject, with the left foot ahead of the right, face straight up toward the head. The knees are slightly bent and your body follows a rocking motion forward and back from leg to leg throughout the movement.

Begin with your hands just above the back of the knee. *Never* apply pressure to the backs of the knees.

Timing: EACH COMPLETE SET OF UP-AND-DOWN MOVEMENTS SHOULD TAKE APPROXIMATELY TWO SECONDS. REPEAT THE MOVEMENT EIGHT OR TEN TIMES.

CORRECTIONS

1. Make sure the bottom hand is completely turned out.
2. Don't place the wrong hand on the bottom.
3. Don't put your weight into the heel of the hand.
4. The hand should go out to the side at the top of the movement, not straight up and down.

With your weight on the hand evenly, stroke up the thigh to the bottom of the hip. Lean your weight; don't push.

At the very end of the stroke, move your hand to the outer thigh and firmly drag back on the outside of the thigh to the starting point.

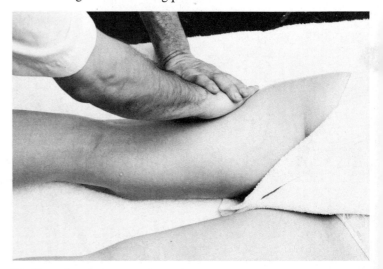

5. Drag back on the side, not the top.
6. Don't jam into the hip bone.
7. Use pressure above the knee, not directly on it.

26. The One-Two Back Thigh

The concept of this movement is identical with the one-two rhythm movement for the lower back. The outside hand leads, the inside follows and catches up, and they drag back together. Learning one hand at a time before putting them together often makes the movement easier to master.

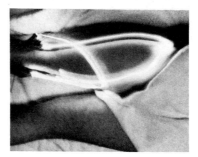

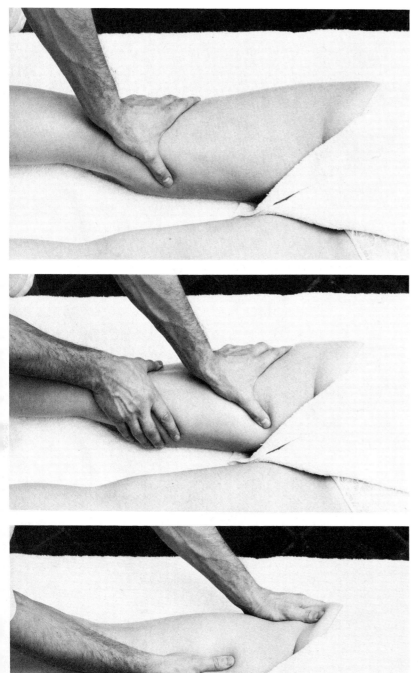

Face in the same direction as in the basic thigh movement. The left hand gently grips the back of the thigh just above the back of the knee, with the center palm in the middle of the thigh.

As the left hand moves up to the middle of the thigh, the right begins at the same place, and follows.

The left hand continues to move up to the top of the thigh, then outward. The right moves up the thigh to three to four inches below the groin, then in. In this last part, the hands move simultaneously and finish together.

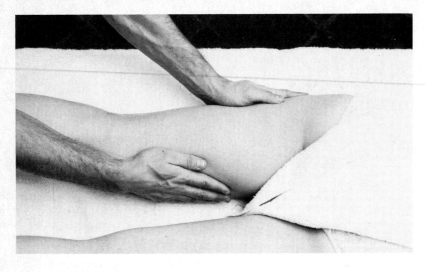

The hands flatten out on the extreme inner and outer parts of the thigh and drag back down with firm pressure. Stop just before the knee, ready to begin again.

One hand quickly follows the other in a one-two rhythm. Both hands are dragged back together as the next beat. The impulse for the movement is led from the thumb curve, which lies between the tip of the index finger and the tip of the thumb. Be sure to have both palms touching the thigh during this movement. If you lift the centers of the palms, the movement will be sharp and painful to the subject. The palms should be on the thigh and the hands should be open and relaxed, with minimal tension in the fingers and thumbs. Most of the movement is done by leaning into the palms and not squeezing the fingers.

> *Timing:* THE TEMPO OF THIS MOVEMENT IS FASTER THAN THAT OF THE BASIC THIGH MOVEMENT. EACH MOVEMENT UNIT, UP AND BACK, TAKES APPROXIMATELY 1½ SECONDS. DO EACH UNIT EIGHT TO TEN TIMES.

CORRECTIONS

1. Make sure you have the right rhythm.
2. The outside hand always leads. On the left leg, start with your left hand.
3. On the way up the hands should be on the top of the thigh, not on the sides; dragging back, they should be on the inner and outer sides.
4. *Don't go up too high with the inner hand.*
5. Make sure you go up high enough with the outer hand.
6. Don't drag back too lightly.
7. Don't lift the hands off the body. Drag back on the thigh.
8. When starting the movement, be sure to start just above the knee, not on it.
9. Put the main pressure on the palms, not the thumb curves or the fingers.

27. Opposition Back Thigh

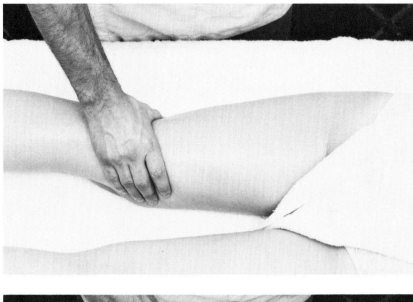

Face directly in toward the center of the thigh. Your feet should be parallel, approximately eighteen inches apart, and your knees slightly bent. The force of the movement is attained by shifting your weight from leg to leg. Begin with the right hand gently gripping the thigh above the knee with the thumb opposing the four fingers.

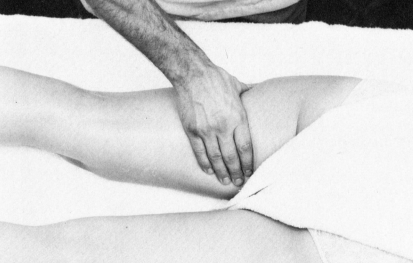

As you move up to about three inches below the top of the thigh, lean into your hand and squeeze with moderate finger pressure.

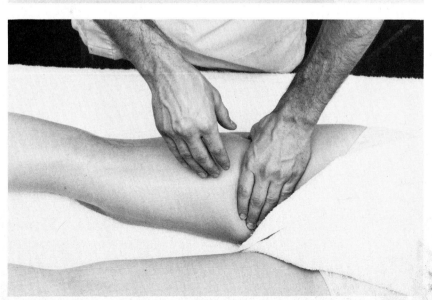

At the top of the thigh the left hand immediately replaces the right.

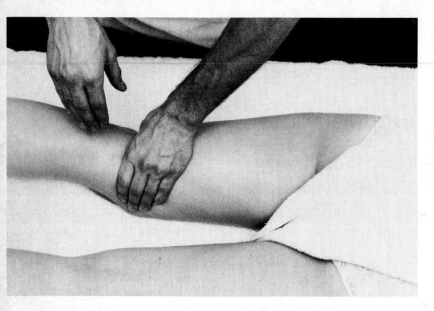

The left hand strokes down with equal pressure to the bottom of the thigh just above the knee. Only the working hand is on the thigh—the other one lifts off the leg and remains in the air just above the thigh.

Make sure you don't jam your fingers into the bones at the sides of the top of the knee. The pressure should result from an equal amount of leaning and squeezing. Pay careful attention to the subject's face for signs of pain or discomfort. If the subject has a large thigh or you have small hands, do the inner, top, and outer parts in sections, but be sure to cover the entire thigh.

CORRECTIONS

1. Start just above the knee.
2. Don't squeeze too much with the fingers.
3. Make sure to lean sufficiently.
4. Don't go too high.
5. Don't jam into the knee on the down movement.

Timing: EACH COMPLETE UNIT, UP AND DOWN, TAKES APPROXIMATELY 1½ SECONDS. DO EACH UNIT SIX TO TEN TIMES, DEPENDING ON THE SENSITIVITY OF THE SUBJECT'S LEG.

28. The Tensor

In most people the outer thigh is one of the tightest areas. Work on this area can be painful, so proceed carefully at first.

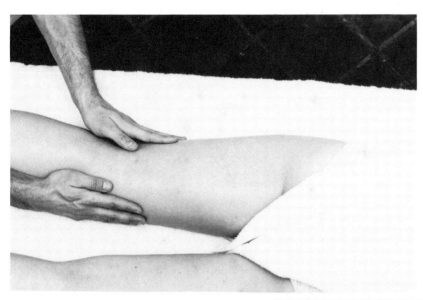

Face directly up toward the subject's head. Your feet should be parallel, with the left foot twelve to eighteen inches ahead of the right. This is another back-and-forth rocking movement but in this case your body is in a crouched position. Remember to relax your head. The center palm of the right hand is cupped directly over the inside of the left knee, with the fingers pointing up toward the head. The hand should be relaxed and exert a slight pressure outward toward your body. The right hand is used as a brace.

Your left hand is placed directly on the outside of the left thigh, with the heel of the hand just above the bone at the outside of the knee.

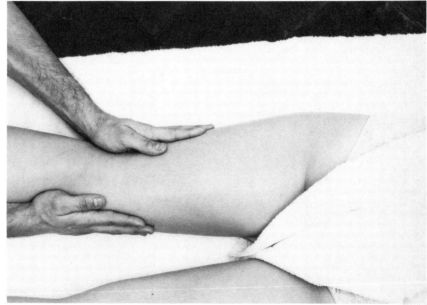

Throughout the movement, the outer edge of your hand should be approximately a half inch above the table. The pressure begins at the start of the movement. With equal pressure of fingers, palm, and heel of the hand, firmly but gently press sideways into the thigh. Be sure to use the right hand to brace the leg so that it doesn't move.

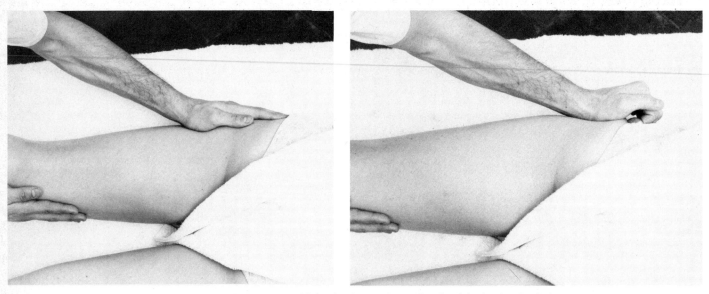

As you move up the outer thigh, don't press too hard with the heel of the hand, and be careful not to hit the prominent bone, the greater trochanter of the femur, which you'll feel at the top of the thigh. When your fingertips hit the subject's underwear, continue the movement with the heel of your hand and curl the fingers into a gentle fist, and finish the movement smoothly.

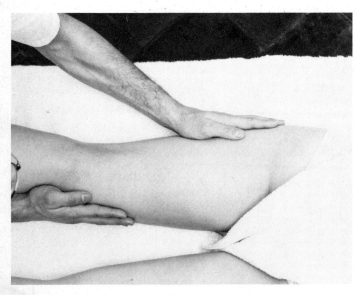

Uncurl your fingers, flatten the palm against the thigh immediately as you drag back to the starting position.

Timing: EACH MOVEMENT SHOULD TAKE ABOUT TWO SECONDS. WORK SLOWLY AND CAREFULLY AT FIRST. DO THIS MOVEMENT FOUR TO EIGHT TIMES.

CORRECTIONS

1. The palm of the left hand should neither touch the table nor be too high off it.
2. Don't press too hard with the heel of the hand.
3. Use pressure from the beginning of the movement.
4. Don't hit the top of the outer thigh bone with the heel of your hand.
5. Make sure you do the finger curl just as you hit the underwear.
6. Remember to uncurl the fist immediately as you drag back.

Now, reversing your own leg and hand positions, repeat all the thigh movements on the subject's other leg. Later in your study of deep massage, the thighs will not be worked on consecutively. You will move from the thigh to the calf of that leg first. After you have mastered these movements it should take three or four minutes to do the back of each thigh. The time to do all the movements thus far would be approximately twenty-five minutes.

Lesson Seven · THE CALVES

The Bones

The function of the muscles is to move and to hold in place the bones that give the body shape. Bones protect the vital organs and nerves, including the brain, heart, lungs, and spinal cord. The marrow housed in the bones produces red blood corpuscles that carry oxygen to the cells, while the bones also act as a reserve calcium supply for the body. The bones must be healthy and properly aligned to support the body against the pull of gravity without undue strain on the ligaments, tendons, and muscles.

Ligaments and Tendons

Ligaments are thick, fibrous connective tissue that connect bones. The thigh bone (femur) is connected to the hip bone (pelvis) by ligaments.

Tendons are also thick, fibrous connective tissue, but they attach muscle to bone. At the lower end of the calf, the Achilles tendon attaches the calf muscles to the heel bone. It is the strongest and thickest tendon in the body. Both ligaments and tendons are stronger than muscle tissue.

Tendons and ligaments are often strained, inflamed, and in some cases torn. Damaged tissue is replaced by scar tissue, composed of cells called fibroblasts. This tissue is inelastic and merely fills space. Where scar tissue exists there is less flexibility. Even without scar tissue, tendons and ligaments have little elasticity. Thus, if you try to stretch a tense

muscle, you may pull the tendon at one or both ends of it. Direct work on the tendons and ligaments comes with more advanced study, and the beginner should treat them gently.

How Movement Is Produced

Think of the bones as basic structural elements in the body set into motion by muscles. Bones don't bend, but the relationship of one bone to another changes at the joint. When the body moves, muscles

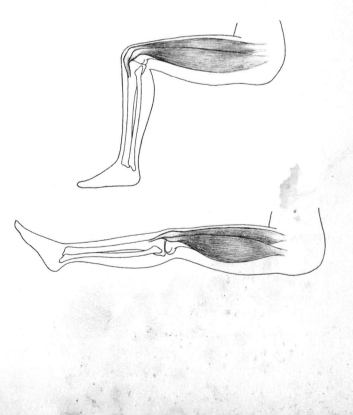

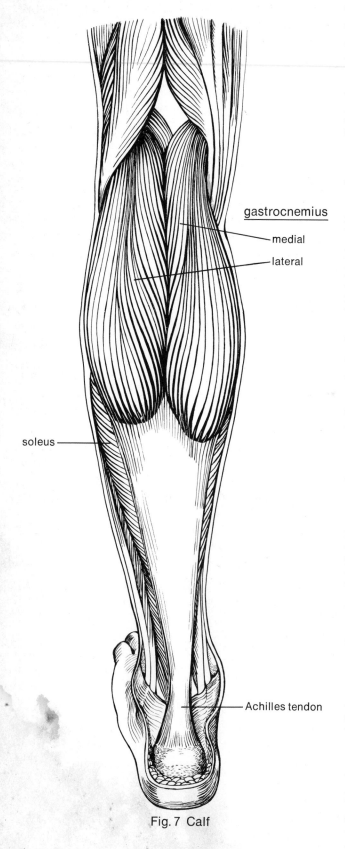

gastrocnemius

— medial

— lateral

soleus —

— Achilles tendon

Fig. 7 Calf

contract to change the relationship of bones. The quadriceps, a muscle on top of the thigh, crosses directly over the front of the knee joint and attaches to the shin just below the knee. When it contracts, the muscle lifts the leg and extends the knee. In order to produce any movement, muscles that cross over joints must contract. Understanding this fact is essential to analyzing movement, muscles, and tension.

Muscles of the Calves

1. *The gastrocnemius* is the most superficial calf muscle. Reaching from the lower end of the thigh bone to the heel, it is used in walking, extending the foot, and raising the heel off the floor. When this muscle is strong and flexible and the calf is well proportioned in relationship to the thigh, it is a sign of healthy development.

2. *The soleus*, just underneath and to the sides of the gastrocnemius muscle, is the major muscle of the calf. It extends from the tibia to the heel. It works in concert with the gastrocnemius and helps to extend and rotate the foot. Both the gastrocnemius and the soleus muscles attach to the heel by the Achilles tendon.

A Torn Cartilage Is Not Tension

A nineteen-year-old football player who was scheduled for a cartilage operation on both legs came to see me. He had been suffering from severe continuous pains deep in the backs of the knees for eight or nine months. With his doctor's consent, he agreed to wait one month, the amount of time I felt necessary to see if the pain was due to tension.

A week after the treatments began the pain was gone on some days but extremely intense on others. Sometimes the pain seemed to depend on the amount of work he did; at other times, it occurred for no apparent reason. The backs of the knees were a little puffy, and the circulation was quite poor in that area. He was extremely tense throughout his body and especially tense in both legs. I treated him three times a week on alternate days so that his muscles had time to recover from the work, which was deep. During the first two visits I worked on his back to get the general circulation going. By the third visit we were concentrating on the legs, the backs of the thighs and the centers of the calves. I never worked on the backs of the knees directly, because it soon became clear to me that the problem was not in the knees but in the calves and the hamstring muscles in the backs of the thighs. For a day or two after I worked on the calves and was able to soften them, he had little or no pain, but after a three-day weekend the calves were tighter and the pain had returned.

When the calf and the thigh are tight, the femur and the tibia are pulled toward each other, creating pressure and irritation in the knee joint, which heals slowly. After three weeks of treatment the pain was about three-quarters diminished, and we reduced treatments to twice weekly. The doctor decided to postpone the operation, since the indications were favorable. At the end of six weeks, the pain was gone and I sent him to a professional to correct his movement patterns. His alignment was poor and he put tremendous strain on his knees. He has continued to take care of himself and the pain has not recurred for seven years.

Injuries and physical pain aren't always what they seem. In this case the pain was in the knees, but the source of the pain was in the calves and, to some extent, in the backs of the thighs.

How to See Tension in the Calves

1. Often, the shape of the calf is angular, but if it juts out from the leg too sharply it is a sign of tension and incorrect or excessive development. There should be a soft, smooth line rather than a bulge from the back of the knee to the ankle.
2. Locked, hyperextended knees, a bad posture habit, mean the knees are bent in the opposite direc-

tion, that is, backward beyond the straight position. This condition severely hampers the circulation and puts continual stress on the area. Standing with your heels together and your feet turned out, try to straighten your knees. If your heels separate, your knees are hyperextended.
3. Frequently, making snapping noises with the toes, squeezing them together, or curling them under are signs of calf tension.
4. A bouncy, tough-guy walk puts stress on the balls of the feet and pushes the weight down into the calves. This is a sure sign of calf tension.
5. When you see someone stamping his feet or grabbing and pressing his legs, you can be reasonably sure he has spastic calves. These actions are an automatic attempt to relax the tension.

Causes of Tension in the Calves

Mechanical Causes

Calf tension can come from a number of problems.
1. The way one walks or moves determines how the weight goes through your leg. Walking with the weight on the heels can produce tension.
2. Poor alignment of the feet, knees, and hips puts stress on the calves, especially if the feet are turned out while the knees are straight ahead.
3. An occupation that requires constant standing often produces calf tension.

Emotional Causes

As in other parts of the body, tension in the calves may be due to repressed emotions.

Calf Movements

29. Opposition Calf

This movement is similar to the opposition-back-thigh movement in lesson 6, with two exceptions. Your feet should now be a little closer together, and a squeezing action rather than a leaning action dominates. The body sways gently from side to side. Squeeze the muscles with the pad of the thumb and the four fingers.

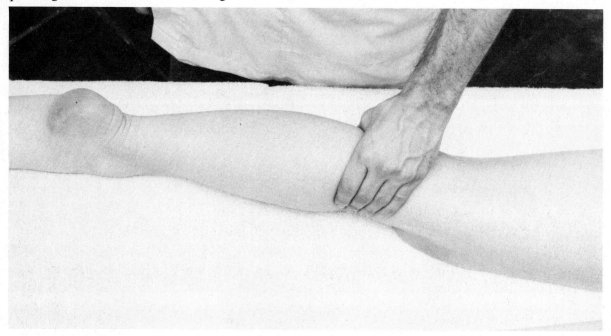

Start with your left hand gripping the left leg at the top of the calf muscle just below the knee.

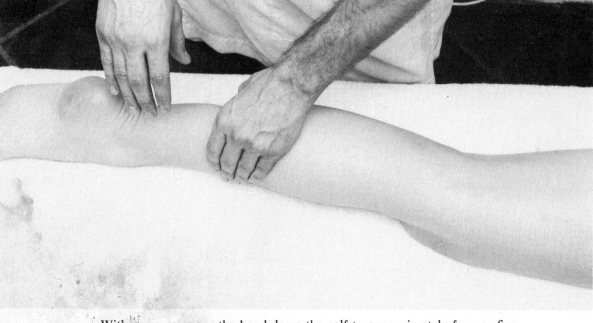

With pressure, move the hand down the calf to approximately four or five inches above the heel of the foot.

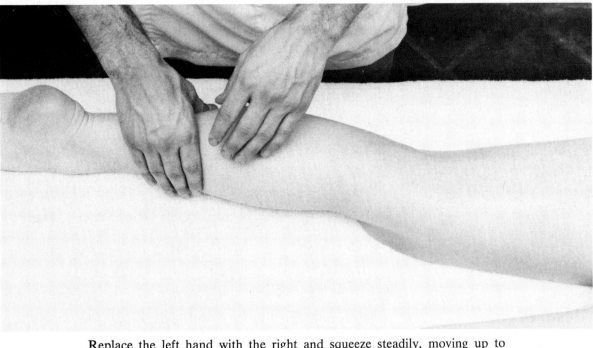

Replace the left hand with the right and squeeze steadily, moving up to just below the knee. Try to maintain equal pressure on up-and-down movements.

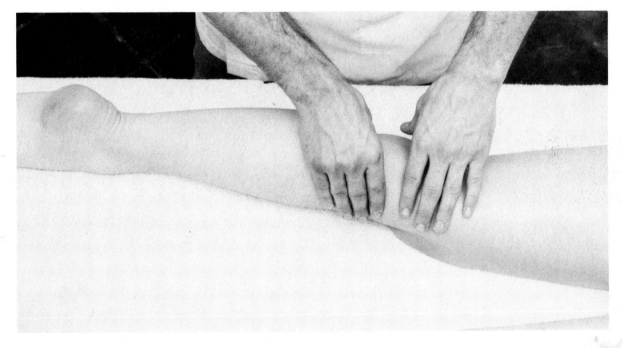

Timing: ONE SET OF MOVEMENTS SHOULD TAKE A SECOND AND A HALF. DO EIGHT TO TWELVE SETS.

CORRECTIONS

1. Don't go too high and jam the knee, or too low and jam the ankle.
2. Be sure to apply enough pressure with the fingers.
3. Make sure you are squarely on top of the calf.

30. Inching

Mastering inching is a prerequisite for the next movement. Both inching and the next movement are based on the opposition principle. Concentrate at first on getting the inching, which may take a few days. Go on to the next movement, small circles, only when you've mastered it.

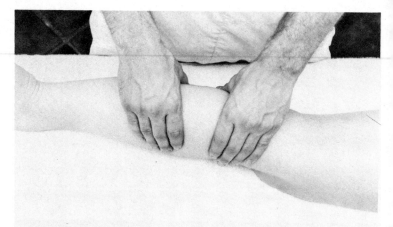

Stand in the same position as for the opposition calf movement. Begin at the top of the calf, just below the knee. With both hands grip the calf. The thumb tips should be opposing the fingertips.

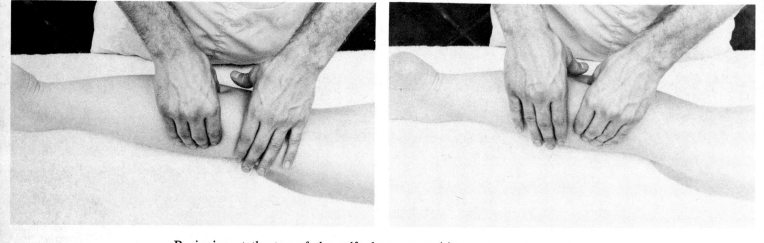

Beginning at the top of the calf, do an opposition movement only in a two-inch or three-inch area, as if those two or three inches were the entire calf. Move in a straight line as if you were on a track.

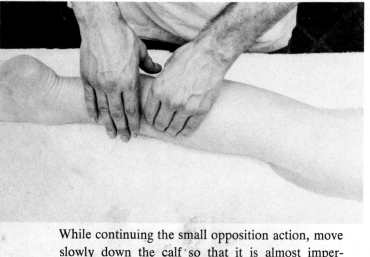

While continuing the small opposition action, move slowly down the calf so that it is almost imperceptible to the subject. When you get about three inches from the heel, begin to move back up to the knee. During this movement, the center palm does not touch the calf unless the calf is unusually large.

Timing: THIS MOVEMENT IS DONE FASTER THAN MOST. DO APPROXIMATELY TWO COMPLETE SETS EVERY SECOND. DO FIFTEEN OR TWENTY SETS.

CORRECTIONS

1. Get the correct speed.
2. Apply pressure as you move toward, not away from, the other hand.
3. Make sure your pressure is even. Don't do all the work with one hand.
4. Don't stay in one place too long. Keep moving.
5. Stay on the leg. Don't pinch off.

31. Small Circles

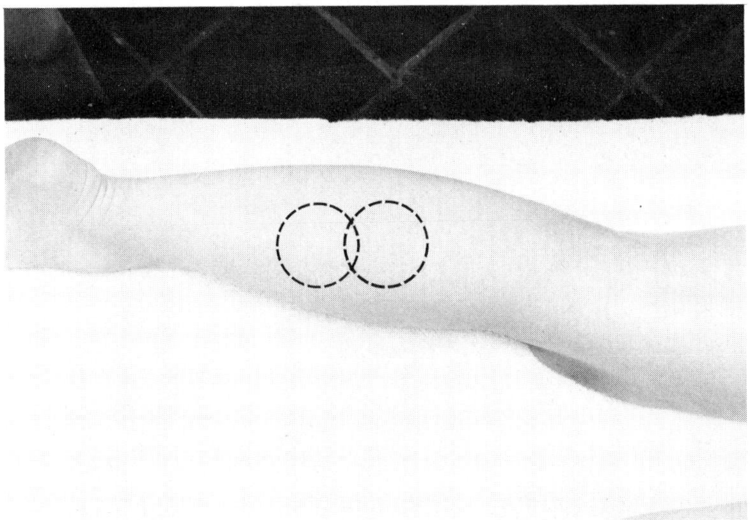

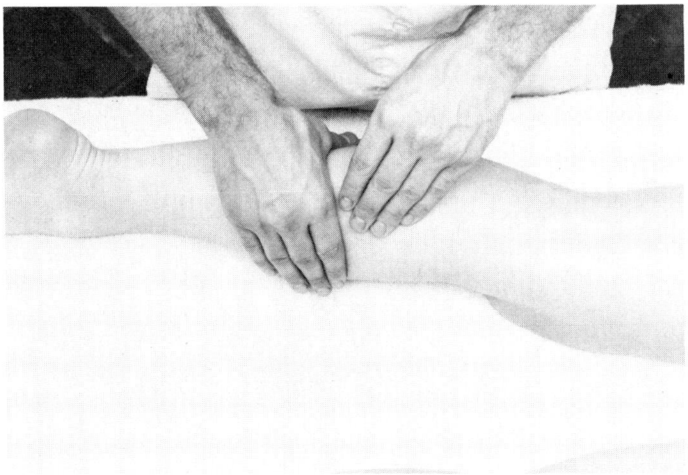

Begin as in movement 30. As each hand begins to move, it dips down toward the table, causing the center palm to touch the calf for a moment. The result is a series of double overlapping circles that move down toward the heel and back up to the calf.

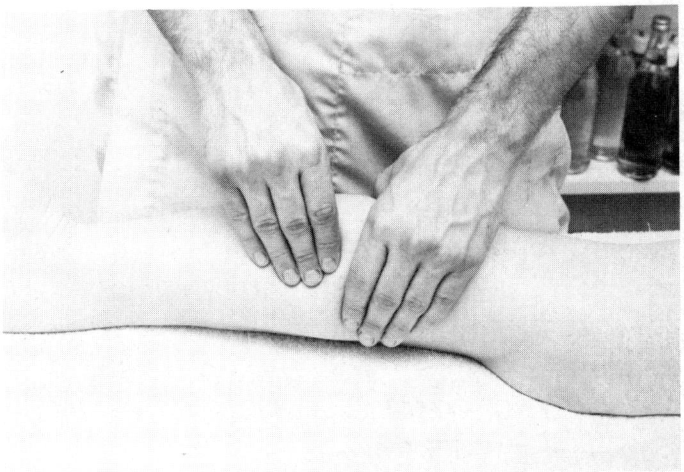

This movement is done primarily with *pads of all the fingers and thumb*. Do not let them leave the leg at any time, and try to lift the muscle up off the leg. This movement often is alternated with the opposition calf movement.

Timing: COMPLETE TWO SETS EVERY SECOND. DO FIFTEEN TO TWENTY SETS.

CORRECTIONS

1. Be sure the circles are consistent in size.
2. Maintain a steady, coordinated rhythm.
3. Don't remove your hands between strokes.

32. Vertical Up

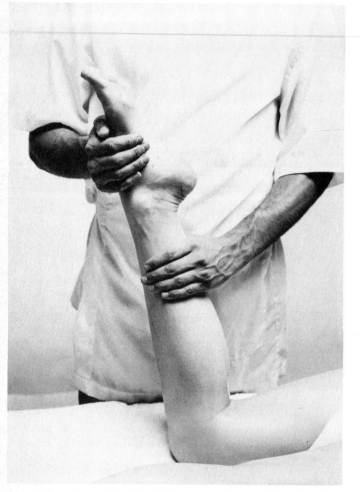
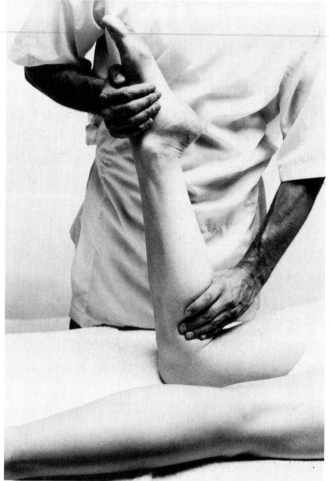

Face the subject's left knee, with your feet about twelve inches apart. With the right hand, lift the subject's leg by the ankle and hold it in a vertical position. Keep the hand relaxed, using just enough pressure to support the leg without gripping the ankle. With the thumb opposing the four fingers, wrap the left hand around the lower part of the calf three or four inches above the heel. You should be gripping with all the fingers and the palm. Throughout the entire movement the palm remains in contact with the calf.

Squeezing your fingers and gently leaning your weight into the palm of your hand, move down toward the table until you are just below the knee. Relax the pressure and drag your hand back to the starting position. Make sure you don't jam your palm into the back of the knee in the middle of the movement.

Timing: ONE MOVEMENT UNIT TAKES TWO SECONDS. DO EIGHT TO TWELVE UNITS.

CORRECTIONS

1. Hold the leg at a right angle to the table.
2. Don't squeeze the ankle.
3. Be sure to start low enough on the leg.
4. Use enough pressure.
5. Don't jam your palm into the back of the knee at the end of the movement.

33. The One-Two Calf

Almost identical with the one-two movement on the back of the thigh, this movement calls for pressure in the fingers, instead of leaning with your weight. You also move both hands equally to the top of the calf.

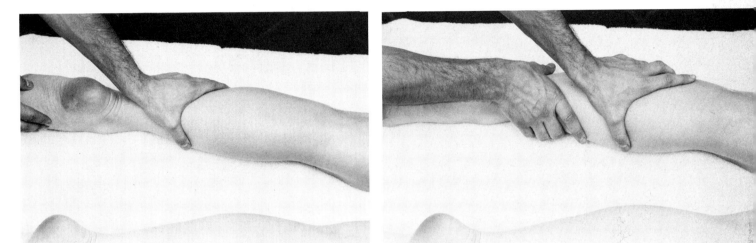

Stand at the foot of the table, facing the bottom of the subject's left foot. Begin with your left hand, the outside hand (above), and do the one-two, left-right action starting at the base of the calf, just above the heel.

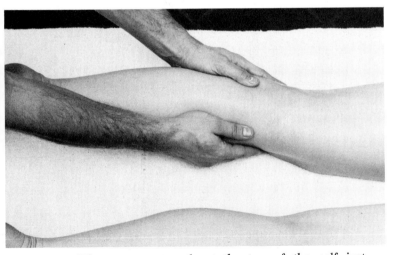

The movement ends at the top of the calf just below the back of the knee. Bring your thumbs across the top of the calf so that they rest next to your other fingers and the hands are facing up on the inner and outer sides of the calf. Drag back down the sides of the calf to the starting position. Be careful *not to run your thumbs across the back of the knee.*

Timing: ONE SET OF MOVEMENTS SHOULD TAKE TWO SECONDS. DO EIGHT TO TEN SETS.

CORRECTIONS

1. Start with the outside hand.
2. Make sure you're using enough thumb and finger pressure.
3. Don't press your thumbs into the back of the knee.
4. Remember to drag back. Don't lift your hands off the leg.

34. *The Whole Leg Movement*

This movement, which puts together the calf and
thigh, encourages blood circulation throughout the
leg. It also acts as a smoothing-out movement for
stronger movements that have been done previously
on the legs.

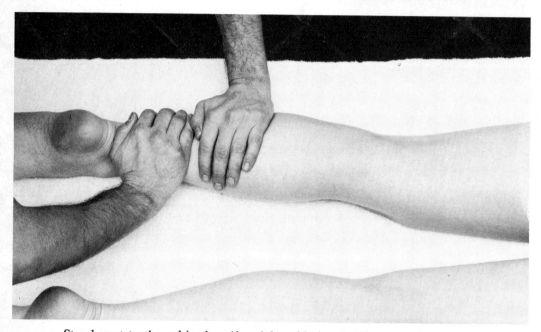

Stand next to the subject's calf and face his head. When working on the
left leg, turn your left hand in, with the palm cupped over the bottom of
the calf, and place your right hand below it in a similar position.

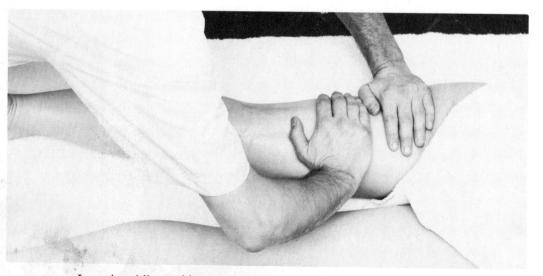

Lean in while stroking up the calf to the top of the thigh. As you go up
over the back of the knee, lighten your pressure. The right hand on the
inner thigh should not go up too high.

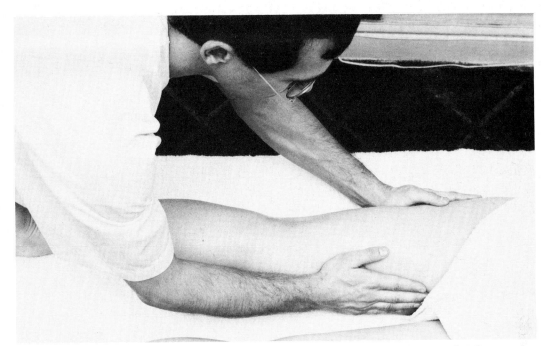

Separate the hands, with the fingers facing toward the head. Drag firmly down the inside and outside of the leg, back to the starting position.

Timing: THE TOTAL MOVEMENT SHOULD TAKE THREE SECONDS—TWO ON THE WAY UP AND ONE ON THE DRAG BACK. DO FOUR TO SIX MOVEMENTS.

Once you have become proficient in doing the calf movements, it should take you about ten minutes to do the backs of both legs and about thirty minutes to do all you have learned thus far.

CORRECTIONS

1. Don't forget to relax the pressure when behind the knee and increase it again above the knee.
2. Don't raise your own shoulders.
3. Don't go up too high with the inner hand.
4. Don't forget to drag back with even, gentle pressure on the sides of the leg.

Run-Through

When you have learned the movements on the back of the thigh and the calf, do the run-through exercise as described in chapter 5.

Lesson Eight · THE FRONT THIGHS

Muscular Compensation

Researchers in kinesiology—the study of muscle function in movement—are finding that movement involves the use of more muscles than was previously thought. Emphasis on a single muscle to perform a given movement, rather than correct use of the body as a whole, will often result in that muscle becoming overdeveloped, less flexible, and prone to injury.

Muscles work in pairs. When one set of muscles contracts, the opposite set expands or stretches. This is the general principle of movement. The contracting muscle does most of the work and produces a lot of tension. The stretched muscle does minimal work and produces little tension.

A muscle has three states: (1) tightened or contracted; (2) stretched or expanded; (3) relaxed, without tension. Both contracted and stretched states have some tension.

The body was meant to be used evenly, so that one muscle balances another. For example, the backbone is in the center of the trunk and is held in place by a series of muscles, ligaments, and tendons. Uneven muscular development and balance can pull the spine out of alignment.

If we don't develop the right and left sides of the body equally, the muscular balance of normal movement is disturbed. If one set develops disproportionately to the other, the paired muscles do not work as efficiently, lose fluidity, and become distorted. Athletes tend to use their "good" side. This tendency perpetuates itself, so the good side becomes stronger and the ignored side is weaker. When exercising or playing at sports, it is best to use both sides, even if it looks and feels awkward at first. In deep massage, too, learn to do everything from both sides. Uneven development can result in actual physical deformities, such as a spine with an exaggerated curve in and out or side to side.

When an injury occurs in one leg, the tendency is to compensate by putting more weight on the other. Extra care is necessary to relax the overworked leg. Exercise to equal the balance in the legs when the injury has passed is crucial, but usually it is overlooked, and injuries arising from the failure to rebalance the muscles are as common and as serious as initial injuries.

If someone gets a pain in the left big toe, he might compensate by tightening the entire leg and putting more weight on the right leg. If you are normally relaxed and squeeze your toes for one or two minutes, you will feel tension rise all the way from your toes up to your shoulder; that is compensating tension. In muscular therapy it is invaluable to be able to analyze the many patterns of muscular compensation so that you know where to work to head off further complications while an injury heals.

Muscle Groups and Knee Pain

A concentration of tension can occur in the middle of a long muscle, at either or both ends, or a combination of these. Often, the greatest tension is felt at the ends of muscles—called muscle attachments or origins and insertions—but remember that tension occurs in groups of muscles rather than in a single muscle. Since muscles are interwoven and layered, tension in an area will affect many muscles. A headache that occurs in the front of the head involves different groups of muscles than one that occurs in the back of the head, although there is some overlap. In the arms and legs, tension usually occurs in straight vertical lines or diagonals.

Knee pains occur in the front, back, inside, outside, deeply in the center, or in a combination of these. Obviously, different pains indicate trouble in different muscle groups when tension is the cause.

If pain is felt in the outside of the knee, the trouble originates at the front outside of the shin and thigh. If the pain is in the back of the knee, the cause usually stems from tension in the calf and the back of the thigh. Many of the muscles of the thigh attach to the bones of the lower leg and similarly a major calf muscle attaches to the thigh bone. When all these muscles contract, they pull the bones of the upper and lower leg together, putting the knee under tremendous pressure and restricting its movements. This pulling together is a major factor of many knee problems.

Pain in the center of the knee or under the kneecap or a knee locked in a straight position can mean a torn cartilage. If the condition and the pain persist, one should consult a physician. However, the most common cause of pain in the knees is muscle tension, especially in the calves.

With sufficient knowledge and training, and sensitive hands, you can feel the tension in particular muscle groups.

Muscles of the Front Thighs

1. *The quadriceps femoris* consists of four large muscles at the front of the thigh—rectus femoris, vastus lateralis, vastus medialis, and vastus intermedius. The rectus femoris starts on the front of the pelvis, while the other muscles begin on the thigh bone. They all attach to the top front of the tibia by the quadriceps or patellar tendon that encases the kneecap. You can feel it just below your kneecap. These four muscles flex the thigh at the hip joint and straighten the knee. Because they are involved in most leg movements, including walking, kicking, jumping, and climbing stairs, these muscles should be among the strongest in the body.

2. *The sartorius* runs from the outside of the hip diagonally over the thigh and attaches to the inner knee. It rotates the leg out and helps bend the knee. This muscle is often involved in knee problems.

3. *The tensor fasciae latae*, described in lesson 6, runs along the outside upper third of the thigh and is visible from the back and front of the thigh.

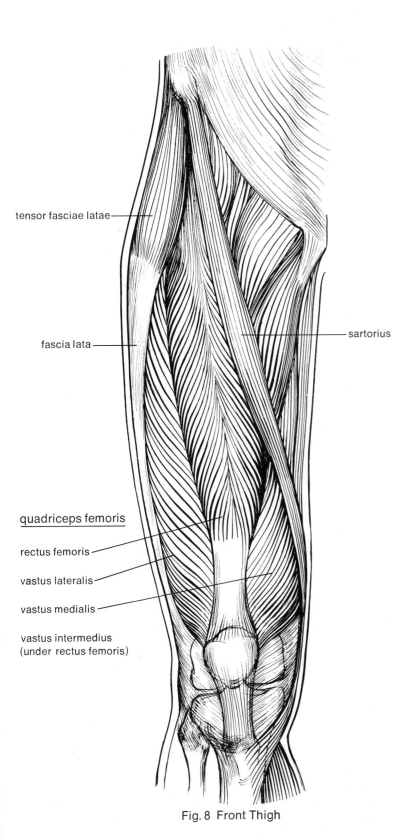

tensor fasciae latae

fascia lata

sartorius

quadriceps femoris

rectus femoris

vastus lateralis

vastus medialis

vastus intermedius
(under rectus femoris)

Fig. 8 Front Thigh

Fascia

The fascia, a type of connective tissue, covers and protects all the muscles. It is particularly thick in the abdomen, the lower back, and the legs. The fascia lata, located on the outer thigh, extends from the hip to the knee, covering the muscles of the outer thigh (not to be confused with the tensor fasciae latae, a muscle under part of it). It is the thickest and strongest fascia in the entire body.

How to See Tension in the Front Thighs

1. A bulky thigh with muscles jutting out in front or at the side is a sign of tension.
2. A pelvis tipped forward with protruding hips puts extra weight on the fronts of the thighs.
3. A bulge on the inner part of the thigh just above the knee often indicates tension or lack of muscular development throughout the front of the thigh.
4. Similarly, standing on one leg more than the other will produce tension.
5. Constant bumping into things indicates tension in the thighs. In this case the thighs have lost their sensitivity, due to excess tension. This clumsiness is often accompanied by an eye problem.

Causes of Tension in the Front Thighs

Mechanical Causes

1. Poor leg and hip posture result in tension.
2. Poor exercise, dance, or sports training causes tight and distorted thighs.
3. Weight lifting creates tension in the thighs.

Emotional Causes

The fronts of the thighs generally hold the most emotionally based tension.

Thigh Movements

Cover the subject with the towel as in lesson 6, the back thigh. Have the subject place his hands on his abdomen so they are not in your way.

35. Basic Front Thigh

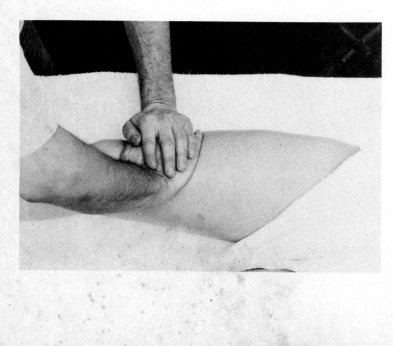

Stand facing the subject's head, just next to the right knee, with your left foot ahead of your right. Place your hands in the altered basic position, (right hand on the bottom), just above the right knee, as you did in the basic back thigh, lesson 6. Make sure that your hand is centered on the front of the thigh and that your fingers are firmly wrapped around it. Do not stiffen your fingers in the air.

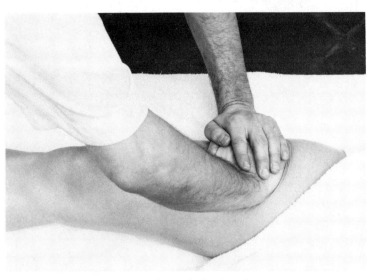

Lean evenly on the whole hand as you move straight up the thigh in this position.

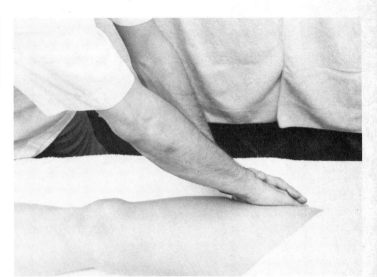

Just before you reach the top of the thigh, move outward to the outer thigh, letting up on your pressure.

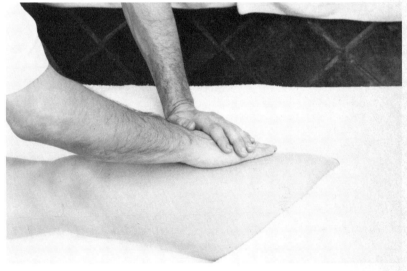

Drag back on the outer part of the thigh to the starting position.

Timing: EACH MOVEMENT UNIT TAKES TWO SECONDS. REPEAT THE MOVEMENT SIX TO TEN TIMES.

CORRECTIONS

1. Do not hit the knee at the beginning or on the drag back. The starting position is just above the knee, not on it.
2. Use the correct hand. Right hand on the bottom for the right leg, left for the left one.
3. Keep your fingers in constant contact with the thigh, but don't bear down on the fingertips.
4. Pressure should be even on the entire hand. Don't bear down on the heel of the hand.
5. Stay on the center of the thigh. Don't go up the inside or outside.
6. Don't go up too high before moving outward.
7. Drag back on the outer thigh, not the top thigh.
8. Be sure to drag back firmly.
9. Relax and drop your shoulders. Don't raise them.
10. Use your body weight, rocking from one leg to the other. Don't push or squeeze.

36. Basic Sartorius

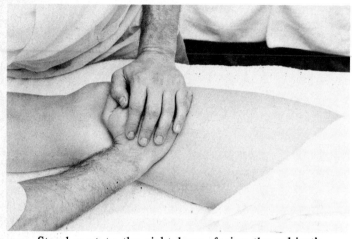

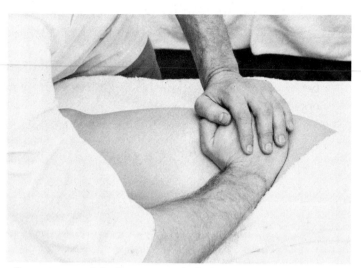

Stand next to the right knee, facing the subject's head, as in the previous movement. Your body should be in a semicrouched position, the hands in the altered basic position, with *the fingers facing out toward you*. The right hand is placed just above the knee, with the heel of the hand on the extreme inner part of the thigh. The elbows should be bent.

Lean your weight into your whole hand and follow the line of the sartorius muscle diagonally across the thigh from the inner part to the outer part. The heel of the hand outlines the sartorius muscle.

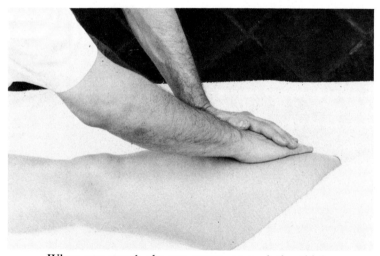

When you reach the top outer part of the thigh, firmly drag your hand back on the outside and cross over to the starting position just above the knee.

CORRECTIONS

1. The hand closest to the body is on the bottom.
2. Be sure the fingers of the hand are turned completely out.
3. Don't go up and out; move diagonally.
4. Don't forget to drag back on the outer leg.
5. Don't hunch your shoulders.

Timing: TAKE TWO SECONDS TO COMPLETE EACH MOVEMENT, BUT WORK MORE SLOWLY AT FIRST. DO ONLY FOUR TO SIX MOVEMENTS.

37. The One-Two Front Thigh

All the one-two movements use an identical rhythm but differ according to the shape of the body part on which you're working. Always begin a one-two movement with the outer hand. Try learning one hand at a time.

Start above the knee, using the palm of your hand. When working on the front thigh, notice if your subject's leg is rotated outward. Adjust the angle of your grip so that you work directly in the top center of the thigh.

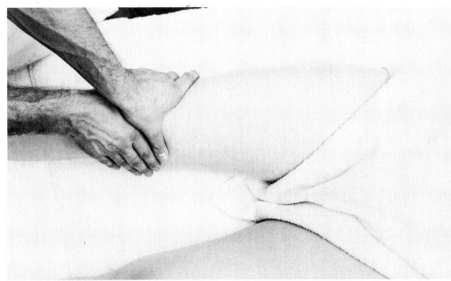

Stand in the same position as for the basic front thigh. Grip the front of the thigh just above the knee, with the left hand in front, exerting moderate pressure.

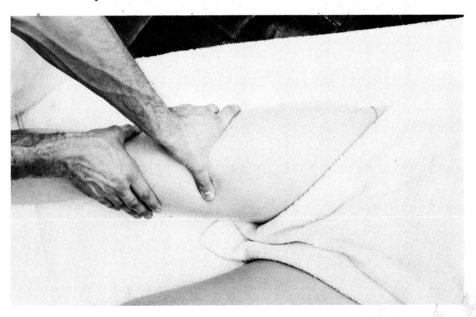

Lean into the palm, moving the left hand up the thigh. As the left hand reaches the middle of the thigh, the right hand follows.

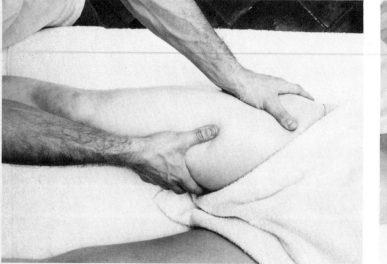

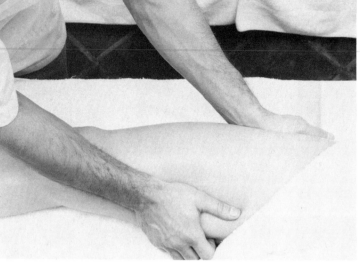

The left hand continues to move up to the top of the thigh and then outward. The right hand moves up and inward, to three or four inches below the groin.

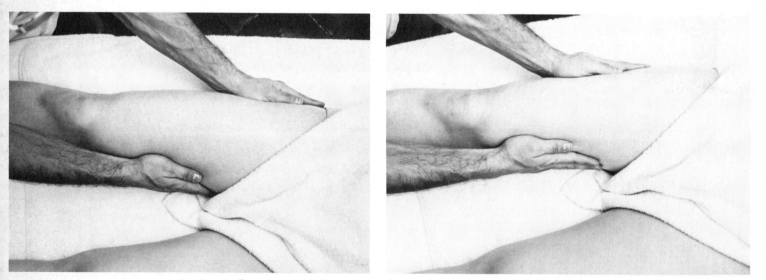

The hands flatten out on the extreme inner and outer parts of the thigh. They drag back down with firm pressure, stopping just before the knee.

Timing: THIS MOVEMENT TAKES ONE AND A HALF SECONDS, ALTHOUGH THE TEMPO DEPENDS ON THE NEEDS OF THE SUBJECT. DO EIGHT TO TEN UNITS.

CORRECTIONS

1. Be sure to use your center palm.
2. Start above the knee, never on it.
3. Don't go too high on the inner thigh.
4. Don't pinch off with the thumb and fingers.
5. Drag hands back together on the sides of the thigh.
6. Don't press in with the thumbs.

38. Opposition Front Thigh

This movement is identical with the opposition on the back thigh.

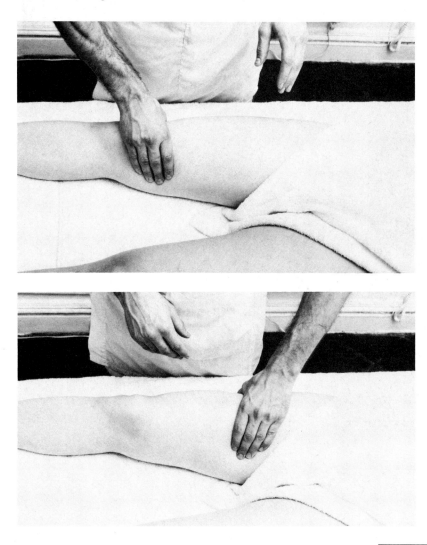

Face the right thigh and grip it above the knee with the right hand.

Use both squeezing and leaning pressures as your hand moves to the top of the thigh. Your left hand replaces it and moves down, stopping just before you hit the knee. The palm of the hand is touching the thigh.

Timing: ONE UNIT OF THIS MOVEMENT TAKES 1½ SECONDS. DO EIGHT TO TEN UNITS.

Try a variation of this movement that works on the tension just above the knees. Every fourth or fifth time, do one or two extra strokes on the downward movement, doubling the pressure with the fingers and thumb. Be careful not to jam into the knee, and watch the subject's face for discomfort.

CORRECTIONS

1. Don't use too much finger pressure.
2. Don't go too high.
3. Don't jam the subject's knee on the downstroke.
4. Be sure your palm is touching the top of the thigh, not raised above it.
5. Don't pinch off the leg; one hand lifts off while the other works.

39. Tensor

This movement on the thigh is often painful, so use extra care in applying the correct amount of pressure for each individual. Done on the outer edge of the tensor, and almost identical with the tensor movement for the back of the thigh, it hits the same muscle at different points.

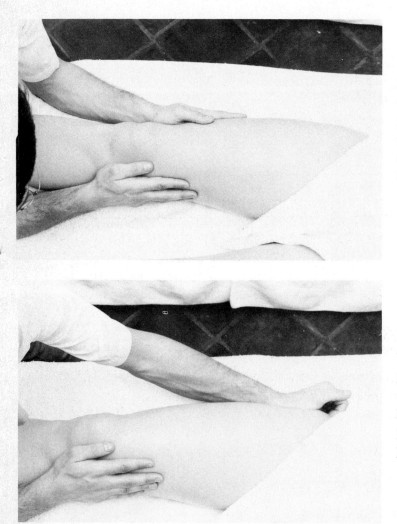

When working on the right leg, cup your right hand around the inner part of the knee, and brace the leg as in lesson 6. Place the left hand just above the outer part of the knee about a half inch from the table surface.

Pressing with the entire left hand, move up the outer part of the thigh, curling your hand into a loose fist at the top. Immediately flattening out your hand at the top, drag back to the starting position.

Timing: ONE SET OF MOVEMENTS TAKES TWO SECONDS. DO FOUR TO EIGHT SETS.

CORRECTIONS

1. Don't forget to use the inner hand as a brace.
2. Be sure to start just above the knee.
3. Put pressure on the whole hand, not just the heel.
4. Curl the hand when your fingers hit the underwear.
5. Don't forget to uncurl the hand for the drag back.

40. Short Tensor

The short tensor is a variation of the tensor movement done in a five-inch space above the knee. It works at the attachment of the largest area of fascia in the body, and the outer quadriceps muscle, the vastus lateralis, which lies beneath it. Begin in the same position as in the preceding movement, but place much greater pressure on your working hand.

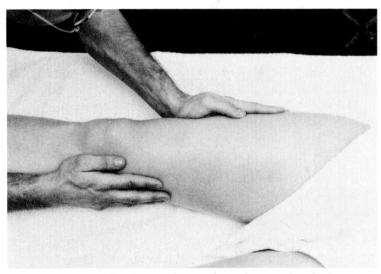

Push in firmly as you go about four or five inches. *Do not curl your hand.* Drag down.

Do this intense movement only three or four times and smooth it out by finishing with a regular tensor movement.

Timing: EACH SHORT TENSOR MOVEMENT SHOULD TAKE 1½ SECONDS—1 ON THE WAY UP AND ½ ON THE DRAG BACK. DO THE MOVEMENT ONLY THREE OR FOUR TIMES.

CORRECTIONS

1. Be sensitive to how much pressure should be used.
2. Don't go more than five inches up the thigh.
3. Don't make a fist.

The front thigh movements should take you approximately four minutes for each leg. If you combine everything you've learned so far, the total time required should be about thirty-five minutes.

Lesson Nine · THE FRONT LOWER LEGS (THE SHINS)

Fatigue

The feeling of muscular fatigue is due to the accumulation of lactic acid in the muscles. Oxygen burns glucose from the food we eat so that energy is provided for the muscles to contract. Since the blood can carry only a certain amount of oxygen to a muscle at a given time, the oxygen available to it will become depleted if the muscle continues to contract. When this happens, glucose will be burned without oxygen, and one of the by-products of this anaerobic (without oxygen) process is lactic acid. As lactic acid accumulates, the muscle is less able to contract. This is what we speak of as muscle fatigue. Lactic acid accumulation may also cause cramps in muscles after vigorous exercise.

When a muscle is fatigued, it must rest until the lactic acid is carried away and enough oxygen is brought to the muscle to compensate for the depletion incurred during contraction. This is sometimes referred to as "repaying the oxygen debt." If the muscles are not permitted to relax, fatigue becomes chronic.

Bones of the Lower Legs

There are two bones in the lower leg—the fibula, on the outside part of the leg, and the tibia, the flat bone in the front of the leg. The tibia lies between the ankle and knee joints and is referred to as the shin bone. It is the only large bone close to the surface of the skin, and it is therefore vulnerable to bruising.

Muscles of the Front Lower Legs (the Shins)

1. *The tibialis anterior* is the large muscle in front of the lower leg, seen at the outside of the shin bone. It attaches at the top of the tibia, runs all along the underside of the shin bone, crosses the ankle by a long tendon, and attaches to the inside of the foot.

2. *The extensor digitorum longus* is located at the outside of the tibialis anterior muscle. It starts at the fibula and attaches by multiple tendons to all toes except the big one.

3. *The peroneus muscles* are a set of three on the outside of the leg; they attach to the fibula and run down to the outside of the foot.

All these muscles are involved in the flexing and rotating of the foot, and the extensor digitorum longus also raises the toes. They are also used in walking, to control the foot between the heel and the flat positions, and in running or landing from a jump.

How to See Tension in the Shins

It is easy to see tension in the shins by watching how people walk. The following are indications of tension:

1. Kicking the feet out and coming down hard on the heels when walking.
2. Walking with the knees completely bent.
3. Standing on one leg more than the other.
4. Frequently twisted and strained ankles and

poorly aligned knees that turn in or out, instead of straight, indicates weakness, or tension in the lower legs.

Causes of Tension in the Shins

1. Generally, the same problems of alignment and stress on the lower legs apply here as in lesson 7, the calves, but in this case there is more stress when the knees are turned in, rather than out, as with the calves.

2. People who walk barefoot on concrete, pebbles, or gravel contract their legs and feet to tolerate the jarring effect. However, walking barefoot on grass, dirt, sand, or at the beach in ankle-deep water, is not injurious.

3. Exercising on a concrete or wooden floor with a concrete base creates tension in the shins. Jumping on any surface with the heels constantly raised can injure the shins also. This can often result in a condition commonly called shin splints, meaning a strain of the muscles in the fronts of the lower legs. This condition makes it difficult to jump, run, or even walk without pain.

Working Blindfolded

Once you have mastered the first nine lessons, and their sequence has become second-nature, try several practice sessions blindfolded. Without your sight, you'll find that your other senses become heightened. When you have to sense with your hands, you feel a lot more. Your concentration increases and your ability to flow from one movement to another becomes apparent. When working blindfolded, concentrate on only one or two of the following concepts at a time:

1. Leaning
2. Breathing
3. Transitions
4. The energy in your hands
5. Rhythms
6. Use of appropriate pressure for the individual
7. Keeping your neck and shoulder relaxed

From time to time try working blindfolded to keep in touch with your progress.

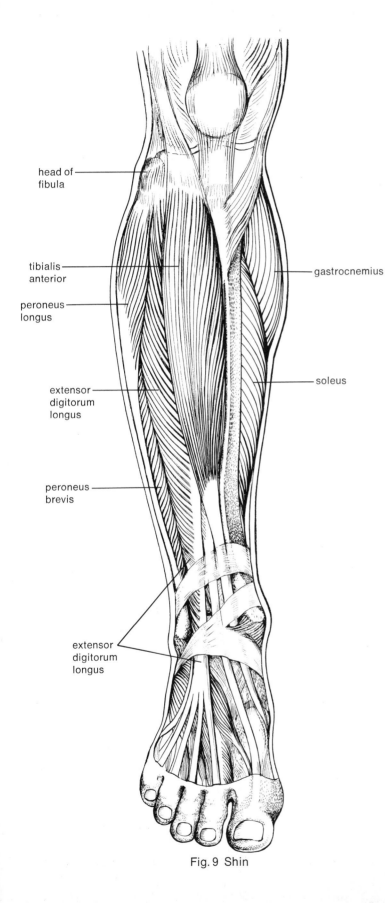

head of fibula

tibialis anterior

peroneus longus

extensor digitorum longus

peroneus brevis

extensor digitorum longus

gastrocnemius

soleus

Fig. 9 Shin

Shin Movements

41. Tibialis Movement

In this movement the pressure is always on the center of the palm. The fingers and thumb are totally relaxed.

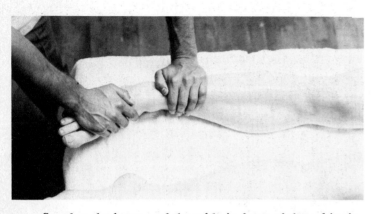

Stand at the bottom of the table in front of the subject's right foot. Place the center of your right palm on top of the right foot and gently rotate the foot in. This enables you to work on the muscles of the shin more easily. Place your left hand on the lower leg just above the ankle, with the fingers pointing inward.

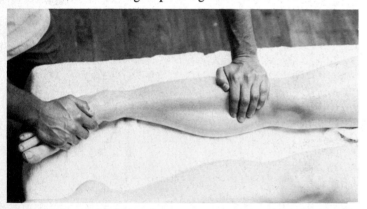

Lean the weight of your body into your palm and move your hand from the top of the ankle up to the base of the knee, being careful not to jam into the knee. Relax your hand and drag it straight down to the starting position.

The proper hand is always the outside one. If you use the wrong hand, you will be pressing your weight onto a bone.

Timing: ONE UNIT OF THIS MOVEMENT TAKES TWO SECONDS. DO SIX TO EIGHT UNITS.

CORRECTIONS

1. Be sure to use the outer hand on the bottom.
2. Be sure to rotate the ankle in far enough.
3. Don't turn the foot in so far that you strain the ankle.
4. Don't grip the ankle so hard that it hurts the foot.
5. Put the pressure on the palm of the hand, not the heel.
6. Do not press on the shin bone.
7. Don't jam your hand into the knee.

42. Two-handed Tibialis Movement

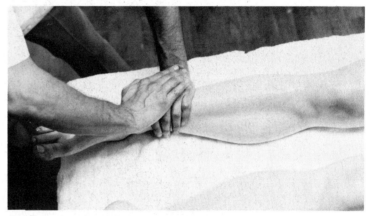

This movement is identical with the last, except the right hand, which was holding the ankle, is now placed on top of the left hand. This allows you to do the same movement with greater force.

The additional pressure usually prevents the leg from rolling outward, but you can brace the right ankle against your right outer thigh if you are working on a table, or against your outer knee if working on the floor.

Timing: ONE MOVEMENT UNIT REQUIRES TWO SECONDS. DO SIX TO EIGHT MOVEMENT UNITS.

CORRECTIONS

They are the same as in the tibialis movements, but without the ankle corrections.

43. Vertical Down

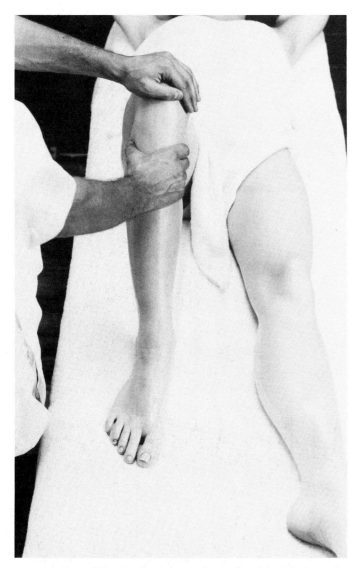 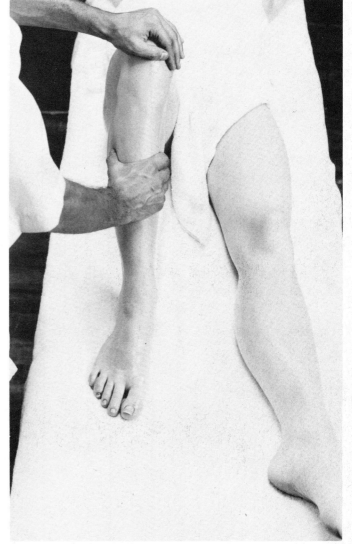

Face the subject's right leg. Place the sole of the subject's foot flat on the ground or table surface. Cup the left hand over the top of the right knee, and exert a slight downward pressure to stabilize the leg. If the foot begins to slip, place a folded towel underneath the ball of the foot. Grip the top of the shin just below the knee with the thumb and four fingers of your right hand, keeping the full palm in complete contact with the leg.

Squeeze your hand and lean as you move down the leg toward the ankle, exerting pressure on the muscles on both sides of the shin bone. The fingertips stay close to the inside of the shin bone.

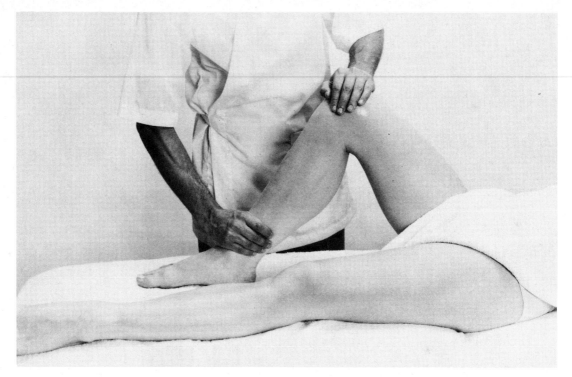

When you reach the ankle, relax your hand and drag it up to the starting position without breaking contact.

The fibula bone is the thin bone you'll feel very close to the surface as you come to the end of the movement. You can run your finger up the outer ankle bone to locate it exactly. Lighten the pressure when you go over the edge of this bone with your thumb.

> *Timing:* ONE MOVEMENT UNIT TAKES TWO SECONDS. DO TEN TO FIFTEEN MOVEMENT UNITS.

CORRECTIONS

1. Be sure to use the hand closest to the ankle for the movement.
2. Don't dig in too hard with the fingertips.
3. Be sure your palm is touching the leg.
4. Go low enough to the ankle.
5. Don't let your thumb hit the lower outer fibula bone.
6. Don't slip or go too fast.
7. Don't hold back on your body weight; use it.
8. Be careful not to raise your shoulders, especially on the working-hand side.

44. Vertical Down with the Tilt

The position and movement pattern is similar to the vertical down.

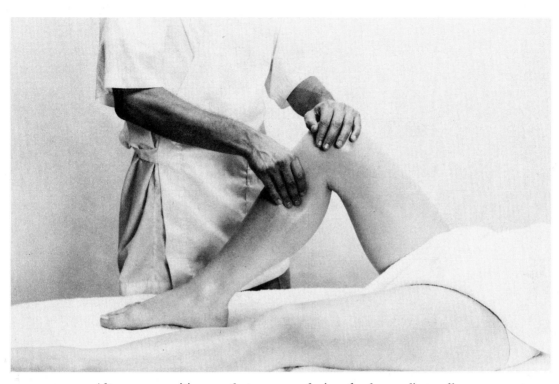

Alter your position so that you are facing the knee, diagonally. You can utilize your weight more efficiently that way. Tilt the hand up so that the palm loses contact with the shin. Press with your thumb and first two or three fingers only, depending on the size of the subject's leg.

Use more pressure both in squeezing and in leaning to go much deeper into the muscles. Perform the movement as you did in the vertical down, being very careful not to jam your thumb into the fibula bone that protrudes above the outer ankle.

> *Timing:* EACH UNIT SHOULD TAKE TWO SECONDS. DO SIX TO EIGHT OF THEM.

CORRECTIONS

1. The same as the corrections for the vertical down.
2. Lean into the leg.
3. Don't use the small finger of the working hand.

45. Fishline Movement

Stand facing the subject's leg just below the knee. Run your hand up the outside part of the lower leg until you hit a small bone that sharply protrudes from the leg about an inch or so below the knee. This bone is the head of the fibula. (Check figure 9, page 143.) The movement is performed horizontally, in a two- or three-inch space next to the head of the fibula. Be careful not to use too much pressure in this movement, because one of the branches of the sciatic nerve runs just beneath the bone where you're working.

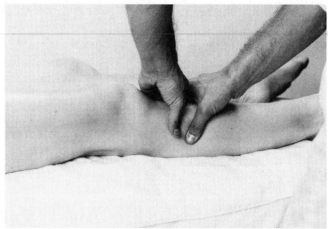

Release the pressure from that thumb and replace it with the other thumb pad, repeating the same motion in the opposite direction. The thumb that is not working should be lifted off the leg slightly.

This movement is done rapidly, and resembles the opposition movement in principle.

Timing: IT TAKES ONE SECOND TO DO ONE COMPLETE SET. DO EIGHT TO TWELVE SETS.

Do a few tibialis movements to smooth out the area and finish the leg.

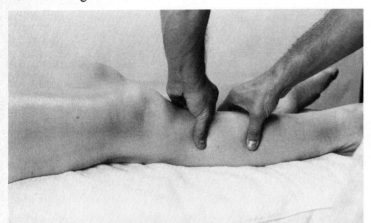

Stand facing the subject's right leg slightly below the knee. Grip the leg below the knee with both hands, the thumbs on the outer part of the leg and the fingers on the inner part. The thumbs should point down to the floor.

The four fingers of each hand do not move but act as a brace to hold the leg still. The movement is executed with the pads of the thumbs exclusively.

CORRECTIONS

1. Work horizontally just below the bone. Don't hit it with the thumb.
2. Work with the pads of your thumbs, not the fingertips.
3. Don't press too hard.

After you've become proficient in the first nine lessons, it should take you thirty-five to forty minutes to complete the back and both sides of the legs. As your technique and efficiency improve, the over-all time will diminish.

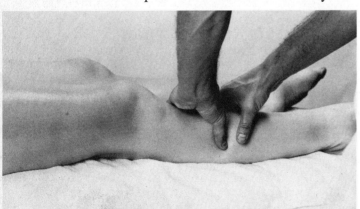

Just below the small bone, push in with the pad of the left thumb and move down the leg about two inches.

Lesson Ten · THE FEET

Customarily, the next step in deep massage is to study in greater detail the parts of the body already covered, and to learn how to treat specific problems, but more-intensive training and most pressure techniques cannot be taught adequately in a book. Moreover, for a beginner, the front of the neck, the chest, the abdomen, and the buttocks are difficult and sensitive areas to work on. Without proper supervision, the novice can produce more harm than good. Therefore, all these movements have also been excluded, and we will proceed to lessons on the feet, arms, and light work on the face.

The movements covered in the previous nine lessons would constitute a complete deep massage. In my experience, this thirty-to-forty-minute treatment is all the average individual can tolerate at first. Additional work on the feet, face, and arms should be done only when appropriate (i.e., for stiff, aching feet). When adding additional movements, eliminate others. For example, if the primary problem is tension in the legs and feet, you might move through the back more swiftly by eliminating some movements or doing fewer of each. Then spend more time on the legs and do some work on the feet.

If the subject's problem is tension in the arms, you might eliminate the fronts or all of the legs, and work longer on the arms and shoulder area.

The Feet

Some people are often embarrassed by their feet. They frequently neglect them, treat them as if they were not part of the body, or distort them with the wrong shoes. The farthest outposts of the body, usually covered by shoes and socks, the feet are rarely thought about unless they hurt.

Muscles of the Feet

Nineteen muscles on the bottom of the foot support the arch and curl and point the toes. One muscle on the top of the foot, the *extensor digitorum brevis*, lifts the toes.

Many muscles of the lower legs extend into the feet by tendons and help to carry out the various foot movements. Thus, the functioning of the feet is closely related to that of the lower legs. When you point or extend the foot, you use the muscles of the calf as well as the muscles underneath the arch. If you have a pain in the top of your foot, it is probably related to tension in the front lower leg, and pain or cramping in the arch is often connected to tension in the calf. As a general principle, tension in the legs, especially the calves, tends to produce tension in the feet.

Since blood flows to the feet through the legs, tension in the legs can hinder circulation in the feet. The feet are also the farthest point from the heart, and the blood returning to the heart has to travel uphill all the way. This is why elevating the legs alleviates tension in the feet.

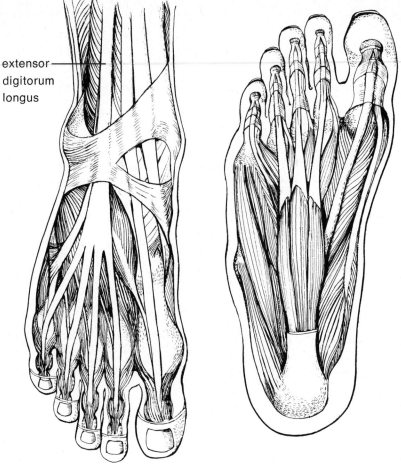

extensor
digitorum
longus

Fig. 10 Foot

How to See Tension in the Feet

1. With hammertoes, the terminal joints of the toes are permanently flexed.

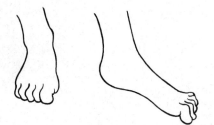

2. With great toe distortion, the big toe is displaced sideways, often above or beneath the adjacent toe.

FALLEN ARCHES   NORMAL   HIGH INSTEP

3. Fallen arches or flat feet indicate tremendous tension in the feet and may result from bad athletic or dance training, although the condition can also be congenital. People with this problem tend to wear out shoes on the inside edge of the sole.

4. A high instep often results in a weak arch, and may be a sign of tension.

5. People who stand with their feet spread far apart and the weight of the body on the feet, rather than on the legs, encourage tension.

6. Pushed-out feet result from standing on the outside of the feet, which causes tension in the front lower legs. In this case, shoes will wear out on the outside edge of the sole.

7. Feet turned in or out when standing indicate tension in the feet.

8. Extreme ticklishness in the feet is always a sign of great tension.

Causes of Tension in the Feet

Mechanical Causes

1. Hammertoes and distorted big toes are often caused by tight or pointed shoes or by chronically contracted legs.

2. Fallen arches, when not congenital, are caused by alignment problems in which the knees are dropped forward and the feet are turned out. This condition occurs when people have a great deal of tension in the inner thighs and lower back, and is often accompanied by a retracted pelvis. In this case, the entire alignment has to be corrected. The rolling-pin exercise on page 42 can be helpful, although if the problem is congenital, little can be done to lift the arches.

3. High insteps indicate that the center of gravity of the feet is higher than average, which makes proper balance more difficult, and a weakness often develops. Sometimes high arches can be exacerbated by bad shoes. People who walk barefoot on rough terrain, i.e., rocky or pebbled ground, often develop contracted high arches, because the feet constantly contract from the pain caused by the surface, until it becomes chronic.

4. Being on your feet too much can cause tension in the feet.

5. Bad knee-foot alignment puts pressure on the feet and can cause tension. For instance, when the knee is turned in and the foot out, the weight is placed on the arch of the foot and the inner ankle joint, instead of the whole leg.

Emotional Causes

We sometimes see people with twitching feet, constantly cracking or snapping their toes, or people who squeeze their feet together. In general, these are nervous habits, an emotional expression coming out in the feet.

Foot Movements

While learning, do all the movements below in sequence on one foot and then on the other. Once you have learned them, however, they can be done on the left foot after the front of the left leg is completed and on the right foot after the right leg.

46. The Pull

Drag your hands back gently to the starting point. Do the movement in a straight line in the center of

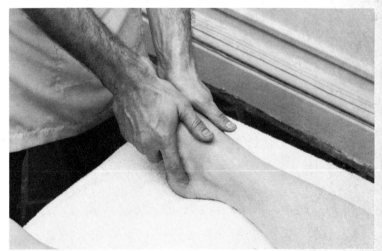

Stand facing the bottom of the subject's foot, while the subject lies on his back. Take hold of the foot with your hands positioned as shown in the photographs above. The pads of the middle, ring, and little fingers will oppose the pressure of the thenar

pad on the top of the foot. Be careful not to press down with the thumbs, since the bones on the top of the foot are close to the surface and sensitive. The forefinger should be relaxed.

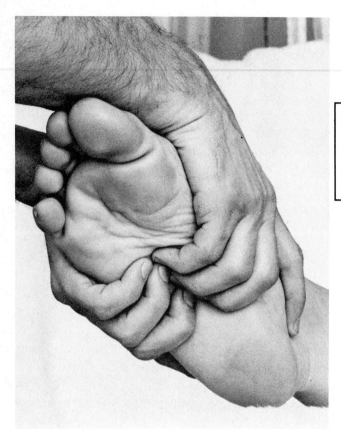

Apply pressure with your three working fingers on the sole of the foot just above the heel.

Leaning slightly away from the foot, squeeze and pull toward the toes. Let up the pressure as you move on to the ball of the foot.

the foot. As you proceed, move to the right and left, so that the whole bottom of the foot is worked. This movement does not include the toes, so be sure to stop short of them.

> *Timing:* EACH MOVEMENT UNIT SHOULD TAKE ONE SECOND WHEN PRACTICING. REPEAT THIS MOVEMENT TEN OR TWENTY TIMES.

If the foot is ticklish from a lot of surface tension, try slapping the bottom of the foot forcefully and then proceed to the movement. If the feet are very ticklish as as a result of tension, they may be too much for you to tackle as a beginner.

CORRECTIONS

1. Don't dig in with your nails on the bottom of the foot.
2. Don't do the movement on the toes. Stop on the ball of the foot.
3. Don't do it in one place. Move slightly to the inside and outside of the foot.
4. Be sure not to press down with the thumbs on the top of the foot.
5. Use pressure only on the pull.
6. Don't use all your fingers, just the last three.
7. Remember to lean back.

47. The Push

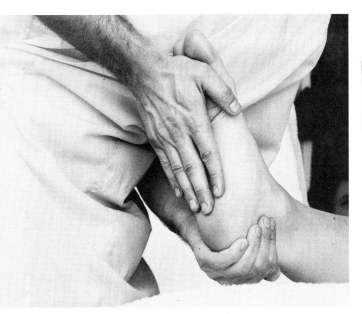

Stand facing the outside of the subject's right foot. Place your left hand under the back of the subject's heel and gently lift the foot an inch or two in the air. Then place the palm of your right hand, fingers facing down, on the sole of the right foot, with the heel of your hand just below the toes on the ball of the foot. In this movement use your whole hand, but accentuate the pressure in the heel of your hand.

Begin this movement in the center line of the foot and slowly move to the outside of the foot. This movement feels pleasant and can be done forcefully.

Timing: TAKE ONE SECOND PER MOVEMENT AND DO IT EIGHT TO TEN TIMES.

CORRECTIONS

1. Make sure your right hand works on the right foot, and left hand on the left foot.
2. Be sure to start with the heel of the hand on the ball of the foot.
3. Remember to lift the foot an inch or two in the air and not to grip it too tightly.
4. Don't stop short. Move the heel of your hand down to the very end of the arch, wrapping your fingers around the heel.
5. Don't forget to move slightly out of the middle line of the foot.

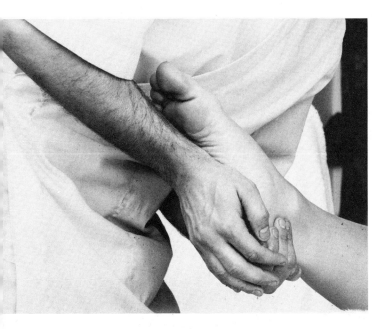

Using your body weight to help, begin by pushing the hand into the foot to make it flex. Exerting a fair amount of pressure, stroke down to the heel. When your fingers come to the heel, they move under it and allow the heel of your hand to finish the movement at the bottom of the subject's heel. Drag your hand back to the starting position, maintaining contact throughout.

48. The Inner Ankle

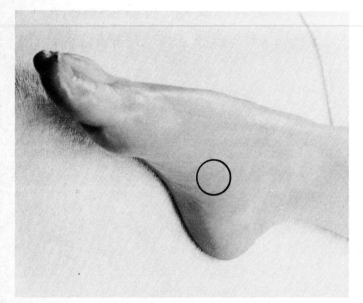

This movement is done directly below the inner ankle bone in a 1-to-1½-inch circle, depending on the size of the foot. Aim for the space between the heel, instep, and ankle bone; if you hit bone, you are in the wrong place.

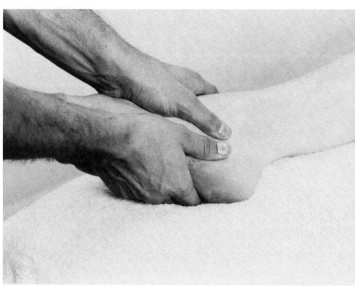

Stand facing the subject's foot as in the pull. Allow the foot and leg to gently roll outward so the inner part of the ankle is exposed. You may have to ask the subject to bend his knee. Hold the foot in your hand, with the thumbs parallel to each other in the starting circle.

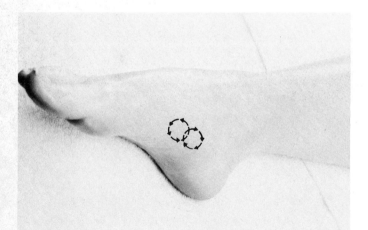

Applying firm pressure with the thumb pads throughout, make alternating, outward-directed circles in an even, continuous manner. The circles should overlap somewhat.

Timing: TWO COMPLETE SETS OF THIS MOVE-MENT SHOULD TAKE ONE SECOND. DO THE MOVEMENT TWENTY OR THIRTY TIMES, WITH MODERATE PRESSURE.

CORRECTIONS

1. Don't squeeze the foot with your other fingers. Hold it gently.
2. Make sure you find the right spot. You shouldn't feel bone.
3. Don't use the thumb tips.
4. Make sure your movement is continuous.
5. Don't apply too much pressure. Watch the subject's face.

49. The Outer Ankle

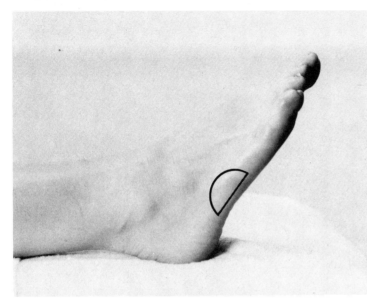

In the same standing position you used for the inner ankle, grasp the front of the right foot with the right hand. Gently rotate the foot inward to expose the outer ankle. Take a moment to find the place to be worked on. Bordered by bone on three sides, it is located in front of the outer heel on the lower outside of the foot directly below the ankle bone.

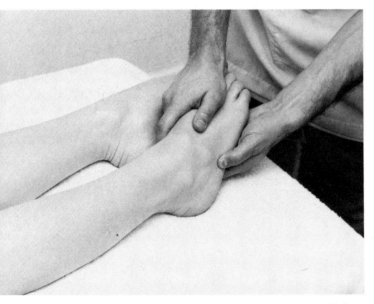

With the foot pointing in, take the pad of your left thumb and place it at the front of the working area.

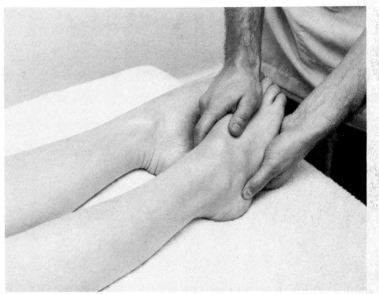

Press in with the thumb pad and push toward the heel. After you cover about an inch of space without jamming into the heel bone, gently drag the thumb back.

Timing: IT SHOULD TAKE ONE SECOND PER MOVEMENT UNIT. REPEAT THE MOVEMENT TEN OR TWENTY TIMES.

CORRECTIONS

1. Don't squeeze the foot. Hold it gently with the supporting hand.

2. Make sure you're not hitting bone. If you do, you're in the wrong place or going too far toward the heel.

3. Don't use the thumb tip.

4. Don't do the movement too hard. Remember to check the subject's face frequently as an indicator of discomfort.

50. *The Interdigital*

This movement can be done with either hand. One hand does the work and the other hand holds the foot still. The work is done with the pad of your thumb on the top of the foot between the base of the toes and the instep.

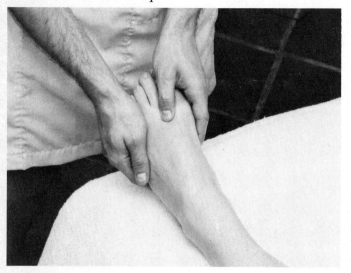

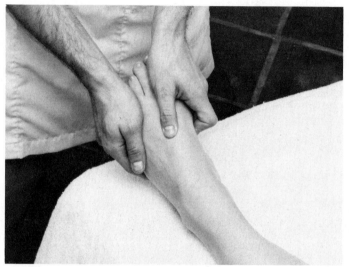

In the same position, facing the bottom of the foot, push in gently with the pad of the thumb and stroke down toward the instep in a straight line

between each of the metatarsals. The metatarsals are extensions of the toe bones. There is about a half-inch space between each of them.

Working your way from the large to the small toes, do three or four complete strokes between each toe before moving on to the next. Use pressure only when moving away from the toes, not dragging back to them. Make sure you use the fleshy pad of the thumb and *not your thumb point or tip*, because this is a very sensitive part of the foot. Go gently.

4. Don't move too fast or too hard. Go gently.
5. Stop when you hit bone, about two inches up from the base of the toes, depending on foot size.

When you finish the interdigital movement, repeat the pull to smooth out and finish off the foot.

After you have mastered these movements, it should take you about five or six minutes to complete both feet.

> *Timing:* EACH STROKE SHOULD TAKE ONE SECOND. GO THROUGH THE ENTIRE PROCEDURE TWO OR THREE TIMES.

CORRECTIONS

1. Be sure to support the foot gently with the other hand, but don't squeeze.
2. Don't work on the metatarsal bones, go between them.
3. Don't press in both directions; press only when going toward the instep.

> When you know the foot movements thoroughly, run through the front thigh, front lower leg, and foot, to make sure you have the sequence down pat.

Lesson Eleven · THE FACE

Our faces are what others see of us. Many people create different faces to act as a cover in situations they cannot deal with openly. If a person's emotional problems lead him to create a multitude of faces, the real face can be replaced by a distorted or masklike look.

Most people are surprised to find that their faces are very tense. Two of the most painful places are inside the tops of the orbits of the eyes, right near the top of the nose, and the masseters of the jaw. The beginner should work very gently on the face and take care not to give pain.

Clumsiness and the Eyes

Clumsiness is often related to tension in the muscles surrounding the eye, which can result in poor eye functioning and an inability to make proper contact with the world. To function properly, the eyes must maintain direct communication with the brain. Even with perfect vision, tension in the area surrounding the eyes can result in failure to register mentally what the eyes see and to react to it appropriately. Accidents like bumping into things, tripping, falling, and injuring oneself while using tools and machinery may indicate too much tension in and around the eyes.

Muscles of the Face

1. *The platysma* is a large sheetlike muscle extending from the lower jaw to the top of the chest. It draws down the lower lip and the ends of the mouth.

2. *The two pterygoideus muscles*, the *masseter muscles*, and the *temporalis* control closing and opening the jaw, and are referred to as the chewing muscles.

3. *The orbicularis oris* encircles the mouth and closes and puckers the lips.

4. *The buccinator* pulls the cheeks in to hold food in the mouth while chewing.

5. *The frontalis* is a thin muscle of the forehead that lifts the eyebrows and produces wrinkling of the forehead.

6. *The orbicularis oculi* encircles the eyes and closes them.

There are many other muscles in the face, but they are thin and not always evident. Raising and lowering the eyebrows while keeping the eyes open and still, opening the eyes wide and closing them tight,

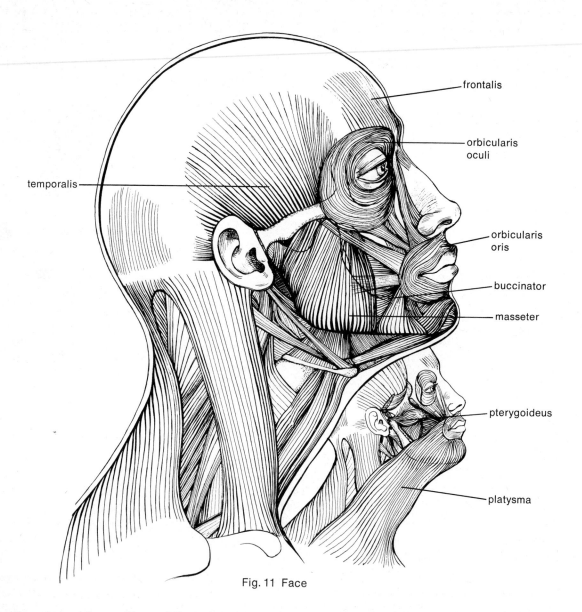

frontalis

orbicularis oculi

temporalis

orbicularis oris

buccinator

masseter

pterygoideus

platysma

Fig. 11 Face

and·moving the nose and nostrils rapidly independently of the face are all simple muscular movements that many people cannot perform because of tension.

How to See Tension in the Face

1. Eyebrows constantly raised, making wrinkles in the forehead.

2. Lines between the eyebrows from a constant frown.

3. The eyes:
   a. bulge out
   b. constantly squinting (although this may be a sight problem)
   c. dropped eyelids
   d. darting from side to side involuntarily
   e. dead stare
   f. twitches
   g. excessively or rarely blinking
   h. poor dilation and contraction of the pupils
   i. light sensitivity, which might be indicated by the wearing of sunglasses indoors
   j. a veiled, dead look, as if the eyes do not see anything or as if they look through you, is a most important sign of tension
   k. stationary eyes where the head must turn to look in another direction
   l. unable to follow a rapidly moving object

4. Lack of mobility and stiff appearance in cheeks.

5. The nose:
   a. constantly flared nostrils
   b. constantly twitching nostrils
   c. the tip of the nose pulled down
6. The jaw:
   a. clamped
   b. constantly flexing jaw muscles
   c. grinding teeth, creating tension at the temples, jaw, and occiput simultaneously
   d. jutted forward or dropped
   e. a jaw that locks when opened wide
7. The lips and mouth:
   a. firmly pressed together
   b. a constant, unchanging smile
   c. lips closed during speech
   d. constant lip biting or tongue biting
   e. constant tooth sucking
   f. playing nervously with the tongue constantly
8. People who are always "making faces" but don't know it.

Premature Wrinkles

Premature wrinkles of the forehead are often caused by tension in the frontalis muscle, which chronically raises the eyebrows unconsciously. When the muscles of the face are held in this position, more chronic tension and poor circulation result. Muscular contraction is important for venous blood circulation but continual contraction causes the skin to become unhealthy and to sag. Many people think working on the face will loosen the skin and cause wrinkling. Actually, the opposite is true. Massage of the forehead improves the circulation, breaks down the tension, increases its ability to move, and results in more elastic, better-toned skin.

Test Yourself

1. Relax your jaw and put your thumb under it and your first finger around the front of it. Push your thumb straight up as hard as you can for about an

inch and a half and move it from side to side. If it hurts, that means that there is tension in the area.

2. Place the tips of your thumbs on the inner part of your eyes and press up into the orbit. If that hurts, there is a good deal of tension.

3. Press into your jaw with your knuckle. If it hurts, it's a sign of tension.

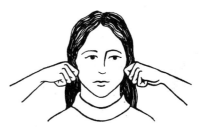

Causes of Tension in the Face

Mechanical Causes

1. Accidents such as a blow to the head or a deep cut can cause tension in the face.
2. Dental braces cause a lot of tension and are often responsible for years of residual tension after they have been removed.
3. Painful dental work can cause tension.
4. Noise and air pollution can cause the face to contract and thus produce tension.
5. Facial surgery can cause muscular trauma.

Emotional Causes

All of the emotions are expressed in the face. Both the voluntary and the involuntary holding back of emotions are therefore a source of tension in the face.

Face Movements

For all the face movements, stand facing the top of the subject's head. Before starting any movements on the face, gently roll the subject's head from side to side ten or fifteen times to make sure he is not holding his head rigid but allowing you to do the movement.

Be sure to execute the movements in this lesson with extreme caution and gentleness. The series should be a totally pleasant experience for the subject. Apply cream sparingly to your fingertips, then rub the cream onto the face. Don't allow the face to get too greasy. A little cream is enough.

51. Opposition Forehead

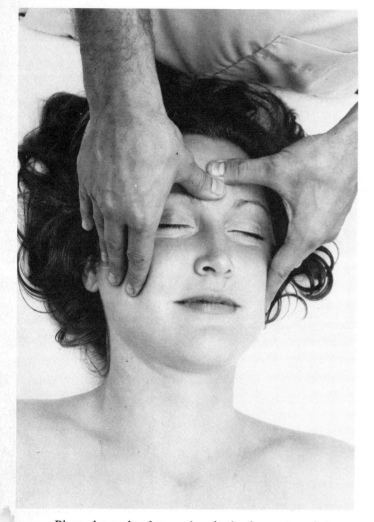

Place the pads of your thumbs in the center of the forehead just above the eyes with one in front of the other. Your four fingers should rest gently on the sides of the head as a brace.

The pads of the thumbs move horizontally toward each other so that they cross, then return to the starting position. There should be constant but moderate pressure on the pads of the thumbs.

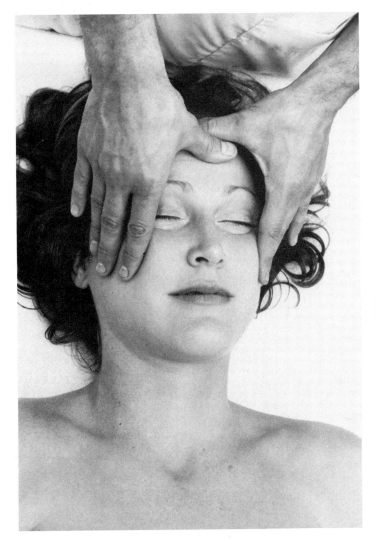

As the movement proceeds, the thumb pads gradually move up the forehead toward the hairline. At the hairline, the thumbs gradually move down toward the eyes.

After repeating this a few times, move your hands to the side about one inch so that you are now working above one eye. Do another complete set, then gradually move back to the center, and finally over to the other side.

> *Timing:* THE RHYTHM IS APPROXIMATELY TWO IN-AND-OUT UNITS PER SECOND. DO ONE OR TWO COMPLETE SETS OF THIS MOVEMENT IN ALL THREE AREAS.

CORRECTIONS

1. Don't put the cream directly on the subject's face. Apply it sparingly to your fingers.
2. Don't grip the sides of the head with the fingers. Rest them gently.
3. Use the thumb pads, not the thumb points or tips.
4. Don't go too hard.
5. Don't go below the eyebrows.
6. Don't go into the hair.
7. Don't stay in one place. Move constantly, but slowly.

52. The Mask

In this movement you are working on the muscles that cover the upper orbits of the eyes.

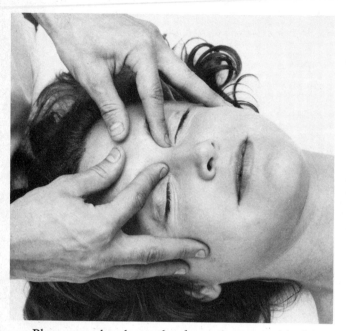

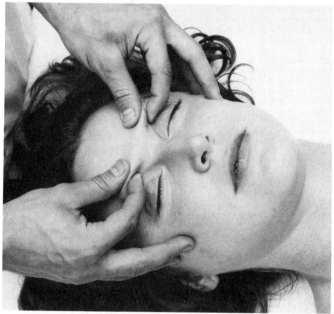

Place your hands gently above the eyes with the forefingers on the inner, upper corners of the eye orbits and the thumbs resting above the eyebrows. The other fingers rest gently on the cheeks.

Gently press the pads of the forefingers up onto the upper orbits above the eyes. At the same time, the thumb pads push lightly downward, so that you are grasping each eyebrow between thumb and forefinger pads. With slight pressure, pull both fingers outward from the nose, following the upper curves of the eye sockets about halfway across the eyebrows. Do this movement with extreme gentleness.

When you complete the movement, lift the thumbs and forefingers in the air and place them in the starting position.

Unlike all other movements, *do not* drag back on this sensitive area. The other fingers maintain contact with the subject's head throughout, but be sure that your forefingers never touch the eyes. Look carefully when doing this movement, so that you always know where your fingers are. The movement is done slowly and should feel pleasurable to the subject.

Timing: EACH MOVEMENT TAKES APPROXIMATELY THREE SECONDS, TWO TO MOVE OUT, ONE TO LIFT BACK. DO EACH MOVEMENT FIFTEEN OR TWENTY TIMES.

CORRECTIONS

1. Be careful of the eyes. Don't let the first joints of your forefingers touch them.
2. Use the forefinger pads, not the tips of the forefingers.
3. Don't lift any of the bracing fingers off the subject's face at any time during the movement.
4. Lift the thumbs and forefingers off the face. Don't drag them back into place.
5. Don't do the movement too hard or too quickly.
6. If the subject is afraid to be touched around the eyes, or if his eyes begin to flutter, omit the movement.

53. The Nose Bridge

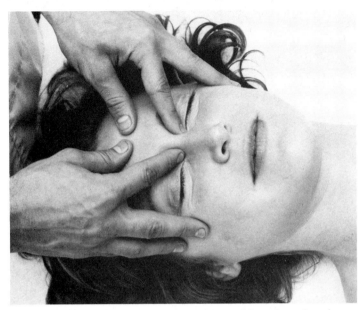

Place your hands in the mask position, but alter it slightly by placing the tips of the forefingers on the sides of the bridge of the nose just below the eyes, at an angle of about forty-five degrees.

The movement is done exclusively with the tips of the forefingers, pressing gently in and down with both fingers at the same time. The thumbs rest gently above the eyebrows. Be careful not to hit the eyes with the rest of the fingers.

Move down the outer section of the bridge of the nose where the nose and cheeks meet, stopping at the end of the nose bone.

Do not continue beyond this point or you will put pressure on the nostrils. The movement is very small, only about half to three-quarters of an inch in length. Push down and drag back.

Be aware of your pressure. Many people have a great deal of tension here but don't realize it, so watch your subject carefully.

> *Timing:* DO ONE COMPLETE SET EVERY TWO SECONDS, AND NO MORE THAN EIGHT OR TEN SETS.

CORRECTIONS

1. Start at the very top of the nose between the eyes.
2. Move both fingers together. Do not alternate.
3. Be careful of the eyes.
4. Don't squeeze the nostrils together. Stop at the lower end of the bridge of the nose.
5. Don't do the movement too hard. Be gentle.

54. Undereye

Rest one hand on either side of the subject's face, with the heel of your hand on his forehead and the fingers resting gently at the sides of the base of the jaw. The thumbs should point toward the mouth, one on either side of the nose.

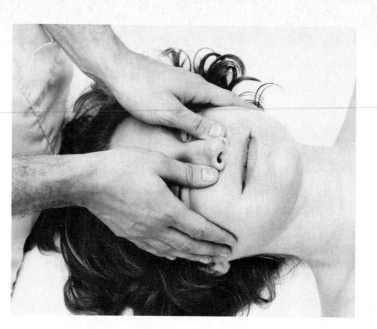

Do this movement only with the pads of the thumbs. As always, be very careful of the eyes. Do not touch them. If your lower thumb hits the eye, raise the heel of your hand off the forehead. You are working on the muscles directly below the eyes, next to the nose.

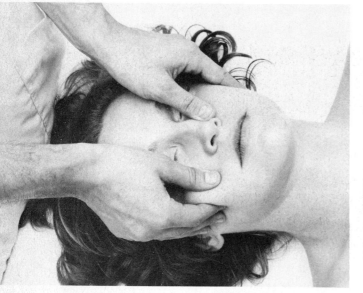
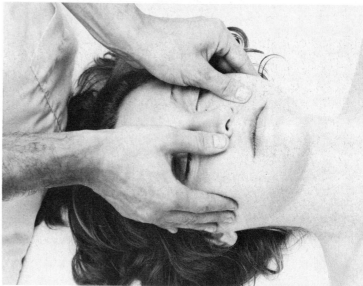

The pad of one thumb presses down right next to the nose and moves out an inch to the side. The second thumb pad repeats the movement on the other side.

When the thumb gets to the outer edge of the movement, it is not dragged back but lifted back into place. While you are lifting one thumb, the other is performing the identical movement on the other side of the nose, so there is a sense of continuity and evenness. This movement is done continuously, alternating right and left. Work gently but firmly.

Timing: ONE SET OF MOVEMENTS RIGHT AND LEFT SHOULD TAKE ONE SECOND. DO ABOUT FIFTEEN OR TWENTY COMPLETE SETS.

CORRECTIONS

1. Be sure you use only the thumb pad, not the point or tip.
2. Be sure you are below the eyes, and are not touching them.
3. Don't go up onto the nose.
4. Don't do the movement fast.
5. Don't press in with your thumbs simultaneously.

55. Jaw Circles

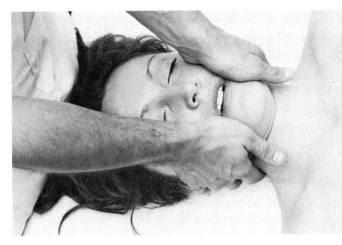

Still facing the top of the subject's head, lean slightly over the face. Have the subject drop his jaw open so the jaw muscles relax. Place one palm on each side of the subject's jaw, with the fingertips gently resting on the neck. Throughout the movement, the fingers do not leave the neck. The movement is done with the centers of the palms and the heels of the hands.

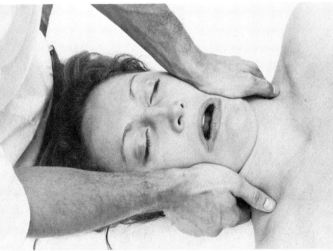

Begin the movement by leaning into the sides of the jaw, with the hands moving down toward the back of the head.

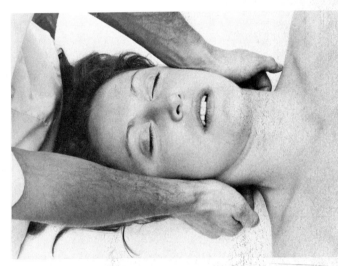

When you pass the jaw hinge, the temporal mandibular joint, with the heels of your hands, move slightly back toward the temples and drag back to the starting position with a circular movement.

In effect, you have made an elongated circular movement, leaning on the downstroke and dragging back up lightly.

Timing: DO ONE COMPLETE CIRCLE EVERY TWO SECONDS. DO EIGHT OR TEN COMPLETE CIRCLES IN AN EVEN, SLOW RHYTHM.

CORRECTIONS

1. Be aware of the subject's tolerance for pressure. The jaw is almost universally tight. Start easy and build pressure slowly.

2. Make sure the subject's jaw is dropped open.
3. Be sure your fingers are pointing straight down toward the back of the head throughout.
4. Don't stick your fingers in the subject's ears on the drag back.
5. Don't lean on the drag back.
6. Don't hit the eyes with the heels of the hands on the drag back.

Once you have thoroughly learned the movements of the face, it should take you about five minutes to complete them.

Lesson Twelve · THE ARMS

Flaccid Tension

Flaccid tension represents an energy withdrawal from the muscles. The muscles seem to be loose, but there is actually deep tension in them, with little energy flow. The muscles feel weak, and people with flaccid tension often have cold hands and feet. This condition is difficult to spot at first, because the only areas that are overtly tight, if any, are the neck and head. The body is flabby. When energy begins to move through the body, it usually gets tighter, and the tension becomes more evident. This is a sign of improvement.

"Even" Tension

An advanced student brought an unusual problem to class one day. A young woman of twenty-five on whom she had been working claimed to have no pain or discomfort except during deep massage. The client had therefore concluded that she didn't need treatment.

There are two possible reasons for this problem. Either the subject was relaxed and the student was working incorrectly by applying pressure in the wrong areas, using irregular rhythms and not dragging correctly, or the subject had an even distribution of tension throughout the entire body. In the case of "even" tension, there is very little sensation. There may be some restriction of movement, but the individual usually functions well physically.

Working on a person with even tension might disturb his or her equilibrium and therefore it may not be a good idea.

People with "even" tension do not usually seek treatment, but you may run across the problem when looking for people on whom to practice.

Cold Hands—Tiring Arms

Certain people have difficulty in their arms and hands. Either they tire quickly, shake, or are always cold. When trying to help these people it is more important to work on the back, especially the shoulders, than it is to work directly on the arms, because the blockage of the blood is most severe at the junction of the shoulder and the arm. Bear in mind that the blood is the distributor of heat in the body. Learning and receiving deep massage can be helpful to people with these problems.

Muscles of the Arms

1. *The biceps* is a muscle with two parts (anatomically called two-headed) that goes from the top of the shoulder girdle to the forearm. It helps hold the shoulder joint together and bend the elbow.

2. *The triceps* is a three-headed muscle that goes from just under the shoulder joint on the scapula and attachments on the upper arm to the back of the elbow. It straightens the arm and works contiguously with the biceps.

There are many muscles between the elbows and the fingers that control flexion and extension of the elbow, wrist, and fingers, as well as the rotation of the forearm. These will not be described in detail.

Within the hand itself, besides the muscles that ex-

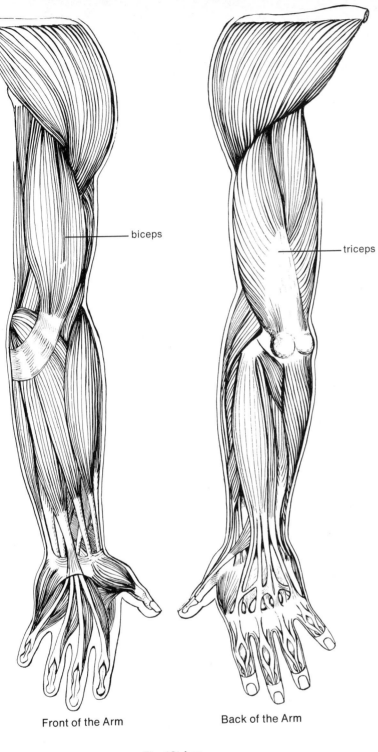

biceps

triceps

Front of the Arm

Back of the Arm

Fig. 12 Arm

Test Yourself

1. Take your fingers and squeeze your triceps very hard. If it hurts, you are tense there.

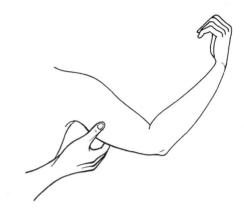

2. Open the thumb and four fingers of one hand and relax it. Take the thumb and middle finger of your other hand and squeeze your inner thumb area. If it hurts, you have tension there.

How to See Tension in the Arms

1. The tension indicators described in the shoulder, lesson 3, apply here.

2. Those with nervous hand habits—banging pencils, picking their fingertips, twitching their fingers, cracking their knuckles, or holding semiclenched fists—indicate not only general anxiety but tension in the muscles of the arms and hands.

3. Those who cannot hold their hands steady are tense.

4. Hands that feel cold, clammy, or sweaty indicate tension.

5. People who always fold their arms on their chest when they stand have tension in their arms.

tend to it from the forearm, are a number of muscles that control the complicated movements of the thumb, and tiny muscles that aid in spreading and closing the fingers.

Causes of Tension in the Arms

Mechanical Causes

1. Many causes are similar to those listed for the shoulder. Whatever is wrong with the shoulders directly affects the arms.

2. Trauma to the arm, such as an accident or an operation, can produce tension.

3. Certain professions and hobbies, such as typing, making fine jewelry, electronics, and sewing, when done with poor body posture can cause tension.

Emotional Causes

As with legs and shoulders, repressed fear and rage are often evident in the arms.

Arm Movements

Do all movements on one arm before going to the other.

56. The Biceps Movement

During this movement, your body rocks forward and backward. Use your body weight to lean into the arm on the upstroke.

Stand on the left side of the table, facing the subject's right arm, with your left leg well ahead of your right leg. Grasp the subject's right wrist with your right hand, and gently lift the arm into the air at a forty-five-degree angle to the ground surface. Grasp the upper arm just above the elbow with your left hand. The whole thumb should be flat across the front of the arm, perpendicular to it, and the other four fingers should grip the arm on the opposite side as a unit.

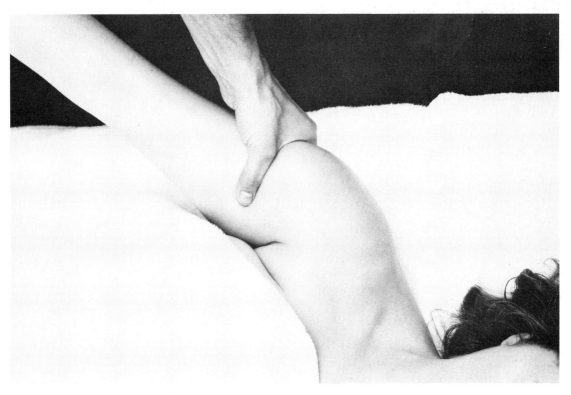

Exerting a moderate squeezing pressure, move your hand up the arm toward the shoulder, compressing the biceps muscle with the entire thumb. As you approach the front top of the arm, the center of your thumb will encounter a bone.

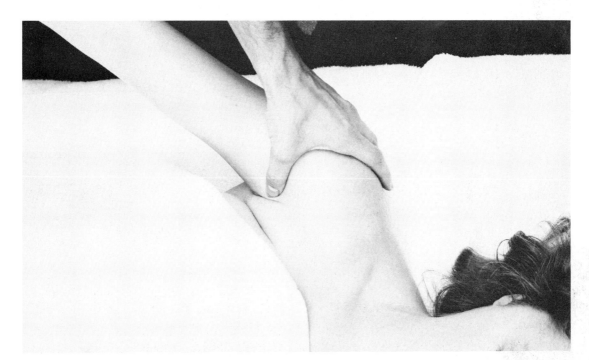

When you reach this part of the bone, lighten the pressure and pivot the four fingers around the top of the shoulder, keeping the thumb stationary.

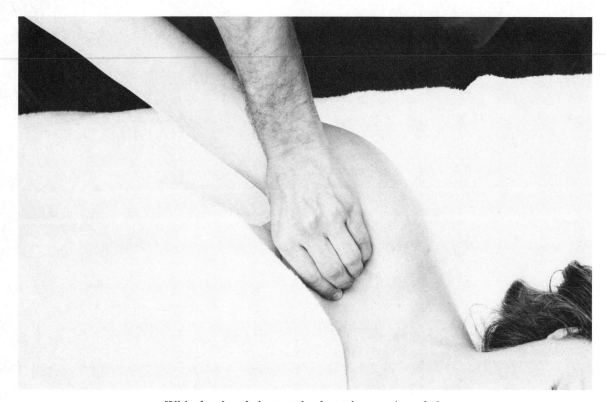

With the thumb just at the front inner edge of the armpit, gently squeeze the four fingers and thumb into the pectoral muscle. Finish with a half inch of skin remaining between your fingers.

Reverse the movement exactly, dragging back to the starting position. Don't pinch off the pectoral muscle. If the subject jumps when you get to the top of the movement where you go into the pectoral, you are either pushing your thumb into his armpit or he is too tense and sensitive for you to work there at this time. If this occurs, omit the pivot and drag back down.

Timing: DO ONE COMPLETE SET EVERY TWO SECONDS. DO EIGHT OR TEN COMPLETE SETS.

CORRECTIONS

1. Remember to have your thumb directly on top of the upper arm, not off on the side.
2. Use the whole thumb. Don't press down on the thumb point.
3. Don't forget to release the pressure when you run into the prominent part of the bone at the top.
4. Don't jam your thumb into the center of the subject's armpit.
5. Don't forget to identically reverse the movement pattern, with no pressure on the drag.
6. Be careful not to raise your own shoulders, especially the one holding up the subject's arm.

57. The Triceps Movement

Make sure the subject is not using his muscles to hold up the arm. If he is, you won't be able to do the movement, because the muscle will be taut. Shake the arm up and down to make sure the subject's muscles are relaxed. During this movement, use the same rocking motion and lean your body weight as in the biceps movement.

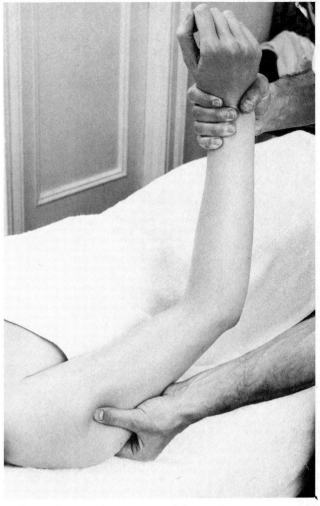

Squeezing gently, move straight up the arm toward the shoulder. The movement ends just before reaching the armpit.

Relax your fingers and drag them back to the starting position. Be careful not to raise your shoulders, especially on the side holding the subject's arm.

Timing: DO ONE COMPLETE UNIT PER SECOND. REPEAT THE MOVEMENT EIGHT OR TEN TIMES.

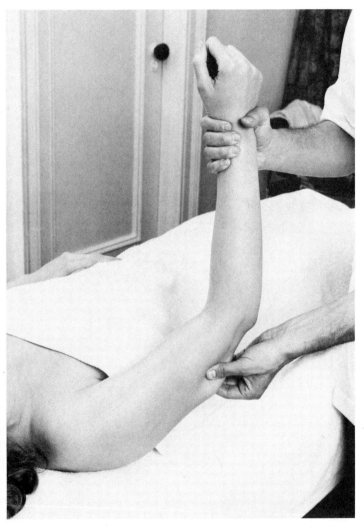

In the same standing position as the last movement, grasp the wrist as shown above and lift the arm a little higher, so that the subject's hand is level with your chest and his elbow is almost straight.

Grasp the triceps muscles, which are on the back side of the arm, just above the elbow, between the thumb pad and the tips of the other four fingers.

CORRECTIONS

1. Make sure that the subject's arm is relaxed and that you are holding it up. Test it periodically.

2. Be sure to lean.

3. Be sure you are using the tips of your fingers and the pads of your thumbs.

4. Don't run into the subject's armpit.

58. The Triceps Ripple

Take the same starting position as for movement 57. When doing this movement, don't lean; use only the strength of your hand. Grasp the triceps muscles just above the elbow between the thumb pad and the fingertips. Try to grip as close to the bone and hold as much of the muscles between your fingers as possible.

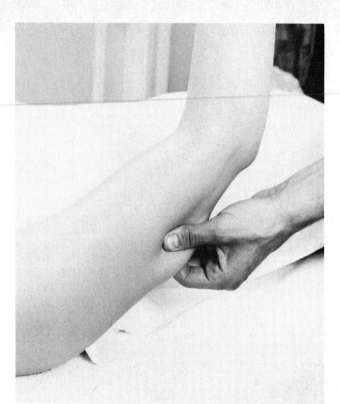

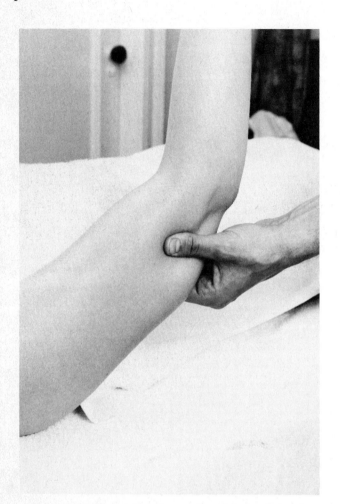

Squeeze firmly and pull your hand away from the subject's arm toward the ground. Allow the muscles to slip through your fingers as pressure is being applied to them. Move up an inch and repeat.

Keep moving up and repeating the movement until you come to the top of the back of the arm, just before the armpit, at which point drag back to the starting position.

Do not apply too much pressure at first, but gradually build it. Be sure to watch the face, since tremendous tension is often present there.

> *Timing:* IT TAKES THREE TO FIVE SECONDS TO GO UP THE ENTIRE ARM. REPEAT THE SERIES FOUR OR FIVE TIMES.

After you complete this movement, repeat the plain triceps movement to smooth out the area. You can also alternate these two movements.

CORRECTIONS

1. Make sure you grasp the muscles. Don't squeeze only the skin.
2. Relax your shoulders.
3. Don't squeeze too hard. Watch the subject's face.
4. Keep the subject's arm slightly bent, not straight.
5. Don't squeeze the subject's wrist; hold it gently.

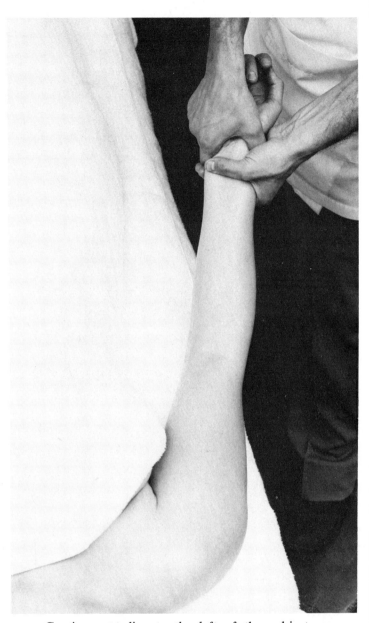

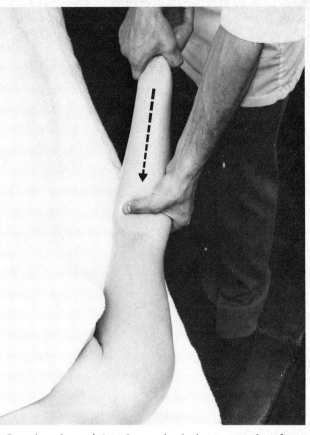

Continue standing to the left of the subject, as shown above. With the subject's arm palm up, gently grasp the subject's right wrist with your right hand, the heel of your hand facing the front of the subject's wrist. The inner part of the subject's forearm is facing the ceiling and the upper arm is resting on the ground or table surface. Grasp the subject's forearm just above the wrist with your left hand, the flat part of the whole thumb across the base of the entire forearm. The four fingers should be pressing against the forearm on the other side. This position is similar to the one in the biceps movement.

Leaning the weight of your body into your thumb, squeeze it against your four fingers and move it in a straight line toward the elbow. When you reach the elbow, relax your hand and drag it back.

As in the biceps and triceps movements, your body should maintain a rocking rhythm during the execution of the movement, with the left foot in front of the right.

Timing: EACH UNIT TAKES ONE SECOND. AS YOU PROGRESS WITH THE MOVEMENT, IN-CREASE YOUR SPEED SLIGHTLY. DO TEN TO FIFTEEN MOVEMENT UNITS.

CORRECTIONS

1. Be sure you are using your outside hand to do the movement.
2. Be sure the thumb is on the inside of the fore-arm.
3. Don't use just the thumb point or tip; use the whole thumb.
4. Begin at the wrist, not at the middle of the arm.
5. Use your body weight to lean.
6. Don't hit the subject's elbow. Stop just before it.

60. The Forearm Extensor Movement

The forearm extensor muscles are on the outside of the lower arm. The standing position is the same as for the previous movement.

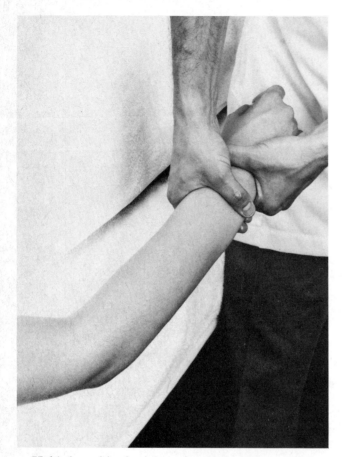

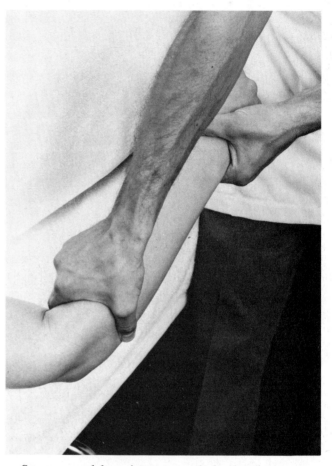

Hold the subject's right wrist gently with your left hand. The back of the subject's hand faces the ceiling, exposing the outer forearm, and the upper arm remains on the surface. Grasp the right forearm just above the wrist with the right hand, the flat part of the thumb on top and the four fingers on the bottom—identical with the last movement, only with a different hand and the subject's forearm turned over.

Squeeze, and lean into your whole thumb as you move your thumb pad along the very outer edge of the forearm, touching the ulna bone. Release pressure when you reach the top of the forearm and drag back to the starting position. Don't jam the elbow.

CORRECTIONS

1. Be sure the back of the subject's hand is facing the ceiling.
2. Don't go too high and hit the top of the elbow.
3. Keep the rhythm even.
4. Don't bear down on the thumb point.
5. Relax your shoulders.

In the last two movements you have been working on both sides of the forearm, but accenting either the inner or outer muscles.

Timing: EACH MOVEMENT TAKES ONE SECOND. DO THE MOVEMENT EIGHT OR TEN TIMES.

61. The Inner Thumb

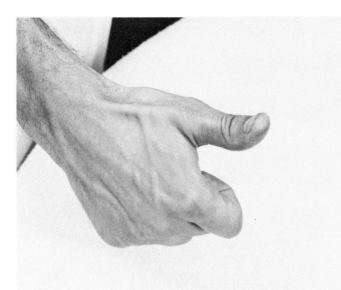

Bend the forefinger of your right hand so that the knuckle points out and the inner part of your forefinger creates a large surface. You will use the pad of your thumb in opposition to the side of your forefinger.

Stand facing the subject's right hand. Lift the subject's right hand with your left hand so that his upper arm remains on the ground surface.

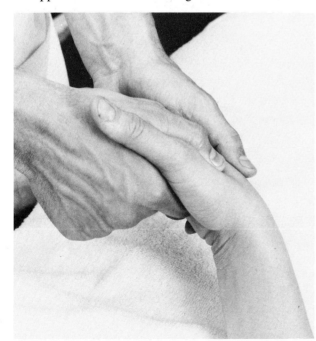

Take hold of the subject's inner thumb muscles, far back behind the center of his thumb curve in the direction of the wrist.

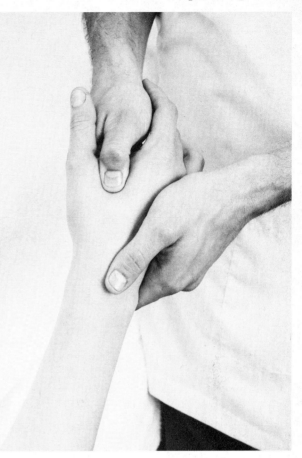

Squeeze the pad of your thumb against your curled forefinger and gently move away from the subject's wrist. Don't squeeze off the skin. The movement is completed when you have a half inch of skin between your fingers. Release the pressure and drag back to the starting position. This is a sensitive area, so go gently at first.

Timing: EACH MOVEMENT TAKES ONE SECOND. DO FIVE OR SIX MOVEMENTS.

CORRECTIONS

1. Make sure you are holding the person's arm up with your other hand.
2. Make sure the subject's arm is relaxed.
3. Use the pad of your thumb. Don't dig in with the tip.
4. Don't do the movements too hard. Gently build the pressure and watch the face.
5. Don't pull off the hand. Remain in contact with it.

62. The Hand Grasp

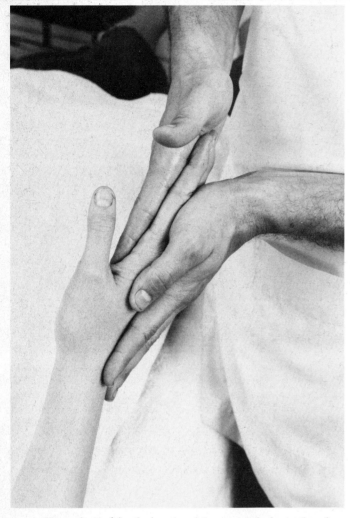 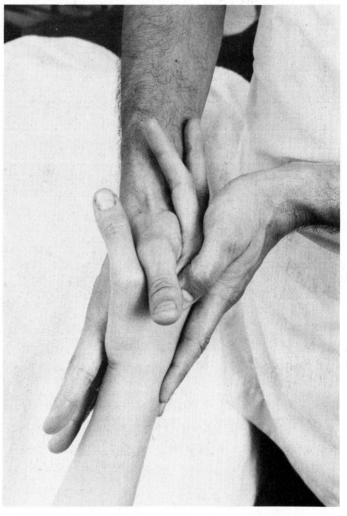

Face the subject's head, with your left foot ahead of your right. Hold the subject's hand, fingers extended, between your palms so that the subject's arm is bent at about a forty-five-degree angle, with the upper arm remaining on the table. Your fingers are facing the subject's elbow. Your left hand, which holds the back of his hand, acts as a brace that you push against with your right.

Push the entire palm and fingers of your right hand directly into the subject's hand as you slide down the fingers into a handshake position.

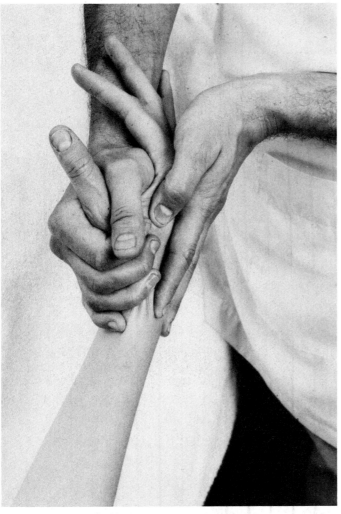 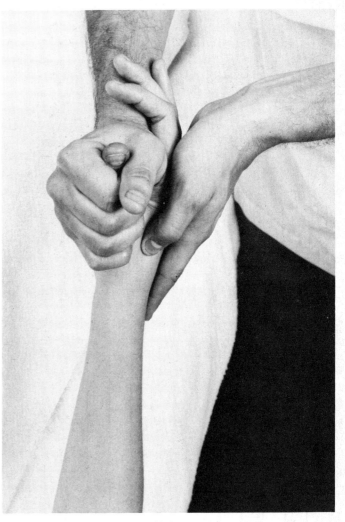

As your thumb locks with the subject's, surround the lower part of his thumb with all the fingers of your right hand, and squeeze, while pulling up the

thumb, as in a cow-milking gesture. When his thumb disappears into your hand, reverse the action identically, but without pressure.

Timing: ONE MOVEMENT SHOULD TAKE TWO SECONDS. DO SIX OR EIGHT OF THEM.

CORRECTIONS

1. Make sure you support the lower arm.
2. Make sure you are bracing the entire hand with your outer hand.
3. Use your whole hand. Don't push in with only the heel of your hand.

4. Remember to return to the starting position by reversing the movement without pressure.

After completing all these movements on one arm, repeat the entire sequence on the other arm.

Once you are thoroughly proficient at the arm and hand movements, it should take approximately eight to ten minutes to complete both arms.

Lesson Thirteen · CHAIR MASSAGE

Chair massage can help relax someone who needs a little relief from tension in a social or work situation where more extensive treatment would be inappropriate. Give a chair massage only when it is requested. But be prepared to soon be the most sought-after person in your office.

Most people who work in an office accumulate tension in the neck, head, shoulders, upper back, and arms, though the problems are most acute in the shoulders and upper back. Those who sit for long periods of time often feel pain in the lower back.

The movements outlined in this chapter increase circulation in the upper body by reducing tension in the head, neck, shoulders, and upper back. It isn't necessary to master the preceding lessons to learn the following material, although it will be easier if you have.

The subject should be sitting in a chair that gives access to the head and shoulders. If your subject is wearing a jacket and tie, ask him to remove them. No cream is necessary.

Movements

The Head Release

The head weighs ten to twelve pounds, so it will be a heavy weight in your hands if the subject lets it go. Gently move the head forward and backward, reminding the subject to breathe and to relax his head. It may take a while for the subject to let go of his head. Once this has happened, begin rotating the head slowly in a circle, making sure that you are holding all the weight of the head. Alternate between the circle and the forward-and-back movements so that the person cannot guess which you are going to do next and will be unable to take control of his head movements. Don't circle the head backward if there is any resistance.

Stand to the side of the subject and place the palm of one hand gently on his forehead, with your fingers pointing away from you. Place your other palm on the back of the subject's head at the lower part of the skull. Ask the subject to release all tension from his neck and allow his head to drop forward into your hands so that he is no longer holding his head up. You are supporting it for him.

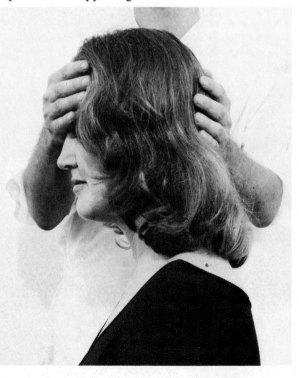

Forehead Press

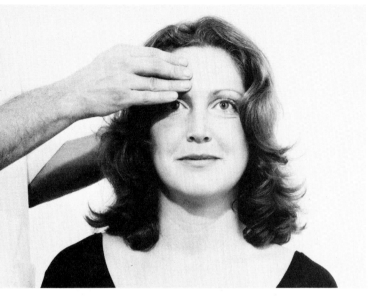

If you are right-handed, stand on your subject's right side so that you can use that hand. Face the subject and place your left hand flat on the back of the subject's head as a support. Place the pads of the three middle fingers of your right hand on the subject's forehead just above the eyebrows.

Press in very gently and begin moving the skin up and down. Do this movement over the entire forehead, lifting your hand and finding a new place every five or six seconds. Do not drag over the skin. Do this for a minute or two.

Temple Circles

The temples are on the sides of the head just in front of the top of the ears. The temporals are strong muscles that aid in jaw movement.

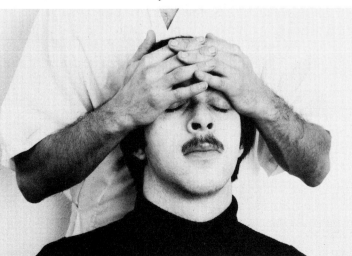

Gently pressing in toward the center of his head with your palms, make a clockwise circular movement, taking the skin along with you but not rubbing over it. Do not press with the heels of your hands and use only slight pressure. This should be a soothing, even-rhythmed, slow movement. Remember, the movement is done with the centers of the palms. Your fingers should remain relaxed.

Neck Squeeze

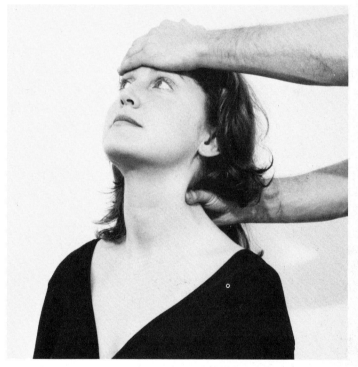

If you are right-handed, stand to the left of the subject. Place your left hand on the forehead to support the head. Grip the center of the neck, with your right thumb opposing the four fingers. Tilt the subject's head slightly backward. Squeeze the neck with the pads of all of your fingers and thumb, drawing your hand backward away from the neck as you do so.

Stand directly behind the subject and place the centers of your palms over his temples. Cross the fronts of your fingers so that they interlock as in a modified praying position. Gently pull the subject's head back so that it rests on your chest. Your body can be slightly bent over if it is more comfortable that way.

Go only as far as the skin will move with you.
Sliding over the skin causes too much irritation from
friction. Release your pressure and return to the original position. Do this movement for a minute or so,
making sure that you are supporting the head. Move
your hand up and repeat the procedure on the upper
neck, return to center momentarily, and finally move
down to the very base of the neck, and repeat.

The Fingertip Grip

Grip the scalp with the fingertips of both hands.
Pressing in rather firmly, make small circles.

After every three or four circles, change your position on the head. This movement can be done rather
strongly, but be careful not to pull the hair by sliding
across the scalp.

The Scalp Scrub

Hold on to the forehead with one hand and vigorously scratch the scalp with your other hand. Use
your fingertips, not your nails.

Do the movement with both hands simultaneously,
alternating between scrubbing firmly and gently.
Hold on to the forehead once again and repeat the
whole process, using your fingernails instead of your
fingertips, but don't scratch too hard.

The Hair Grip

This is an effective movement for head and scalp
tension; however, some people will find it intolerable, while others will love it. Tell the subject what
you are going to do before you begin, and if he or
she has objections, skip it.

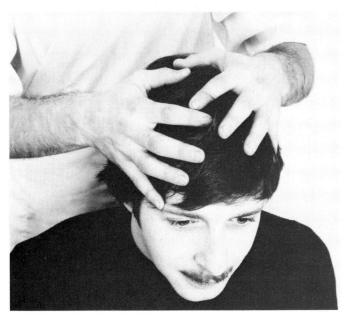

Place both hands on top of the subject's head, palms down.

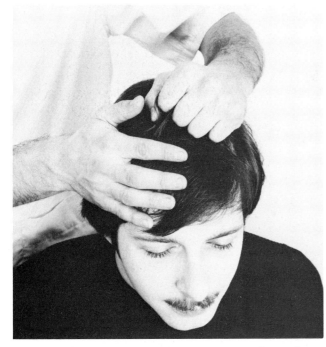

Keeping the tips of your four fingers on the scalp, make a gentle fist *with one hand* so that you pull the hair slightly with your grip.

Don't pull your fist off the head, leave it always in contact with the scalp. As you flatten the first hand out on the head, the other hand repeats the movement so that the two hands alternate. This is done quickly, and gradually increases in vigor depending on the subject's tolerance.

The Deltoid Drop

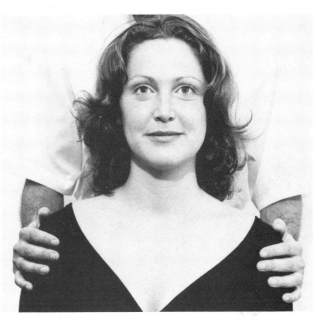

Standing behind the subject, grip the tops of the arms just below the tips of the shoulders. Use your four fingers opposing the heels of your hands. Do not use your thumbs at all. You should now have the deltoid muscles in your hands. Squeeze the muscles between your fingers and the heels of your hands forcefully eight or ten times.

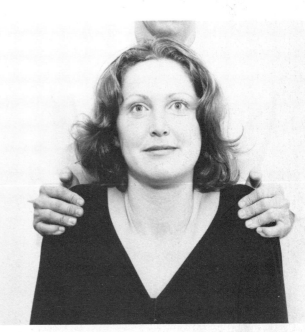

Now squeeze and lift the shoulders as high as they will go, then drop them.

Check to see that you are doing all the work and that the subject is not helping you. Release your pressure and allow the shoulders to drop suddenly. If they stay up, the subject is tightening the shoulders. Do this ten or fifteen times, slowly at first, then a little faster.

The Trapezius Lift

Still standing behind the subject, grip the tops of the shoulder muscles, fingers opposing the heels of the hands. Your hands should be between the neck and the tips of the shoulders, grasping the trapezius muscle.

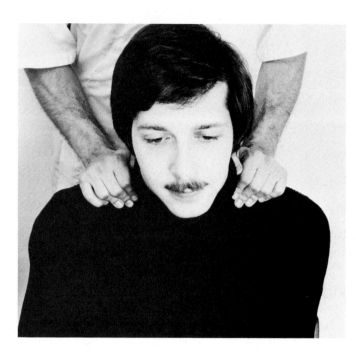

Squeeze the trapezius between your fingers and the heels of your hands, without using the thumbs. Lift slightly as you squeeze, then release. Do this slowly and rhythmically fifteen or twenty times.

Now, instead of using the heels of your hands, use the pads of your thumbs to oppose your four fingers. This makes the movement deeper. Squeeze the trapezius muscles and release them, moving gradually away from the neck, fifteen or twenty times.

The Trapezius V

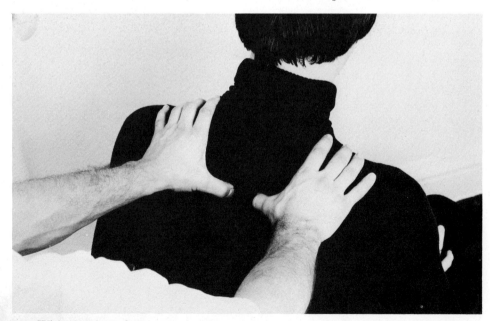

With the four fingers wrapped around the front of the shoulders in the position shown above, drop your thumbs down as far as they will go and place the tips of your thumbs on either side of the spine.

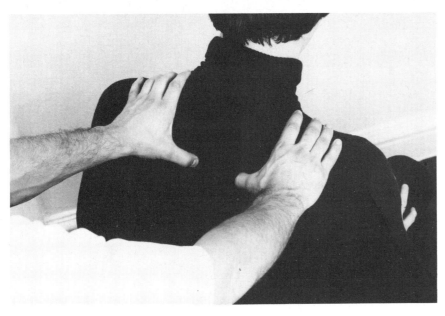

Press in firmly with the thumb tips and move outward from the spine one inch or as far as the skin will move without rubbing across it.

Lift the thumbs slightly and insert the tips just above where you left off.

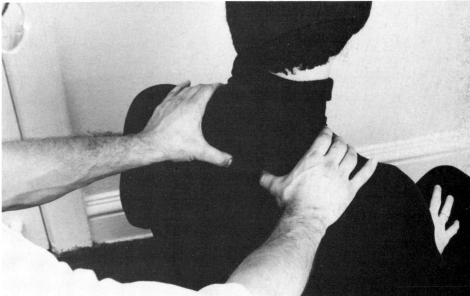

Continue the movement with the thumb tips rising upward and outward so that they form a **V** pattern from the upper back to the tips of the shoulders.

As you move out, don't hit the shoulder blades. If you do, you've gone too far. It will take about five or six movements to complete the **V** pattern.

Do the whole pattern several times. Then reverse it so that you move down from the tips of the shoulders to the sides of the upper spine. Alternate, doing the **V** up and then down, eight or ten times.

Paraspinal Push

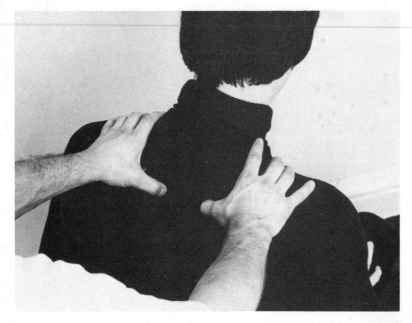

Place your hands in a position similar to that of the beginning of the trapezius **V**, only this time the thumb tips are one inch away from the spine on either side.

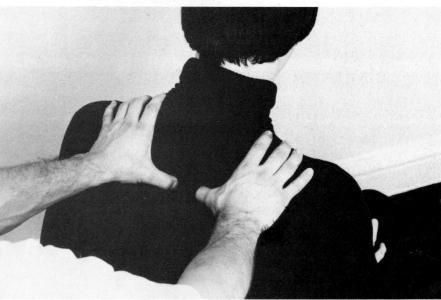

Press in firmly with the thumb tips and move them toward the spine so that they are next to it.

Move the thumb tips out one inch to the original position, keeping the same strong pressure. Repeat this two or three times. When doing this movement you horizontally cross and recross a long vertical muscle called the paraspinal muscle or erector spinae. Move up a half inch and repeat the movement. Con-tinue to move upward in half-inch steps until you arrive at the base of the neck. Then move down in the same manner until you reach the beginning position. Don't exert so much pressure that you cause the subject to jump or to feel pain.

General Pressure Circles

Pressure circles are done with either the first two fingers or the middle three fingers, whichever is easier for you. Press one point on the body firmly and make a small circular movement. Move the skin along with you, don't rub over it. The size of this movement varies, because different areas of skin can be moved different amounts.

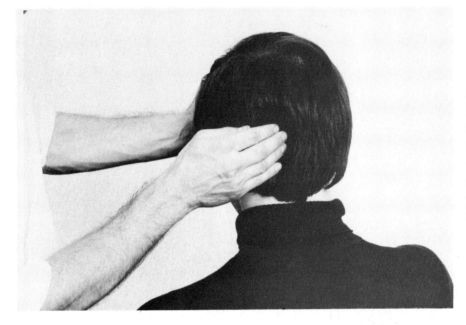

Stand to the side of the subject. Begin by holding his forehead in your left hand and doing pressure circles with your right hand straight across the occiput, which is where the back of the skull meets the neck. Do it right on the lower part of the skull bone, but be careful not to pull the hair.

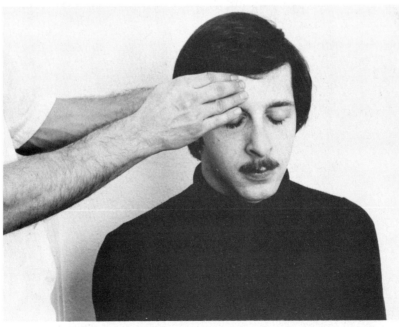

Walk to the other side and do pressure circles on the forehead with the right hand while the left hand supports the back of the head.

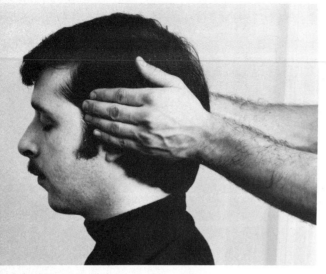

Standing in back of the subject, supporting the head on one side with one hand, do pressure circles gently on the other temple. Reverse hands and do the other temple.

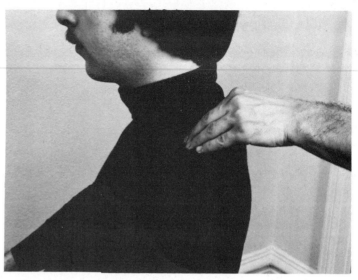

Try pressure circles on the top of the trapezius on both sides.

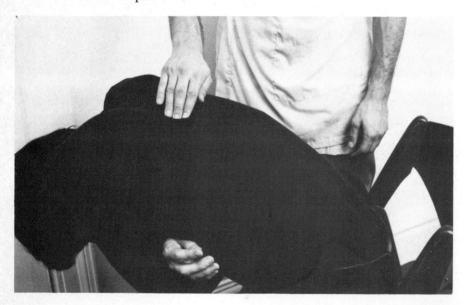

Have the subject cross his arms in his lap and bend forward in a relaxed position so that the paraspinal muscles are stretched out. Begin at the top of the back and do pressure circles directly on the paraspinal muscles.

Travel slowly all the way down one side of the spine until you are just above the hip bone. Move to the opposite side and travel back up. Repeat this process on the paraspinals three or four times.

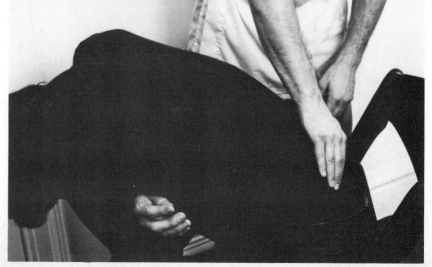

The Arm Pull

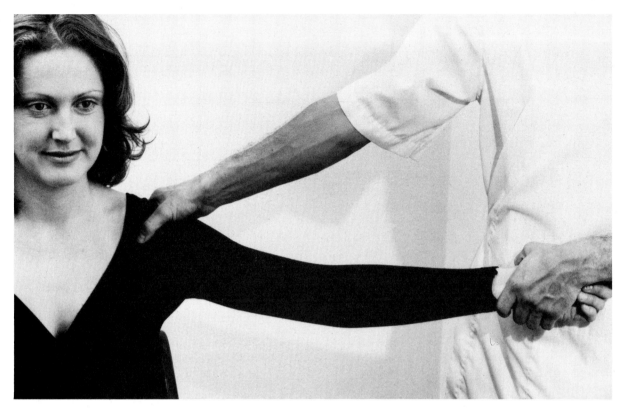

Standing to the left of the subject, take hold of the subject's left wrist with your left hand and extend his wrist toward you. Grip his shoulder joint with your thumb and four fingers and press into it slightly. As you press in, pull the arm out to the side gently with your other hand.

Hold it for a few seconds, then stop pulling and allow the subject's arm to relax. Do this very slowly and repeat five or six times before proceeding to the other side.

The Arm Shake

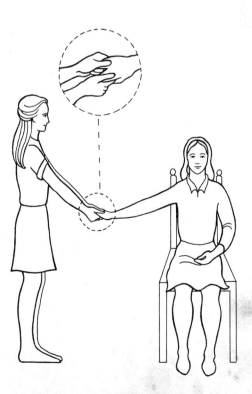

Standing on the left side, take hold of the fingers of the subject's left hand by holding two of his fingers with each of your own hands.

Very gently shake the arm up and down so that it makes a gentle, small, wavelike motion through its whole length. Repeat this movement on the other arm.

CONCLUSION

These thirteen lessons present a comprehensive introduction to the practice of deep massage and muscular therapy. They should enable you to work responsibly in a manner beneficial to the subject. You should be able to enjoy giving deep massage to your friends, and, through continual practice and study, advance a considerable distance. However, in order to practice deep massage or muscular therapy professionally, you would have to study with a qualified teacher.

APPENDIX

THE TENSION TEST

Tension is the forerunner of pain. Test yourself and your friends for how much tension you have. Take the whole test before you look at the scoring. Don't cheat. Write down your answers, numbered 1 through 61, on a separate paper. Answer yes or no.

1. Have you ever had a serious muscular injury of any kind?
2. Do you crack the knuckles of your fingers or the joints of your toes several times a day?
3. Do you get tired easily?
4. Have you ever had an operation?
5. Do you have, or have you had, a serious disease, whether chronic, contagious, or psychosomatic?
6. Do you use medical or illegal drugs or alcoholic beverages regularly?
7. Do you have chronic pain anywhere in your body?
8. Is it easy for you to express your anger?
9. Do you need more than 8 hours of sleep to feel rested?
10. Are your hands and feet often cold?
11. Do you get cramps in your arms, hands, legs, or feet?
12. For men: When you cough, do you ever get pain in the scrotum?
13. Do you sometimes have trouble breathing?
14. Do you get colds or sore throats more than four times a year?
15. Is your blood pressure normal?
16. Do you dance for pleasure?
17. Do you ever get a twitch or a tic?
18. Are you very ticklish?
19. Do you bump into things a lot?
20. Do you cough a lot when you're not sick?
21. Do you sneeze a lot for no apparent reason?
22. Do you bite on things a lot of the time? Your fingernails, pens, erasers, etc.?
23. Do you enjoy sex with someone you love?
24. Do you live in a city?
25. Do you eat a lot of sugar (including sugar found in prepared foods such as ice cream, cake, and commercial bread)?
26. Are you round-shouldered?
27. Are you light-sensitive? (Does bright light hurt your eyes?)
28. Do you have difficulty in sleeping at least three nights a week?
29. Do you get a headache more than 5 or 6 times a year?
30. Do your eyes often get red and bloodshot?
31. Did you ever wear dental braces?
32. Do you turn your ankles accidentally and strain them fairly frequently?
33. Are your feet particularly ticklish?
34. Is it easy for you to cry when you feel sad?
35. Do you have flat feet (fallen arches)? When you are standing barefoot, does the inside bottom of your foot touch the floor?
36. Do your legs ache or hurt after walking ten or twenty blocks?
37. Does one or both of your knees hurt when it rains or before it rains?

38. Do you walk with one or both feet turned out? Walk around naturally and look at your feet.

39. When you sit for a long period of time, does your back hurt?

40. For women: Do you get menstrual cramps?

41. When you stand, do you tend to stand with your weight on one leg?

42. Does it bother you to scream really loud or to hear other people yell?

43. Place the tips of your thumbs in the inner upper corner of the orbits of your eyes next to your nose. Then push up fairly forcefully. Does that hurt? (See page 159.)

44. Keep your head stationary and look up as high as you can to the extreme upper left corner of your vision. Then, without moving your head, roll your eyes to the right upper corner. Do this 8 or 10 times. Does it hurt while you do it or after?

45. Place your fingers on the sides of your jaw. Clench your teeth for a moment and feel your main jaw muscles flexing. Relax your jaw, and press those muscles firmly with the knuckles of your index fingers. Does that hurt? (See page 159.)

46. When you open your mouth as wide as you can, does it lock, make a cracking sound, or go into spasm?

47. Wrap your index finger around the front of your chin and push the tip of your thumb up under your jaw, the index finger acting as a brace to push against. Push with your thumb and move it back and forth horizontally, exerting a lot of pressure. Does it hurt?

48. Take your hand and squeeze the back of your neck very hard with your thumb opposing your forefingers. Does that hurt?

49. Let your head drop to the side; roll your head all the way around to the back, the other side, and the front a few times. Does it hurt to do that? Especially in the *back*?

50. Lie down on the floor on your stomach and place your hands, palms up, on your lower back. Allow the tips of your middle fingers to touch each other and your elbows to drop. Do your elbows touch the floor?

51. Squeeze the top of your shoulder. This is the muscle between the base of your neck and the tip of your shoulder. Use your thumb opposing your index and middle fingers. Press firmly. Does that hurt?

52. Lift one arm up to the side. Grasp the triceps muscles (which are located on the underside of the upper arm) with the thumb and four fingers of your other hand as close to the bone as you can. When you squeeze firmly, does it hurt?

53. Grasp your left chest muscle (the pectoral) with the thumb opposing the four fingers of your right hand, just between the front of your armpit and the beginning of the chest. Does it hurt? Try the other side too.

54. Stand sideways in front of a mirror, disrobed, and observe your breathing. Is most of the movement in your lower abdomen?

55. While in the same position as in question 54, is your head projected forward?

56. Stand sideways in front of the mirror, with your feet parallel, about 3 inches apart. Does your abdomen drop forward, do your buttocks protrude in the back, and is there an accentuated curve in the small of the back (swayback)?

57. Lie on the floor on your back and relax. Is there more than a 1-inch space between your lower back and the floor?

58. Stand disrobed with your feet absolutely parallel about 2 inches apart. Keeping your back erect, bend your knees as far as you can with your heels remaining on the ground. When you look down can you see the first two inner toes on each foot completely? (See diagram on page 27.)

59. When you or someone else forcefully grips and squeezes your thigh just above the front of the knee, does it hurt, tickle or make you jump?

60. Cross your right leg over your left with the right ankle resting just above the left knee. Forcefully press your left thumb straight into the center of your calf. Does that hurt?

61. Place your index finger between your first two toes and wrap it around the top of your big toe. Press the tip of your thumb firmly into the bottom center part of the toe. Does that hurt?

Now that you have finished the test, turn to page 191 and calculate your score.

TENSION TEST KEY

61. Yes — 1		
60. Yes — 1	40. Yes — 2	20. Yes — 1
59. Yes — 2	39. Yes — 2	19. Yes — 2
58. No — 1	38. Yes — 1	18. Yes — 2
57. Yes — 1	37. Yes — 1	17. Yes — 2
56. Yes — 2	36. Yes — 2	16. No — 1
55. Yes — 1	35. Yes — 1	15. No — 2
54. Yes — 2	34. No — 3	14. Yes — 1
53. Yes — 1	33. Yes — 1	13. Yes — 3
52. Yes — 1	32. Yes — 1	12. Yes — 1
51. Yes — 2	31. Yes — 1	11. Yes — 2
50. No — 1	30. Yes — 1	10. Yes — 2
49. Yes — 2	29. Yes — 2	9. Yes — 2
48. Yes — 2	28. Yes — 3	8. No — 3
47. Yes — 1	27. Yes — 1	7. Yes — 2
46. Yes — 2	26. Yes — 2	6. Yes — 2
45. Yes — 2	25. Yes — 2	5. Yes — 1
44. Yes — 2	24. Yes — 2	4. Yes — 1
43. Yes — 3	23. No — 3	3. Yes — 2
42. Yes — 3	22. Yes — 1	2. Yes — 1
41. Yes — 1	21. Yes — 1	1. Yes — 2

TEST RESULTS ANALYSIS

(1) *0 points*: Perfection.

(2) *1–10 points*: Totally free of excess tension. Very few people will fall into this category. This is the ideal state that we try to approach.

(3) *11–30 points*: Relaxed. This person may have a few areas of tension but would be muscularly in pretty good shape.

(4) *31–50 points*: Moderately tense. This score would reflect a person with some physical problems and occasional areas of pain.

(5) *51–80 points*: Very tense. Depending on this person's age, he either has or will have many physical injuries and pain. This person could probably use a lot of help.

(6) *81–100 points*: Extremely tense. If your score falls in this category, your body is in serious trouble. The tension is severe and is likely to be present throughout the entire body. There is probably fairly constant pain in one place or another. The likelihood of serious physical injury or organic disorder is extremely high. These people may find it difficult to express their emotions.

INDEX

About the Author

Ben E. Benjamin is the founder and director of the
Muscular Therapy Institute, which has training centers
in New York City, Boston, and Washington, D.C. He
received his Ph.D. from Union Graduate School, and
has taught the Benjamin System at leading universities
across the country.

Also by Ben E. Benjamin

Sports Without Pain